Education

Made Simple

The Made Simple series
has been created
especially for self-education
but can equally well
be used as
an aid to group study.
However complex the subject,
the reader is taken
step by step,
clearly and methodically,
through the course. Each volume
has been prepared by experts,
taking account of
modern educational requirements,
to ensure the most
effective way of
acquiring knowledge.

In the same series

Accounting
Acting and Stagecraft
Additional Mathematics
Administration in Business
Advertising
Anthropology
Applied Economics
Applied Mathematics
Applied Mechanics
Art Appreciation
Art of Speaking
Art of Writing
Basic
Biology
Book-keeping
Britain and the European Community
British Constitution
Business and Administrative Organisation
Business Calculations
Business Economics
Business Statistics and Accounting
Business Law
Calculus
Chemistry
Childcare
Child Development
Commerce
Company Law
Computer Electronics
Computer Programming
Computer Programming Languages in Practice
Computers and Microprocessors
Cookery
Cost and Management Accounting
Data Processing
Dressmaking
Economics and Social Geography
Economics
Effective Communication
Electricity
Electronic Computers
Electronics
English
English Literature
Financial Management
First Aid
French
Geology

German
Graphic Communication
Human Anatomy
Human Biology
Italian
Journalism
Latin
Law
Management
Marketing
Marketing Analysis and Forecasting
Mathematics
Modelling and Beauty Care
Modern Biology
Modern European History
Modern Mathematics
Money and Banking
MSX
Music
New Mathematics
Office Administration
Office Practice
Personnel Management
Philosophy
Photography
Physical Geography
Physics
Practical Typewriting
Psychiatry
Psychology
Public Relations
Public Sector Economics
Rapid Reading
Religious Studies
Russian
Salesmanship
Secretarial Practice
Social Services
Sociology
Spanish
Statistics
Taxation
Technology
Teeline Shorthand
Twentieth-Century British History
Typing
Woodwork

Education

Made Simple

A. V. Kelly

MADE SIMPLE
BOOKS

HEINEMANN : London

Made and printed in Great Britain by
Richard Clay Ltd, Bungay, Suffolk
for the publishers, William Heinemann Ltd,
10 Upper Grosvenor Street, London W1X 9PA

First published 1987

British Library Cataloguing in Publication Data

Kelly, A. V.
    Education Made Simple. – (Made simple books,
    ISSN 0265–0541)
    I. Title   II. Series
    370   LB17

ISBN 0 434 98494 9

Contents

Foreword

This book is aimed at students who are about to embark on courses of preparation for teaching, at either undergraduate or post-graduate level, and at the interested layperson, especially that ever-growing group of people who are involved, as parents, as school governors, or in both capacities, in decision-making in education. It is not, therefore, offered as a parents' guide to the education system – there are several books of that kind already available. Rather it is intended to assist everyone who has an interest in education, whether professional or lay, to engage in more productive thinking about education.

To this end it attempts to do two things. First, it sets out to provide some background information to assist towards the development of an understanding of key educational issues. Second, however, and perhaps more importantly, it stresses the problematic nature of all educational decisions, and tries to demonstrate that these are always so much matters of opinion and preference that many different views can, quite legitimately, be held on them. Too often it is assumed that education is a form of science and that teaching is the practical application of that science. Nothing could be further from the truth. A major purpose of this book is to reveal the importance of a full appreciation of this.

My thanks are due to Jill Thorn for her invaluable assistance in the production of the typescript of this book from scribblings which I myself often had difficulty in deciphering.

A. V. Kelly
Goldsmiths' College
April 1986

Introduction

'What kind of education, then, shall we give them?' With these simple and, indeed, largely unmemorable words, Plato in *The Republic* launched the study of education in the Western world. In doing so, he not only drew attention to the central concern of that study, the question to which all others are peripheral, but also demonstrated the importance of this question for social living as a whole, since his reason for posing it was that at an early stage in his search for 'justice', the cohesive principle of civilized society, he found it necessary to consider what kind of education would be most likely to promote it. Few since that time have wished to quarrel with the basic truth that he had grasped, that the kind of education a society provides for its young will determine to a large degree both the nature of that society and the quality of life of the individuals within it.

It will be clear, then, both that the study of education is as old as most areas of study and that to a large extent this is because thinkers have realized that it holds the key to many wider issues of social living.

It is thus an area of human endeavour and exploration which is of importance for, and should, therefore, be of interest to, not only those who are professionally engaged in it but also all who have the interests of society at heart. Indeed, this creates many problems for the professional, who, unlike colleagues in fields such as medicine and the law, finds that everyone has a view on how the job should be done and that many feel that they could do it better. It is right that everyone should feel entitled to hold views about education, but it is also desirable that such views should be informed and thoughtful, soundly based on knowledge, on understanding and on clarity of thinking. This book is an attempt to help both future professionals and laypersons to acquire the beginnings of that solid base.

Education is also an area in which theory and practice have often been widely separated – to the detriment of both. It is clearly important that here, as much as in any other field, the two should go much more closely hand in hand. There are signs that in this respect there has recently been some improvement and it will be a further aim of this book to assist that process, if only by concentrating attention on those issues which are of current importance to educational practice.

Finally, education is also a field of study in which there has been, and still is, continuous debate and disagreement, from the dialogues of Plato through to present-day disputes over issues such as comprehensive education, mixed-ability classes, standards in the 'basic skills' and the establishment of a common core to the curriculum. It is right and proper that this should be so, since without such debate and dialogue there cannot be that continuous development which a rapidly changing society requires. A further aim of this book will be to emphasize the open-ended nature of educational questions by throwing light on them rather than by offering final solutions to them, for it is important to be clear about the kind of study we are engaged in, and the degree of certainty or uncertainty to which it is susceptible. The student of education must realize from the outset that he or she will find few hard and fast answers to his or her questioning, and this one must learn to live with. Education theory is not a body of knowledge; it is rather a collection of issues on which there can be many legitimate views.

It is for this reason that the book's opening chapter offers a review of the major views which have been expressed about the nature and purposes of education during the 2000 years over which these questions have been debated in the Western world. The discussion there also reveals that most of these views continue to be held and that the debate goes on. Subsequent chapters then set out in detail the form in which these same questions appear in current educational discussions.

Chapter 2 traces the development of the education system of England and Wales and, in particular, explores some of the questions which have continued to arise from the attempt to establish some form of mass education and to provide equality of educational opportunity.

Chapter 3 looks at the present political scene and examines the impact on schools and on the educational system as a whole of recent moves towards more direct political intervention in the school curriculum.

Against that background, chapter 4 considers some of the many aspects of the school curriculum which must be fully analysed and explored if curriculum planning is to be soundly based and effectively carried into practice.

One major concern of the curriculum planner must be with the ways in which children's minds and personalities develop, and chapter 5 outlines some of the theories of development in childhood and in adolescence which psychologists have offered. The emphasis in these theories is largely on intellectual or cognitive development, but this chapter goes on to suggest that emotional development is equally important and to identify some of the implications of that.

Chapter 6 takes the discussion further by considering the personal, social and moral education of children. It examines some important theoretical questions which this issue raises, looks at some of the psychological theories of moral development and considers some of the practical steps which need to be taken by schools and teachers in this area of their work.

The closing chapter attempts to summarize what has gone before and to say a little about what it implies for the education of the teachers themselves. As was suggested at the outset, however, this can only take the form of picking out the issues which have emerged and suggesting that the true student of education, and especially the teacher, must go on exploring these. The study of education must always involve uncertainty and constant review and revision of one's thinking. For teachers, this process also requires a similar review and revision of their practice. It is this which gives it its fascination. And it is the appreciation of this which constitutes the first step towards making that study simple.

1
What is education?

Introductory texts to most subjects are likely to begin with some discussion of what the subject is, what it sets out to explore, its scope, its limitations and so on. Most kinds of study involve more than a mere denotation of their subject matter. To understand them fully we must understand *how* they explore the world as well as *what* particular aspect or aspects of the world they do explore.

However, there are other, peculiar reasons why we must begin the study of education with a discussion of what education is. Here we must begin by familiarizing ourselves not only with what kind of study it is, nor merely with those things which constitute its subject matter. We must also ask questions about **what education itself is**, what it is people are or might be referring to when they speak of education, what it is that the student of education is setting out to study. And the main reason why we must begin by asking this is that there is **no one answer** to this question but **several**, no one view of what education is but a plethora of views, no one fixed concept of education but many.

The biologist or the historian or the philosopher may have difficulties apprising us of the complexities of his or her study but the subject matter is not difficult to identify. The subject-matter of the educationists' study is itself uncertain and shifting; it is itself **problematic** and thus renders the study of it that much more difficult to define.

This opening chapter sets out both to demonstrate the truth of that claim and to shed some light on the issues lying behind it by exploring some of the views which have been expressed throughout the ages on this question of what education is – some of the differing (sometimes widely differing) theories of education which have been offered. It goes on to explore what is fundamentally the same question by comparing education with other kinds of teaching and asking what it is that makes us call some kinds of teaching education and others not. And then, having made it clear that the question 'what is education?' is a highly complex and far from straight-forward one, it ends by considering some of the implications of that for the study of education. The main conclusions are that the study of education is **not the scientific or pseudo-scientific kind of activity** that many people have attempted to claim; that it is an activity **riddled with the values** of those practising it and those theorizing about it; and that the main quality the student of education needs is the ability to live with **uncertainty** and to cope with a study which will seldom offer him or her anything that might be called 'a truth'.

For there are very few areas of educational study where our concern is to discover what are the facts of the case. Perhaps we might be said to be engaged in that kind of fact-finding exercise when we study the history of education or explore the educational systems of other countries. But even then our main concern is with the light such exploration throws on our **understanding** of our own practice, with the degree to which it helps us to make our own **judgments**. The study of the systems of schooling in other countries is usually called 'comparative education' and that very name suggests that we are undertaking that study in order to compare what we find with what we know of our own system and thus to be in a better position again to make educational judgments. There are no such things as 'educational facts' or 'educational truths'. The study of education, then, is not a search for such facts or truths; it is rather a search for the kind of knowledge and understanding which will help us to see educational problems more clearly and thus to make sounder judgments concerning them, whether as practitioners or as observers of the practice of others.

The truth of this will emerge as we look at some of the theories of education which have been offered us over the centuries.

The traditional view

The view of education which has had longest currency in the Western world is that which was first stated in the works of the Greek philosopher, Plato (428–347 BC), which has been restated by many subsequent theorists and which is still at the root of many people's attitude to education today. Its main features will emerge in the brief discussion of it which follows, but it will help to note them now so that the reader can be on the look-out for manifestations of these. This will be of advantage when we pick them up again after that discussion.

This is a theory of education which is based on a very **strong view of knowledge and truth**, one which believes that there are **univer-**

sal truths to be found even in areas such as those of aesthetic and moral values. It thus regards education as concerned primarily to inculcate in children a firm sense of what these moral values or moral truths are. It also often sees education as a process by which certain valuable aspects of high culture are transmitted. Another main emphasis is on education as **intellectual development**, the development of man's powers of reason. And this in turn leads it to ignore, and even to devalue, all or most practical activities, and to have the greatest difficulty in accommodating aspects of development other than the intellectual aspects, such as emotional development. Finally, it is also a view that requires educational planning to begin from some notion of its **end product**, some conception of what kinds of people the education system should produce.

It will be clear from this not only what the main features of this view are but also what its opponents have found unsatisfactory about it. The significance of these features will quickly become apparent if we look at the views of the first proponent of this kind of education theory, Plato.

Plato's theory of education

Plato's main aim was to devise a theory and a scheme of education which would result in a balanced and harmonious individual and a balanced and harmonious society. For his concern is not with education in itself but with its **social function**, and, as we saw in the introduction, he develops his theory of education in support of his political theory, his view of society. It is only when he has reached a clear view of what a 'just' society might look like that he asks what kind of education would be likely to achieve this. For justice is his main concern, and he sees it in terms of the kind of **balance or harmony** which is reached when all the constituent elements of any organism are working together, each performing its own function and not interfering in that of the others. This is the kind of balance and harmony, then, that he is looking for both in the state and in the individual and it is to education he looks to produce this.

He develops this idea in a somewhat simplistic manner through his theory of the **tripartite state** and its parallel, **the tripartite soul**. Briefly, he regards all human societies as having three prime needs – economic welfare, safety from dangers, both internal and external, and government. His principle of 'one person – one job' leads him to the view that society should be seen as consisting of three kinds of citizen – **the artisans**, who will attend to the economic needs of the society, **'the auxiliaries'**, whose role it is to ensure the implementation of the law and to protect the society from external aggression and **the rulers**, who make the laws and all other kinds of governmental decision. The prime function of education is to select people for their most appropriate roles and to prepare them to fulfil them properly. A just society will only be achieved when each sector performs its own function and no other.

At the same time, he wishes education to meet the needs of the individual and to create a comparable harmony within the individual's 'soul'. Again he sees **the soul of man as tripartite**, its three sections corresponding to the three divisions in society. First there are **the appetites**, clamouring for attention to the needs of the organism; these he likens at one point to a beast with many heads. Then there is **'spirit'**, a kind of aggressiveness which, properly educated, becomes self-control or self-discipline; this he compares to a lion. Finally, there is **reason**, that which distinguishes man from other animals; this he likens to man himself. In a just, balanced, harmonious, properly educated soul, as in the state, reason will be in control and will take all the decisions, 'spirit' will see that those decisions are properly carried out and the appetites will be made to accept them without question or challenge. Again it is the role of education to bring about this kind of harmony.

It will be clear from this brief description of his view of the soul and of the state that, for a large proportion of the population, education will consist of little more than a **training in obedience**. He says at one point of the appetites that the only form of education they are responsive to is **taming**, and that must suggest a similar approach to the education of the artisan class in the state. They will, of course, need some kind of vocational training to enable them to develop whatever skills their trade or profession needs, but such vocational training does not lie within the scope of Plato's notion of education.

His recommendation, then, for the early stages of education (by which he means from birth to twenty years of age) is that education should consist largely of experiences which will promote in the individual an **acceptance of the society** in which he or she lives and a knowledge of those **moral principles** which will lead to right behaviour. He or she is to have a programme of 'music' (by which he means all the arts) and 'gymnastic', a balanced diet of physical and intellectual experiences which will lead to that balance and harmony within the soul which constitutes the just person. The elements within 'music' will be carefully chosen so that they promote the right moral attitudes. And the arts in society too will be closely censored to ensure that they reinforce this process and do not work against it.

This is the only form of education which most of the citizens will receive. At the age of twenty, however, **some** will be **selected for further education** designed to prepare them to take on the task of government. Selection at this stage is **by merit**, both **moral** and **intellectual**, and certainly not by birth or privilege.

This second stage of education consists of a series of academic pursuits of an increasingly abstract nature – arithmetic, geometry, three-dimensional geometry, harmonics and, finally, dialectic. The latter is a somewhat complex notion and Plato is never totally clear about it, but fundamentally it is a form of philosophical study or enquiry which ultimately brings one to an understanding of all knowledge and of all truth, to an appreciation of what he calls the **'form of beauty, truth and goodness'**, a somewhat mystical concept which is somehow intended to encapsulate **complete and perfect knowledge** of all things. It is this knowledge that the ruler must have if he or she is to be able always to make right decisions, as he or she must if we are to justify the imposition of those decisions on the mass of citizens who have been trained to accept them un-critically.

There is much more, of course, to Plato's theory than this, but perhaps enough has been said for the reader to be able to see its main elements, its basic principles. We must now turn to some elucidation of these.

The main features and implications of this view

Theory of knowledge

The first thing to notice about this theory of education is that, as we suggested at the beginning, it is firmly based on a particular and **strong view of knowledge and of truth**. It believes that knowledge of a kind which is **absolute and certain** can be attained in all spheres. It believes in the **supremacy of reason** over all other human attributes. And it believes that through reason man can attain knowledge and establish truth not only in the fields of science and mathematics, but in those of morals, aesthetics and, indeed, politics too. It is this view that enables Plato, without flinching, to advocate the right of those who have attained this kind of supreme and complete know-ledge to make all decisions, moral, aesthetic and political for those of their fellow citizens who have not, and to decide how they must behave, what kinds of artistic experience are appropriate for them and so on.

It is this kind of view which, in a far less stark but perhaps no less sinister form, underpins the attitudes of many people to edu-cation today. For to look to the school to promote right behaviour in its pupils is to assume that one knows what right behaviour is. To plan a curriculum in terms of a selection of that which is valuable from the culture of society is to assume that we know what valuable culture is. To see education merely as **the transmission of knowledge** is to assume that knowledge enjoys the kind of certainty this particular theory of knowledge claims for it.

This view of knowledge, then, first articulated by Plato, is still very much in vogue, albeit seldom recognized or acknowledged. It is the fundamental principle not only of his theory of education but of many current views of education. Its implications, therefore, need to be fully appreciated. All the points which follow stem directly from the adoption of this basic view of knowledge, and they are relevant not only to Plato's theory but also to similar theories held today.

Moral education

The first of these implications is the emphasis on education as fundamentally **moral education**. The whole elaborate system Plato outlines for us is designed to bring the individual ruler to a recognition of the supreme principle of morality, to ensure that he or she will personally behave according to this, and to enable him or her to make what will be objectively the right decisions for their fellow citizens. The earlier upbringing of the rest of the citizens too, their exposure only to certain kinds of art, those which promote these objectively right moral values, and their diet of 'music' and 'gymnastic' 'for the sake of the soul', are all designed to ensure an acceptance of the decisions made by the rulers. Fundamentally, the concern is with right behaviour, but in the interests of the society rather than that of the individual.

However, there are two very important questions we must ask about this aspect of his scheme – both of them as relevant to us today as they were to those of Plato's day. The first of these is 'Can we be sure that we know what the good is with the kind of certainty that Plato is claiming?' There is a conviction in Plato's writing not just **that moral values are absolute** but that philosophical enquiry will reveal to us what those moral values are; that there are moral 'truths' which enjoy the same kind of validity and status as mathematical or scientific 'truths'. This is the fundamental tenet of that philosophy or theory of knowledge known as **rationalism**, and it leads not only to this kind of view of morality but also to a quite distinctive view of education. For it is only if one is convinced of the certainty of one's values – not merely moral values but aesthetic and cultural values too – that one can justify imposing them on others. This is a debate we will find ourselves returning to throughout this book.

The second question we must ask may be even more important than the first: 'Even if these values are absolute, are we justified in depriving a majority of people from proper access to them?' For Plato's plan is that a few citizens, those who demonstrate the ability to become rulers, should have full access to this moral and other knowledge, to the 'form of beauty, truth and goodness', while **the rest are trained merely to obey them**. This means that if education is the process by which people are helped to that full development of their intellectual powers which Plato's second system of education is designed to promote, then only a minority will be educated. Thus, while perhaps acknowledging some of the attractions of Plato's notion of what education is, we must not lose sight of this particular implication, namely that, on this theory, education in the full sense is **available only to a chosen few**.

If we remain in any doubt as to the present-day relevance of this, we have only to consider the debates over the concept of **mass education**, **secondary school selection procedures**, **comprehensive schools**, **mixed-ability classes**, **the multi-ethnic curriculum**, and all those current issues which focus on the notion of **equality of educational opportunity**. Plato's system, like that still advocated by many, gives everyone the opportunity to enter the second stage of education if they prove good enough, but offers nothing to those who do not succeed in being selected at that level. It is clearly based on a particular interpretation, what has been called **the 'strong' interpretation, of equality** – equality of **access** but not equality of provision. And, although the kind of society it envisages is more properly called **meritocratic** than aristocratic, it is questionable whether one could describe it as democratic. It is well worth bearing this aspect of his theory in mind. It may well be endemic to all theories of this kind.

Education as intellectual development

The conviction of man's ability to attain knowledge which is certain, which we saw underpins Plato's view of morality and of moral education, leads him also to emphasize **intellectual or cognitive development** to the exclusion of all other forms of development. For everything, including moral behaviour and aesthetic experience is conceived in terms of some form of cognition.

This kind of theory can take **no account of other aspects** of human development, in particular those which would form part of **emotional development**. For example, the emphasis in his theory of moral education is on moral development as the acquisition of 'moral knowledge' and no proper account can be taken of the emotional aspects of moral behaviour. Most of us are only too well aware of the role our emotions play in our moral behaviour. How we *feel* about a particular situation or problem is at least as important as how we *think* about it. Yet Plato's only answer to this is to say that our feelings will get in the way of our reaching properly thought out rational conclusions. These feelings therefore must be suppressed, tamed, reduced to a subordinate role or even to no role at all in our lives. They are 'the beast with many heads'.

This is typical again of that school of philosophy which makes rationality the basis of everything. It generates theories – of morals, of politics, of education – which are for *rational* beings rather than for *human* beings, for creatures such as those terrifying Daleks with which Dr Who has had to battle from time to time, creatures which are terrifying precisely because they are impersonal, without trace of emotion, lacking any kind of human warmth. Yet this kind of view has been fundamental to much Western philosophy, which has assumed a definition or **model of man as a rational animal** and, like Aristotle, has gone on to argue that he ought to develop that aspect of his being which distinguishes him from other animals. It is the possession of **reason**, it is claimed which distinguishes humans from other animals so that this is the aspect of human existence which must be given priority. It thus adopts a model or view of humanity as primarily and essentially rational. For this philosophy, what makes human beings human is not their powers of compassion, or the ability to consider the interests of others, or their moral potential, but their powers of reason. The development of these powers then takes priority over all else. Taking up this view, for example, Aristotle claimed that the art of contemplation was the supreme form of human activity, transcending all forms of moral behaviour, a view which has prompted countless examination questions along the lines of 'Would Aristotle break off his contemplation to save a drowning child?'.

This view has a long and unhappy history in the Western world. Most of our educational practice has demonstrated an allegiance to the idea of **education as intellectual development**, or, worse, **education as the acquisition of knowledge**. And little attention has been paid to the kind of emotional development which children might be experiencing as a result of the practices adopted to fill their heads with this knowledge. Furthermore, too often the concern has been to repress their emotional responses in the interests of developing their power of reason with all of the consequent ill-effects on them of that kind of policy.

Again too, we do not have to look far around the present-day scene to see manifestations of this view. There are many still who see the school's role as **the transmission of knowledge**, who look to schools to teach pupils the 'basic skills' and to help them to obtain as many examination passes as possible. Current attempts to evaluate the work of schools and to open them up to some form of public accountability, as we shall see in chapter 3, are for the most part predicated on this kind of view, stressing as they do **perform-ance testing** and **examination results** as the major criteria of success. The emphasis for some people then continues to be on the intellectual or cognitive dimension of education.

The consequence of this is that **other forms of development are devalued**. Few among present-day politicians or even theorists of education are as ready as Plato was to state this explicitly, openly to deny this aspect of human development (although I did once hear a well-known philosopher of education say – he has never to my knowledge put it into print – that it was of no concern to him whether children were happy or not, provided that their intellectual development was proceeding satisfactorily). Yet this is the effect of the kind of emphasis on the cognitive I am describing. In the face of this devaluing of activities whose intellectual content might not be immediately apparent, it is difficult for any school or any teacher to develop an alternative philosophical stance or even to maintain such. If the effectiveness of a school is being measured by tests of its pupils' intellectual attainments, then it is on those attainments that schools and teachers will inevitably concentrate.

Again, therefore, we see that a major feature of Plato's theory of education is also a major feature of the theory adopted, or at least assumed, by many in the present day. Again too we can see its consequences. And again we must note that it is endemic to the philosophical view upon which this kind of education theory is built.

Practical subjects

Practical activities are also devalued in Plato's scheme and continue to be so. Plato, like those who came after him, was concerned to distinguish **education** from **training**, study for its own sake or 'for the sake of the soul' from utilitarian or instrumental study aimed at achieving certain kinds of ends extrinsic to the study itself. Thus he placed a high premium on purely intellectual activities like mathematics and philosophy and no value at all on practical activities such as art and crafts of various kinds. For example, he is at some pains to make clear that, although geometry is a useful subject, it is not for that reason that he advocates the study of it. Similarly, Aristotle, who followed Plato, recommends 'a little drawing' as part of his curriculum but is at pains to disclaim any association with the useful aspects of that skill.

Again we can see that this view of education is essentially that of those who over the years, indeed over the centuries, have wished to argue the merits of what they have called a **liberal education** and to condemn the converse of that, a **vocational education**. And we can see why emphasis has been placed on the kinds of study which seemed to extend the mind, in the rather narrow sense in which this kind of philosophy conceives of it, and why there has been the greatest reluctance to include useful or practical subjects in an educational curriculum. It is worth noting that even the study of science had great difficulty in establishing its right to be included in an educational curriculum, especially at a time when that curriculum was dominated by the manifestly non-useful study of Classics.

It will also be clear that it is this kind of educational philosophy which is responsible for the fact that so many people still regard subjects such as Latin or Greek or even science as superior in some way to subjects like art, Home Economics or Craft Design and Technology. Those that take this view – and there are many – are subscribing to precisely the view of knowledge and of education which Plato was advocating.

We must note, however, what a limited and limiting view of education this is. For, on the one hand, it **denies the educational merits** which are clearly to be discerned in the study of art, of Home Economics, of Craft Design and Technology or of any other subject which currently has a low status in the school curriculum. And, on the other hand, like that view of morality we discussed earlier, it **restricts educational opportunity** to those pupils who have the ability and, what is perhaps more important, the interest and inclination to succeed in the study of those subjects which satisfy the kind of academic and intellectual criteria which Plato set up and which many people continue to adopt. Again, therefore, we note a further barrier to the achievement of educational equality.

The pupil as a 'man-in-the-making'

The last aspect of Plato's theory which we need to note is his concern with **the end product** of the educational process, his clear conviction that we must begin with a blueprint of the kind of person we wish to see as the product of education and plan according to that. Again we must note that he adopts this position because of his other conviction that he can define without fear of contradiction what is a good or educated person, so that he feels he has every justification for planning education in such a way as to produce good or educated persons of this kind.

But what are the consequences of even asking 'What if that conviction is misplaced?', 'What if our blue-print is wrong?' This, of course, is something Plato cannot conceive of, so confident is he of his view of moral truth and moral knowledge. If, however, he is wrong, if, as subsequent writers have claimed, there is no such thing as a moral truth or as moral knowledge, then to impose any particular view of morality is to **indoctrinate** rather than to educate; it is to produce the kinds of person we – or those in power – wish to see rather than persons who can make up their own minds about what they want to be or to do; it is to plan education **in the interests of society** rather than to take account of the interests of the individual. It is for this reason that Plato has been charged with **totalitarianism**, a preference for the welfare of society over that of its individual members.

Again, we can see that this is an inevitable corollary of his view of knowledge and especially of moral knowledge. If we are convinced that we know what the good is, what is right – objectively and absolutely – we can have no qualms in imposing that on others. In fact, we would be doing less than our duty if we did not attempt to impose it on others. Thus this kind of philosophical position leads inexorably away from the notion of **individual freedom** and away from the idea that education must concern itself with the **individual pupil**.

We must also note that the very notion of educating people according to the blue-print, like its underpinning idea of a single all-embracing concept of morality and aesthetics, implies **a denial of individuality**. If we *know* what the good and educated person – the perfect human being – *is* then we must try to make everyone into such a person, and that necessitates attempting to make everyone the same. For there can be only one version of perfection and any variation of this must logically imply imperfection. Thus, as the work of later rationalist philosophers makes very clear, there is no room in such a theory for any notion of individuality.

The relevance of this for present-day educational practice is not difficult to see. Many contributions to the current debate over the school curriculum reflect this same attitude. Demands for an increased emphasis on science and technology are made not because of the educational advantage of these for the individual pupil or student but because of **the supposed needs of society**. And, in a different sphere, there is much pressure on schools to attend to the moral upbringing of pupils, not by encouraging them to think for themselves and to learn to make their own moral judgments, but by **teaching them 'right behaviour'**.

Furthermore, pressures for **a common curriculum** for all pupils, centrally determined by government agencies, can only be predicated on this kind of view of knowledge and thus on a denial of individuality. An advertisement for children's shoes recently seen on British television was at pains to stress the individuality of children's feet; it is odd that some people continue to assume that this does not apply equally to their minds and their personalities.

Subsequent developments

All these features, and more, are to be found reflected in the work of the major educational theorists who followed Plato. The **liberal/vocational distinction** is there throughout – in the works of the Roman educationists, such as Cicero and Quintilian, in that of the early Christian theorists such as St Augustine and St Thomas Aquinas, in the ideas of the Humanists, in the tradition of the British public and grammar schools and in much of the education debate of the present day. The preference for **intellectual studies** over the practical subjects has also been a continuing trend and can be seen in those **subject hierarchies** which are a feature of the curricula of today's secondary schools. Parents are never as unhappy to discover their children have dropped art or Home Economics from their programme as they are if they discover they are no longer studying mathematics or science; and they are often strangely proud if their offspring are felt capable of studying Latin.

The notion that education should concern itself with **the development of the intellect** and that the emotions should be suppressed or 'tamed' has also been a continuing one. Clearly it fitted very well with Christian notions of upbringing, Christian theology having gone so far as to embrace the notion of **original sin**, the idea that all children are born inherently evil and must be purged of that by their educational experiences. Few today would perhaps wish to go as far as that, but the idea that education should curb some of the natural tendencies of children in the interests of developing their powers of reason is still prevalent. So too is the associated idea that education must concern itself with **moral upbringing** and that this should take the form of teaching children **right behaviour and proper moral values**. Finally, the view of the child as **'man-in-the-making'** (or 'woman-in-the-making or 'person-in-the-making') has also persisted throughout the ages and into the present day – the idea that educationists should start with a blueprint of the kind of adult they ought to be endeavouring to produce and work towards that. This has clearly always been the Christian view of the role of education – it is for the production of good Christian adults – so that kind of view has permeated much of our thinking about education.

The theory of Plato in all its major manifestations, then, has endured to the present day. For a long time, it went unchallenged, largely because in its essential principles it had the full support of the Christian church which dominated man's thinking for many centuries. In more recent times, however, there has emerged **an alternative view**, a view which challenges the traditional view at all of those major points we have identified, a view, therefore, which not only leads to **a different concept of education** but also to **quite different educational practices**, and a view which in turn is based on a quite different theory of knowledge and a quite different conception of what it means to be human.

We must now look at that alternative view.

The alternative view

In the eighteenth century, there began that process of revolution in many areas of thought, which has subsequently been termed the 'Enlightenment', the emergence of what David Hume called 'the science of man'. In the arts, it took the form of the Romantic movement whose main characteristic was the emphasis it placed on the imagination. In science, it saw the beginnings of that experimental approach to scientific exploration which led to many quite dramatic developments in our knowledge of and control over our physical environment. In philosophy, it sparked off **a challenge to many of the traditional assumptions** inherited from Plato, especially those about **the nature and status of knowledge**. In politics, it placed the emphasis on the individuality of the human personality and the need to liberate this from the chains of social convention. And consequent on this, in education, it led to the emergence of a totally new and different concept of what education is and what it should be concerned to bring about.

Theory of knowledge

We saw that Plato's theory of knowledge, which dominated thinking until this time, had claimed a very secure status for knowledge and had believed that there are eternal truths to be found, that these are to be found also in the areas of aesthetics, morals and even politics, and that the way to find them is through the application of the human being's powers of reason. We saw further that this theory involves a view of humans as primarily rational rather than feeling beings and that it leads to a concept of education as the transmission of those eternal truths to pupils – or at least to those who have the capacity to absorb them.

All of those claims are now to be disputed. The challenge to this view of the nature and source of human knowledge came first from John Locke (1632–1704), whose assertion that all knowledge comes into the mind **through the gates of the senses** turned philosophy on its head. For on this theory it is **experience** rather than reason which is the source of knowledge, we learn from what our **senses** tell us and not from the use of our intellect divorced from sense-experience, and, since our sense-experience is notoriously uncertain, since our senses often deceive us, we must now accept that knowledge is far more **tentative and provisional** than those eternal truths of rationalism, and that this is especially the case in the spheres of morals, aesthetics and politics. There is much that has occurred in the present century, even in the area of science and mathematics, which has reinforced this view.

'Progressive' education

Such a view of knowledge clearly has equally revolutionary implications for education and these were soon to be asserted. With these assertions there began what has come to be called **the 'progressive' movement in education** – an odd term in many ways, not least because many of those who have used it have intended it in a pejorative sense. The essences of this view are made clear by its first exponent, Jean Jacques Rousseau, and it will be helpful if we begin by looking at his first simple version of it.

Jean Jacques Rousseau (1712–78)

Jean Jacques Rousseau has been described as a born revolutionary, a man who believed that in many spheres of human life and thinking it was time for a completely fresh start. He was thus well at home in the period of the Enlightenment. His views on most matters were new and even startling. His theory of education was quite **revolutionary**.

   This is apparent from the outset of *Émile*, the work he devoted to a discussion of education. In the second paragraph of its Preface he tells us, 'I shall say very little about the value of a good education, nor shall I stop to prove that the customary method of education is bad; this has been done again and again, and I do not wish to fill my book with things which everyone knows. I will merely state that, go as far back as you will, you will find a continual outcry against the established method, but no attempt to suggest one better'. This tone is starkly reinforced by the opening sentence of the book proper – 'God makes all things good; man meddles with them and they become evil'.

   Several features of this view emerge clearly from that short sentence. First, he is **opposing** the Christian doctrine of **original sin** which was a feature of traditional approaches to education. Education, he is telling us, should not be seen as the means by which we suppress and inhibit the natural tendencies of children towards evil. Rather, since, in his view, their natural tendencies are towards good, education must seek to **protect them from the corrupting in-**

fluence of society. One might of course feel that to claim that children are born inherently good is as unjustifiable as to claim they are born with inherent propensities towards evil, but one must recognize this as a useful counterblast to those theories of education well summed up in the barbaric phrase 'Spare the rod and spoil the child'.

Second, it is clear that, since man's 'meddling' is the source of evil, education cannot be seen as the transmission of knowledge and the imposition of values on the Platonic, rationalist model. Rather the educational policy must be one of **non-interference** with children's **natural development**, 'Tender, anxious mother, I appeal to you,' he says. 'You can remove this young tree from the highway and shield it from the crushing force of social conventions. . . . From the outset raise a wall round your child's soul.'

Third, the emphasis must be on **learning rather than teaching**. The distinction is crucial since it draws our attention to a very important feature of this view of education. It is the teacher's task to guide the learning and the development of the pupils through providing experiences and opportunities for experience through which this kind of development may occur. 'Give your scholar no verbal lessons; he should be taught by experience alone', he tells us. And, 'Let him know nothing because you have told him, but because he has learnt it for himself. Let him not be taught science, let him discover it'.

Thus we see that the focus of attention has switched from the knowledge and the eternal truths to be transmitted by the teacher and absorbed by the pupil, to **the subject of the educational process**, the child himself or herself, and education begins to be seen in terms not of its knowledge-content but of **the processes of development** it is concerned to promote. Furthermore, the pupil is seen for what he or she is here and now and not viewed in relation to what he or she is to become. In Rousseau's terms, the pupil is to be seen not as a 'man-in-the-making' but as a child, with childish interests and characteristics. 'We know nothing of childhood; and with our mistaken notions the further we advance the further we go astray. The wisest writers devote themselves to what a man ought to know, without asking what a child is capable of learning. They are always looking for the man in the child, without considering what he is before he becomes a man.' Thus attention is drawn **away from the end product** of the educational process and **centred on that process itself**, away from what is to be learnt and on to the individual who is to do the learning. We can see too the invitation here, which was soon to become important, to explore more fully aspects of child psychology as an aid to developing more effective approaches to teaching and learning.

The 'great educators' of the nineteenth century

These themes were taken up by a number of major educational theorists during the next century. It is not necessary to look at their work in detail, since at root they were merely elaborating on the ideas first expressed by Rousseau. People such as Pestalozzi (1746–1827), Herbart (1776–1841), Froebel (1782–1842) and Maria Montessori (1870–1952), all in slightly different ways and with slightly different emphases asserted and developed what was to all intents and purposes the same basic educational philosophy. What is more they also endeavoured, again in different ways, to translate that philosophy into practice.

It was this more than anything else which paved the way for several well-known **practical exponents** of 'progressive' education in the twentieth century, people such as J. H. Badley at Bedales School, A. S. Neill at Summerhill, Susan Isaacs at Malting House and Kurt Haan, first at Salem School and later at Gordonstoun. It was through the work of people like this in the field that this view of education came to be asserted in practice and their examples, allied to the theories of those 'great educators' we have just listed, came to exercise a great influence on practices in the **primary sector** of the state system in the United Kingdom.

That we will consider briefly in a moment. First, however, we must look at the work of another major theorist, whose influence spanned both the nineteenth and the twentieth centuries – the American philosopher and educationist, John Dewey.

John Dewey (1859–1952)

The importance of John Dewey stems largely from the fact that he brought a number of different threads together into a single theory of knowledge, of man, of society and of education. That theory he called **pragmatism**. It was important within philosophy since it represented one of the major reactions against the restatement of the basic principles of Plato's theory of knowledge by the major figures of the German Idealist movement, especially Kant and Hegel. It was important within educational theory because it also related its view of knowledge directly to educational theory and practice. Indeed, Dewey's view of philosophy was 'that it is the theory of education in its most general phases', by which he meant that there is little point in theorizing about knowledge, about man or about society if one does not at the same time attempt to develop a theory about how one's views of these are to be translated into reality, a view about education. The point of this may become clearer if we consider what was a major influence on his thinking and also a major feature of his philosophy.

In the year in which Dewey was born (1859), Darwin published his *Origin of Species*. The **theory of evolution** which he offered there became a very important influence on the thinking of people in most fields in the years that followed. Dewey was no exception. For from this notion of evolution he developed the view that nothing in human experience can properly be seen as fixed, static or eternal, that everything must be recognized as being in **a state of continuous change**, development, or evolution. We can immediately see how this led him in all spheres to views which were the exact opposite of those of Plato, whose concern, as we saw earlier, had been with permanence and with the arresting of change.

Thus, in the first place, Dewey saw **knowledge as in a state of continuous evolution**. For him it is not that body of fixed eternal truths that it was for Plato and for many who have come after him and, indeed, for many of our contemporaries. Knowledge, like all else, develops. It is **a creation of man** not a gift he receives from some divine or metaphysical source and, like all creations of man, and like man himself, it must be seen to evolve, to change, to develop.

It must also be seen as evolving to meet the changing and evolving needs of man and society. For man has created and continues to **create**, or to **modify** and **adapt**, knowledge to solve the ever-changing problems with which his environment presents him. Hence, knowledge is seen as 'what works' in relation to these problems or what helps us to solve these problems. This is the essence of pragmatism; it offers us a new and evolutionary view of 'truth' as well as of knowledge, a view which would appear to make much more sense in the context of the rapid technological and social changes that recent years have witnessed. There has been much evidence in the present century of the validity of this view, since we have witnessed revolutionary approaches to knowledge, especially in the fields of mathematics and physics, which have turned traditional views of these subjects on their head. Furthermore, it is these revolutionary approaches which have made possible much, if not all, of the technological advance this century has seen.

Several important things follow from this view of knowledge. First, Dewey argues that it necessitates **a democratic organization for society**. This evolutionary process will be inhibited by any totalitarian social organization, such as that recommended by Plato, whose concern is to maintain the *status quo* on the grounds that that reflects perfection of knowledge. Conversely, it is not any particular version of democracy that he is wishing to advocate but rather **the notion of democracy**, the idea of a society which is itself open to change and evolution. 'The very idea of democracy, the meaning of democracy, must be continually explored afresh; ...

while the political and economic and social institutions in which it is embodied have to be remade and reorganized. . . . No form of life either does or can stand still; it either goes forward or it goes backward, and the end of the backward road is death. Democracy as a form of life cannot stand still. It, too, if it is to live must go forward to meet the changes that are here and that are coming.'

The consequences of this view for education are quite considerable. As with Rousseau, we see that the idea of education as the transmission of eternal truths must be completely abandoned since there are no such truths. Furthermore, any attempt to transmit knowledge as though it does have this status will, first, be a form of **indoctrination** rather than education, since it will include also **the imposition of the values** implicit in that knowledge on the next generation, and will, second, by its very nature **inhibit the further development of knowledge**, since it will encourage in pupils a view of knowledge as fixed and not as evolutionary and open to change.

How, then, is education to be viewed and planned? Dewey's answer is simple but at the same time extremely complex. Education is to be seen as **experience**. Pupils are to be helped to develop their own knowledge and their own understanding rather than encouraged to acquire and accept that of their teachers. They must learn primarily how to generate new knowledge, **how to contribute to the evolution of knowledge**. Thus they must be helped to see it not as something fixed and static to be learned, but as something **to be used in solving problems** and to be developed through such use.

On this view we must plan education not by reference to the knowledge to be transmitted by the teacher and assimilated by the pupil, but in terms of the provision of experience through which the pupil will develop many different kinds of capacity. Thus education is to be seen and planned in terms of the **developmental processes** it is designed to promote, and the main criterion of judgment to be used in educational decision-making is those processes of development, what Dewey called **'the experiential continuum'**. The value of an educational experience is judged by reference not to the supposed value of the knowledge-content involved but to its effectiveness in supporting continuous development. This view, then, reinforces that shift of focus from the knowledge to the pupil which we saw earlier had been a major feature of the work of Rousseau and those who followed him, and which is the central feature of this view of education.

Some further developments

There are three subsequent developments we must note as adding support to this view of education at both the theoretical and the practical levels.

The first of these is the formal adoption and advocacy of this approach to educational planning in the **primary sector** of schooling in the United Kingdom by two major reports, that of the Hadow Committee, *Primary Education*, in 1931 and that of the Plowden Committee, *Children and Their Primary Schools*, in 1967. It has been claimed on the evidence of recent research that the influence of these reports on the actual practice of primary schools has not been as extensive as was once thought. This may well be true and we will consider some possible reasons for this when we look at political influences on the curriculum in chapter 3.

We must note here, however, the impetus these two reports have given to this conception of education **at the theoretical level**; and the extent to which the view of education adopted by them reflects the basic principles of that philosophical stance we have just been exploring. The Hadow Report tells us, for example, that the curriculum must be developed from the experiences of the pupils, that in this way 'knowledge will be acquired in the process, not, indeed, without effort, but by an effort whose value will be enhanced by the fact that its purpose and significance can be appreciated, at least in part, by the children themselves' and that to achieve this we must adopt methods 'which take as the starting point of the work of the primary school the experience, the curiosity, and the awakening powers and interests of the children themselves'. In its most often quoted words, 'the curriculum is to be thought of in terms of activity and experience rather than knowledge to be acquired and facts to be stored'.

More than thirty years later, the Plowden Report reiterated these principles. The school, it tells us, 'is a community in which children learn to live first and foremost as children and not as future adults. . . . The school sets out deliberately to devise the right environment for children, to allow them to be themselves and to develop in the way and at the pace appropriate to them. . . . It lays special stress on individual discovery, on first hand experience and on opportunities for creative work.' 'A school,' it tells us at the beginning of this passage, 'is not merely a teaching shop.'

We can see in these two reports, an official recommendation that, not least in the primary sector of schooling, we should adopt that view of education which we have seen emerging and growing in the work of Rousseau, Pestalozzi, Froebel, Montessori and Dewey.

A second factor which has given impetus to the growth of this view of education is **the work of the developmental psychologists**. This we shall discuss in much greater detail in chapter 5, but we must note here that, in devoting its attention to an examination of how children think and learn and how their capacities for thinking and learning change and develop, it has come to stress that children's thinking is **qualitatively different** from that of adults, that children see and view the world in ways quite different from adults, that it is mistaken to see them merely as 'adults-in-the-making'. It can thus be seen as responding to that challenge of Rousseau that we have gone wrong by 'always looking for the man in the child, without considering what he is before he becomes a man'. We must note, therefore, the support that has come from this source for this view of education. Its full force will become more apparent when we explore this work in greater detail in chapter 5.

Finally, we must note the support that has come for this view from certain recent developments in **the sociology of education**. For recent years have seen the emergence of **new directions** for the sociology of education, and those new directions have taken it very positively towards the generation of a **sociology of knowledge**. Most of the proponents of these 'new directions' would not see themselves as supporting the idea of 'progressive' education; their concern has been much more to criticize and attack those approaches to education which are based on a view of knowledge as fixed, as static, as a body of eternal truths. Nevertheless, in attacking such approaches they have added their weight to that move away from this form of education which we have seen began with Rousseau.

In particular, they have argued strongly and convincingly that knowledge is **socially constructed**, a product of the work of man rather than of God, and that, since it thus does not enjoy any kind of objective status, there is no justification for a view of education as the transmission of such knowledge to pupils. Indeed, they would agree with the claim we made earlier that such transmission of knowledge, along with the values implicit in that knowledge, is a form of **indoctrination** rather than education. Again, we can see why this has been taken by some as another argument in support of the view of education as a series of developmental processes and why, consequently, this development within the sociology of education has contributed to the emergence of such a view.

We can thus see how there has emerged a second and quite different view of education, a second and quite different answer to the question 'What is education?'. It might be helpful if, before moving on to discuss a different kind of approach to that question, we attempt to summarize the major differences between the two views we have examined.

The two views compared

The most fundamental differences between these theories lie in the view they take of **human knowledge**, the traditional theory regarding it as fixed, as objective, as true in a very strong sense, even in some theories as God-given, the alternative view seeing it as tentative, as in a permanent state of development and evolution, as true in only a provisional way, as man-made or 'socially constructed'.

As a consequence the traditional view sees education primarily in terms of the **transmission** of this certain knowledge and the objective values implicit in it and regards the content of the curriculum as the starting point for educational planning. The alternative view sees education as **a process of development** through which children will come to be able to develop their own knowledge and values rather than acquire those of their teachers, and shifts the focus of curriculum planning from its content to its subjects, the children, and from a concern with the knowledge to be transmitted to a concern with the processes of development to be promoted.

Third, the traditional view, because of its emphasis on rationality as the supreme principle and on human beings as rational animals, has had to emphasize the notion of education as **cognitive or intellectual development**, while the alternative view has been at pains to stress the importance of **other forms of development**, particularly those of an emotional or 'affective' kind; it has been concerned with how children **feel** as well as with how they **think**.

Lastly, a point we will take up at some length in chapter 2, the traditional theory, again because of the view it has adopted of knowledge, or reason, and of their central role in education, has led to the emergence of notions of education which, from whatever angle one views them, are essentially **élitist**, stressing different levels of ability, valuing them differently, and seeing a meritocratic form of selection as a prime function and purpose of the school system. The alternative view, because of its looser, less certain and less dogmatic view of knowledge and values, has found it easier to develop a genuine theory of **educational equality**.

We must stress again that both of these views can be identified in **the current educational scene**, not always in the 'pure' form we have outlined here, in fact too often in a muddled and thus less easily identifiable form. Nevertheless, they are there and that is what makes it important for us to be clear about their major features and implications.

We must now turn to a rather different kind of attempt to answer the question 'What is education?', that which has attempted to use the more recently developed device of philosophical or conceptual analysis.

The concept of education

The present century has witnessed the arrival of a new approach to philosophy, not entirely unconnected with the kind of thinking we considered in the previous section of this chapter. This 'revolution in philosophy' has consisted of a move away from the attempt to define notions such as education in terms of theories concerning what **ought** to be, how we **ought** to behave, what we **ought** to be doing, and away from the idea that we can derive **prescriptions** from an analysis of the essences of things, that we can analyse man and define him as a rational being and then deduce from that how he ought to behave and how we ought to treat him. Instead there has been a move towards the claim that this is a mistaken view of the role and scope of philosophy, that it is wrong to expect philosophy to answer for us questions about how we ought to behave or, indeed, how we ought to set about educational planning, and that the most we can expect of philosophy is that it will assist us to **clarify our thinking** by helping us to **analyse the concepts** we are using in that thinking. Thus philosophical or **conceptual analysis** has been the watchword and in all spheres of human knowledge and thought philosophers have turned their attention to seeking enhanced understanding and, indeed, improved communication, through the device of achieving conceptual clarity.

In the field of education, the burden of this development is that instead of attempting to answer the question 'What is education?' by developing theories of how we ought to set about it, like those of Plato, or of Rousseau, or even of Dewey, we should be asking what is distinctive about the concept, what it actually means, **what it is that distinguishes it** from other related concepts.

Many of the attempts to do this have quickly led people back into some form of prescriptivism – perhaps inevitably in an area where the central concern is with practice. To be so led, however, is to be taken back to the kind of approach this device was deliberately invented to replace, and thus represents a degree of muddled thinking which is particularly inappropriate and unacceptable in a specific attempt to achieve conceptual clarity.

We must recognize that this approach will offer us an answer or answers to our question of 'What is education?' not by telling us what we ought to do and how we ought to set about planning it, but by objectively drawing our attention to what seems to be involved in our use of the term, what people seem **to mean** by it. And it will also be the case that we must recognize that it may mean different things to different people. At the most, therefore, we can look to this approach to explicate for us some of the **different things** we might be doing when we set about **teaching** children. It will or should seek merely to tell us what educaton is and how it differs from other forms of teaching rather than to advocate it.

In general terms, what this kind of approach leads us to is a recognition that teaching can take a number of different forms, **training**, for example, or **indoctrination** or **conditioning** or straight-forward, plain **instruction**, and that it may be helpful to try to differentiate between these and to identify their essential differences.

Thus it is suggested that, while the term 'teaching' itself can be seen as a purely neutral term, describing a kind of transaction between teacher and taught, the nature of that transaction must be explored very closely before we are able to use any of those other terms to denote what is occurring. If it is a matter of a straight transmission of knowledge then we might call it an act of **instruction**. If the concern is to help the pupil to develop certain useful skills or to improve on these, if, in other words, the point of the exercise is not to be found in what is being taught in itself but on what it is being taught *for*, then **training** may be the appropriate term. If the intention is to implant certain values or beliefs in the pupil in such a way as to discourage any critical reflection on these, then we would be inclined to describe this kind of act as **indoctrination**.

The term 'education', it is claimed, is best defined by **contrasting** it with these other forms of teaching, in particular by recognizing that it is a term which introduces certain **considerations of value** into our analysis. Thus it is contrasted with 'instruction' in terms of the **value** of what is being transmitted – we might *instruct* someone in the art of torture but it would be odd to claim we were *educating* him or her in doing so. It is contrasted with 'training' on the grounds that the prime concern of education is with **the intrinsic value** of what is taught rather than its usefulness – we might train someone to operate a lathe but we would be unlikely to argue that this in itself was a part of his or her education. It is contrasted with indoctrination on the grounds that education is concerned to encourage **critical reflection** on the part of the pupil and certainly not to discourage it. We might *indoctrinate* someone to a belief in Marxism or Christianity, but if it were our intention that this belief was to be adopted whether the individual accepted it freely or not, we would hardly speak of this as *education*.

Thus there emerges the concept of a form of teaching which has several particular distinguishing features which enable us and encourage us to call it education. Education, it is claimed, on this analysis is a form of teaching which is concerned to develop **understanding** in the pupil rather than the mere assimilation of knowledge, to encourage **critical appraisal** of what is offered and to

promote some kind of **individual autonomy** rather than blind acceptance of the view of others. Furthermore, it is suggested that the use
of this term implies that the experience or knowledge offered is
positively regarded as being **valuable**, that it is felt to be valuable in
some sense in its own right, **intrinsically worthwhile**, desirable for
itself and not merely as instrumentally useful to the attainment of
purposes extrinsic to the educational activity itself. A major part of
the process is the attempt to ensure that pupils come to recognize
this value for themselves, that they not only acquire the knowledge
but learn to value it in the process.

To make these claims is not, of course, in itself to prescribe this
kind of approach for teachers and schools. It is merely to identify
this as one particular kind of teaching. It is also to identify it as the
kind of teaching most people have in mind when they use the term
'education'. For, as the examples just offered reveal, we do tend to
reserve the term for the kind of schooling which goes beyond mere
training or instruction and which is free of the kinds of deficiency
most of us would associate with indoctrination. We do tend to use
it only of forms of teaching of which we genuinely **approve** and,
even when we use it in ways which the above analysis might suggest
were inappropriate, it is often because we hope our use of it
will win the approval of others for what we are doing or describing.

This kind of analytical approach to the concept of education,
while not telling us what education is in the prescriptive sense in
which the two major views we explored earlier have attempted to
do, does draw our attention to the main fatures of **a particular
approach to schooling**, features which we might find appealing and
attractive and which we might therefore wish to adopt for these
reasons. At the very least it should help us to clarify our thinking
about schooling and to recognize several of the very different things
that that term embraces.

There are **many different things** which teachers do in schools and
which are thus included in the general and generic term 'schooling'.
They instruct children in certain things; they train them in certain
ways; they develop certain skills; they may even 'condition' or
indoctrinate them, intentionally or unintentionally. They also often
claim, however, that they are engaged in educating them and by
that they usually mean something different from those other things.
There is something different from those other things that some
teachers, and parents too, attempt to do in bringing up children,
something that goes far beyond mere instruction or training, and
which is certainly very different from, in fact diametrically opposed
to, indoctrination.

It is this that is normally called 'education' and it is that form of schooling which is not any form of 'programming' but, on the contrary, is specifically concerned to help the individual to resist and to defeat all attempts at such programming. It is concerned to develop **understanding, critical awareness, the ability to think for oneself**. It is important to recognize that such a form of upbringing is possible and that we need to evaluate its merits against those other possible kinds of schooling. This is the meaning given to the term education in this book and it is this form of schooling that it will be the main concern to explore.

This discussion may have reinforced our earlier claim about the **complexities** of the question 'What is education?' and may have explained and justified the devotion of a whole chapter to an exploration of that question. It will also have revealed some of the complexities of the study of education which were also mentioned earlier. It is with a brief discussion of that that this chapter concludes.

The study of education

It will be clear from what has been said in this chapter so far about the several views which can and have been taken on the question of what education is that it is going to be equally difficult to give one answer to the question of what the study of education entails. In part, this is also of course because in many respects it is a study which is still in its infancy, at least as a study in its own right and not as a sub-branch of philosophy or psychology or sociology. In the main, however, it is due to that **problematic nature** of educational theory and practice we have identified.

In many respects, therefore, it may be more productive to indicate what the study of education *is not* than to define what it is. Certainly it is easier to identify ways in which it has gone wrong, approaches which have proved to be not only unhelpful but also quite often damaging and inhibiting to educational practice.

First, we should note that the study of education **can never be a scientific activity**, not at least in the usual sense in which we describe certain kinds of study as science. Many people have attempted to study it in this way and to undertake research into educational practice of a supposedly scientific kind, but such approaches have never been capable of getting to grips with the essence of educational activity, so that they have seldom been very helpful to teachers wishing to improve their educational practice and have often even had the effect of inhibiting and restricting their practice. For while one can and might quite usefully make a study of teaching methods, one can only do this if the purposes of these methods, the principles underlying them and the value positions adopted are already agreed, since these purposes, principles and values cannot of themselves be the objects of scientific study. Science can explore and inform us about what *is* the case; it can never tell us what *ought* to be. In education, it cannot resolve for us the question of what kinds of thing we ought to be doing or which of those views of education we identified earlier we should adopt; it can only help us to decide, once we have made that kind of choice for other reasons, whether our practice is effective or not.

Too often, however, once the scientific stance is adopted those other issues tend to be ignored, so that a view of the study of education as a scientific activity is usually associated with **a failure to ask those important questions** about what education is that this chapter has raised. Scientific explorations may tell us, for example, how effective our approaches have been in helping children to learn to read. They can never help us with the questions of what it actually *means* to be able to read (just mouthing words, 'barking at print', understanding what we read and appreciating its quality, or whatever) or what are the purposes of helping children to acquire such abilities. They often as a result cause these aspects of teaching to be ignored and forgotten.

Scientific approaches to the study of education, then, may be helpful in some circumstances but they cannot and do not enable us to study education itself, and, indeed, they often lead to situations in which its very essence escapes us and what is really of value in it runs through our fingers. If they are to have any value at all, they must be **supplemented** by other kinds of approach.

It is for this reason that attempts have been made to see and to approach the study of education as something which must be tackled from several different perspectives, in particular from the perspectives of what have been called its **major contributory disciplines** – philosophy, psychology, sociology and, in some people's lists, history of education. There is no doubt that all of these disciplines have much light to throw on educational issues. That will be apparent from the earlier sections of this chapter, where all four of these kinds of study have been used or appealed to.

However, we must note at least three major weaknesses of this kind of approach. First, it offers us no basis upon which we can put together the different perspectives these disciplines offer into **a coherent whole**. Most of the schemes we are offered for this are simplistic in the extreme and reflect very little understanding of the disciplines themselves. Second, as a result, much of what is offered becomes **irrelevant** to educational practice, or at least comes to be regarded as such by students and teachers. It is the art of relating this to practice that is the most crucial element in the study of education – at least as far as practising teachers are concerned – if we are studying it with a view to developing and improving the practice of it and not merely as a particular sociological or historical phenomenon. This cannot be achieved by those contributory disciplines either collectively or individually. Third, it is again **the value dimension** which eludes this approach, since none of these disciplines can offer a satisfactory answer to the questions of how we are to decide on what we ought to be doing, what theory of education we ought to adopt, what our educational purposes should be. Therefore, this approach jeopardizes that central element, since, because it cannot itself cope with it, it more often than not leaves it out of consideration.

Some, of course, see it as the role of the philosopher in this kind of collaborative undertaking to answer those questions for us. We have already seen, however, that to take that line is to adopt a view of philosophy which mainstream philosophers have long been inclined – for very good reasons – to reject. It is also to invite a return to a very simplistic view of the study of education as having two elements, one concerned with ends, the other with means – idealist notions of what education ought to be coming from one quarter and scientific advice on how to make it so coming from the other. The view then is of educational theory as a body of 'beautiful thoughts' and of methodological 'know-how' or expertise – ideas, on the one hand, and devices for translating them into practice on the other. There are many problems with this rather naive view, the main one being that it **discourages any really critical appraisal** of those 'beautiful thoughts', largely because it sees them as given, as **non-problematic** and thus as beyond the scope of this debate. It thus pushes us very much towards that traditional view of education as a process of initiation into some kind of timelessly and eternally true knowledge and values.

What else, then, might the study of education be? The answer to that must be found in seeing it not as a device for generating any kind of universal knowledge about education in the way that the study of science aims to attain universal knowledge about the physical world and psychology even attempts to produce similar knowledge about our mental processes. Rather we must see it as a much more **individual matter**, a means by which we each come to a clearer notion of what *we* mean by education and how those of us who are teachers can practise it more effectively and those of us who are not can understand and evaluate what we see teachers doing or attempting to do. Education is more a matter of **values** than of knowledge; its practice depends more on **individual judgment** than on factual know-how'; it is an **art** rather than – or perhaps as well as – a science. In any sphere where judgments must be made, the aim must be to ensure that those judgments are as well informed as possible and thus as sound as possible, and the generation of theoretical perspectives must have as its central purpose assisting individuals to make such informed and sound judgments.

The study of education, then, is much more akin to modern approaches to philosophy than it is to any science. Its concern must be with **conceptual clarity** rather than with the generation of universal knowledge, and with assisting people to make **sound judgments** based on clear understanding rather than scientific applications of 'factual' knowledge. And the final proof of that must lie in the inadequacy of all that has been offered as universal knowledge in this field, its failure to have any kind of productive impact on education practice, and the continued debate about educational values which has proceeded for more than 2000 years unaffected by it.

Summary and conclusions

This chapter has attempted to reveal some of the complexities and uncertainties surrounding the study of education. It did this first by outlining the **two main views** of what education is and how we ought to set about practising it which have emerged during the period of more than 2000 years during which the debate has continued. The first of these, that which started with Plato's theory of education, takes a strong view of knowledge and of values, regarding these as firm and not subject to real disagreement or dispute, and thus sees education as the initiation of the young into this knowledge and those values. The second, which began with Rousseau's attempt to get away from the traditional view and which was taken up more recently by John Dewey, bases itself on a far more tentative view of knowledge and values, either as in a continuous state of evolution and change or even as perpetually shifting and uncertain. Thus it sees education more in terms of experience and of the development of powers of thinking than as the assimilation of largely fixed bodies of knowledge. It thus begins its educational planning from the point of view of the pupil to be educated rather than that of the knowledge to be transmitted.

We then considered a rather different approach to the question of what education is, that of the twentieth-century philosopher's technique of **conceptual analysis**. We saw that this, while no longer confidently leading us to any particular view of how education ought to be practised, was able to show us that there are and can be several different approaches to schooling, several different kinds and purposes of teaching, and that of those the one we are most inclined to use the term 'education' of is that whose purpose is to develop pupils' understanding, to help them to learn how to view matters critically and to come to their own conclusions on them, and to encourage them to value certain kinds of human activity for their own sake rather than in utilitarian or instrumental terms.

We next turned to a brief consideration of what all of that debate implies for **the study of education**, and we suggested that, because it is clearly a matter of values, because large areas of it are problematic, because there is much scope for the adoption of different views of and approaches to it, it can never be a form of scientific study. We also noted some of the inadequacies of attempting to study it as if it were a sub-branch of other disciplines, particularly again the failure of that kind of approach to capture that essential value element.

We finally concluded that the study of education is not a means of generating universal knowledge on educational issues but more a matter of developing personal understanding of the complexities of those issues as a basis for making informed judgments on them, whether as teachers concerned with educational practice or as laypersons concerned to evaluate, and even in some circumstances to advise, on such practice.

It is from that perspective and in that spirit that subsequent chapters will undertake to offer some further thoughts for the reader's consideration. For it is that form of education and its associated approach to the study of it that this book is concerned to elucidate.

Suggested further reading

Blenkin, G. M. and Kelly, A. V., *The Primary Curriculum*, second edition, Harper & Row: London, 1987, Ch. 1.

Curtis, S. J. and Boultwood, M. E. A., *A Short History of Educational Ideas*, University Tutorial Press: London, 1953.

Peters, R. S., *Ethics and Education*, Allen and Unwin: London, 1966, Ch. 1.

Rusk, R. R., *The Doctrines of the Great Educators*, Macmillan: London, 1957

Thompson, K., *Education and Philosophy: A Practical Approach*, Blackwell: Oxford, 1972.

Whitehead, A. N., *The Aims of Education*, Williams & Norgate: London, 1932.

2
The development of the educational system in England and Wales

The debate which we outlined in chapter 1 over what education is and how it should be planned and put into practice is one which will constantly be brought back to our minds as we look at the development of the educational system in England and Wales. (The Scots have a somewhat different system and are slightly touchy when this is not acknowledged, so that it will be the picture in England and Wales, and more recently Northern Ireland, we will be mainly concerned with here.) The perspectives we noted in chapter 1 will quickly emerge again as we consider the kinds of thinking which have underpinned the major developments – as, indeed, they do when one considers any aspect of education, as subsequent chapters will reveal.

Furthermore, the advent and development of state education for all, which will be our major concern, will soon be seen as bringing **a further complication** to that debate. For once education was extended to the masses and, further, made compulsory for them, the central question ceased to be 'What is education?' and came to be **'What form of schooling should we be providing for the whole of the child population?'**. It thus focused not so much on the theoretical debate over what education is but rather more on the practical issues of whether education as such should be provided for all pupils or whether the school system should not be used to provide most of them merely with basic literacy and numeracy along with some form of vocational training. This latter debate continues even today, although it is usually to be found in a far less stark form, and it is thus something we must keep well in mind as we review the growth of the state system over the last 100 years or so.

This chapter will begin with a brief outline of those different interpretations of, and suggested plans for, **mass education** which can be detected in the history of education in England and Wales since the advent of compulsory schooling in 1870. It will suggest that these different interpretations can be seen both in theoretical discussions of education, such as those offered by major government reports, and in the practical provision of schooling, and especially the legislation which has governed this. Against this backcloth, a review will be offered of the **major landmarks** in the development of the system up to the 1944 Education Act, a major bill which attempted to set both the scene and the tone for the post-war development of **an egalitarian system**. A brief discussion of the major features of that Act will then be undertaken as a basis for an examination of what has occurred since then, not least in order to see how far the idealism of that Act has been achieved, or even maintained, in subsequent developments.

Mass education

The issue of the form and content of education was not a subject for much heated debate until the advent of the notion of **education for all**. While access to education remained the privilege of those who could afford to pay for it, then, almost by definition, the form of educational provision they wished to purchase was not one that would provide children with vocational skills but rather one that would turn them into cultured gentlemen, give them access to the high culture of society – what Matthew Arnold, the great Head of Rugby School, called 'the best that has been thought and said' – and prepare them both for their responsibilities in government at whatever level and for a satisfying and productive use of the leisure which their wealth gave them. The industrial revolution changed to some extent the clientele of the public schools, since it produced many *nouveaux riches*, men who, with little education themselves, had made their wealth from the new industrial processes. These men, far from wanting their sons to learn skills and trades from which they would also make money, were much more concerned to give them the entrée to that leisured and cultured world of the upper classes.

The industrial revolution did, however, have its impact on society and on education in other respects. It emphasized **class distinctions**, not least by the emergence of a middle class. It raised questions about **the notion of 'high culture'** and its value. And it led ultimately to a recognition of the need to institute arrangements which would provide **educational opportunities for all** pupils, rather than just for those whose parents could afford to buy an education for them.

The notion of 'education for all'

It was this establishment of 'education for all' that heightened the debate about the form such education should take. For, from the outset, there were several different views which could be discerned. First, there were those who saw the introduction of mass education as a device for providing the working classes with the **basic skills and capabilities** that would enable them to make productive contributions to the industrial processes to which their subsequent lives would be devoted. The new industries required a workforce which had achieved basic literacy and numeracy, albeit of a somewhat minimal level, and it was claimed that the provision of the population with these basic skills was the prime purpose of the new schooling.

It is clear that most of those who advocated this view took it rather further and saw this as an opportunity to instil in all children certain kinds of moral value and attitude, in particular an acceptance of authority, as a device for ensuring law and order, as a **'gentling of the masses'**, as a means of attempting to ensure that the excesses of the French revolution should not be repeated in his country. Conversely, they were opposed to any kind of education which would encourage the masses to think too much for themselves.

Thus one major, and largely dominant, influence on the development of state education was that of those who saw it largely as **a preparation for industry and for good citizenship**, as a means towards industrial efficiency and the maintenance of the social order. This group has been called by Raymond Williams, in his very interesting book, *The Long Revolution*, **'the industrial trainers'**. It is perhaps worth commenting here that this is a view which still claims many adherents in the current educational debate.

The second group of people identified by Raymond Williams is that of those he calls **'the old humanists'**. These are those who argued for that more traditional view of education as the means of **access to the high culture** of society. Education is more than training for some industrial role, they claimed. Education is a process by which people come to appreciate in the full sense the greatest achievements of man, especially in literature and the arts. Schools exist to promote this process and to provide such access.

Again, we must note that this is a view which continues to be **prevalent**. There are still those who deplore the suggestion that schooling should be overtly utilitarian or vocational, who are saddened by the slow disappearance of Classical Studies from the school curriculum, by the increased emphasis on science and technology and the corresponding decrease of interest in the Humanities. We must also note, however, that this kind of view, while having much appeal – indeed, very few of those who press most strongly the vocational dimensions of schooling are prepared to advocate the complete denial of this view – must inevitably lead to some form of **élitism**, to a system of schooling which values and rewards only those pupils who are able to profit from the kinds of experience which satisfy the criterion of 'high culture', and thus to a loss of opportunities to those who, whether from ability or interest, cannot do so. This latter group will, of course, include a large proportion of pupils from **working class** backgrounds or from **ethnic minorities**, whose notions of culture are often very different from those encapsulated in the kind of curriculum 'the old humanists' would advocate.

It is this kind of consideration which led to the emergence of a third view of the purpose of mass education, that of the group which Raymond Williams calls **'the public educators'**. These take the view that everyone has **a natural right** to be educated and that the introduction of education for all reflects a determination on the part of society to recognize that right and to attempt to respect and to respond to it. They wish to see schooling as **a form of education** rather than training, but they further wish to define education in terms that go some way **beyond** the rather narrow concept of **access to high culture**. They are thus pressing for the establishment of a form of popular education based on a **new notion** of what education is, a notion which takes full account that such education is now to be offered to all pupils and not merely those who come from a certain kind of leisured and privileged background.

This is another view which one can still detect in the current debate. It is a form of education which successive Labour governments have endeavoured to attain in the years since 1944, most notably through the establishment of **comprehensive secondary schooling**, but it has to be confessed that it is a form of education which we seem to be as far from attaining in 1986 as we were in 1870. In part, this may well be owing to the fact that generations of educational theorists and practitioners and of politicians have failed to put flesh on the idea, to give it any kind of substance, so that educational provision has continued to be seen in terms of either its vocational usefulness or its cultural content.

This analysis of the major influences on the development of and thinking about mass education may be somewhat oversimplified, and it certainly makes no allowance for shifts of influence in response to particular circumstances, but there is no doubt that these three kinds of influence can be seen as one traces the development of the educatonal system of England and Wales. There is no doubt too that the system which has emerged reflects **a compromise**, an attempt to reconcile the essential differences of these views. Nor is there any doubt that the most significant influence has been, and continues to be, that of those whose emphasis is on **training and industrial efficiency**.

The presence and the significance of these influences will emerge very clearly as we now turn, against the backcloth they provide, to look at some major landmarks in the development of our system of schooling.

The development of the system up to 1944

The picture before 1870

Before the establishment of schools for all the nation's children in 1870, there existed in England and Wales no schools which were owned or maintained or staffed by any public body.   And no child was educated exclusively at the public expense. This was not the picture in all other European countries, since long before 1870 many other countries had established systems of state education. It was, however, the position in this country.

Two quite different kinds of education were available, neither of them provided by the state. The first was **the public school system**, oddly so called since it was a private system open only to those who could pay the fees demanded. This was the only form of secondary education available anywhere (and this in fact continued to be the case even after 1870).

The second kind of education was known as **'elementary' education** and was very much an inferior variety. It was essentially a product of isolated pockets of philanthropy and many of the schools were provided by one charitable organization or another. The largest of these were the British & Foreign Schools Society, established in 1810 by Joseph Lancaster, and The National Society, established in 1861 by Andrew Bell. The Church – or, rather, the churches, since more than one denomination was involved – also played a major role, as can be seen today from the many church schools which still exist and which still owe a direct allegiance to one religious foundation or another.

There were also **private schools** of other kinds. These included the so-called 'Dame' schools, which were intended for very young children and were usually little more than child-minding establishments, and some industrial schools in which children were taught the basic skills of reading and a variety of useful occupations – knitting and sewing, for example, for girls, and often carpentry for boys. The work of the children was sold to obtain money for the maintenance of these schools, so that often this led to an emphasis on that aspect of the curriculum at the expense of the teaching of reading and writing. As the demand for child labour in the factories increased so the opportunities for children from poor backgrounds to attend such schools diminished and this led to the appearance of the first **Sunday schools**, designed to take advantage of the one day of leisure these children had and also to keep them off the streets, to prevent the wild and unruly behaviour many of them were not unnaturally inclined to indulge in on their one day of relative freedom. We can see here both aspects of the early thinking of Williams's 'industrial trainers'.

The teaching in all of these elementary schools was usually of **a very low level**. The 'Dames', as was suggested earlier, were little more than baby-minders and the older children were often taught by men whose major characteristic was a failure to succeed in any other occupation (a very likely source of the low esteem in which schoolteachers continue often to be held), and whose teaching was sometimes a spare-time activity which had to fit in with the demands of other forms of employment. It is also worth noting that the early part of the nineteenth century saw the introduction of the **monitorial system** whereby older pupils were given the task of teaching the younger ones.

However, for a variety of reasons, **a very small proportion** of the child population had access to these schools. In 1820, it was claimed in the House of Commons that only one fourteenth to one fifteenth of children had access to any kind of formal education in England, and in Wales only one twentieth (the figure for Scotland given at the same time was between one ninth and one tenth). It must also be noted that for many of those children who did have some educational experience that experience was often **minimal**, rarely amounting to more than eighteen months or so and often being marked by **highly irregular attendance**.

State intervention

It was probably this paucity of provision as much as any other factor which led to the beginnings of **state intervention** in education with the decision taken by Parliament in 1833 to provide a sum of **public money** to support private subscriptions for the erection of schools for the education of the poorer classes. This was the first penny of public money (the actual sum was £20,000) spent on education in England and Wales, and subsequent years saw increasing amounts voted to support educational provision in a similar way. By 1846, the figure was £100,000 and by 1859, £836,900.

In spite of this, however, the provision remained **meagre**. The state did not own a single school; most children left school before they were eleven years old; education was not compulsory; attendance continued to be irregular; the average length of time spent by children at school was no more than four years; and there was general dissatisfaction with the provision the state was making, a dissatisfaction which was exacerbated when the government spent £78 million in the two years between June 1854 and March 1856 on the Crimean War.

This dissatisfaction led to the setting up of the **Newcastle Commission** which reported in 1861. Its task was 'to inquire into the present state of education in England, and to consider and report what measures, if any, are required for the extension of sound and cheap elementary instruction to all classes of people'. The Report expressed much of the prevalent dissatisfactions. In the schools inspected, the attendance amounted only to 76.1 per cent of the pupils on roll. As many as 17 per cent of pupils attended for less than fifty days per year. Attendance, even as irregular as this, was to be found only over about 4 years in the case of children between six and twelve years old. Only a minority remained at school after the age of ten. And the Commission considered that only about a quarter of pupils were receiving a satisfactory education, even as that was conceived and defined at that time. The evaluations it made of the quality of what its inspections revealed were as depressing and critical as its statistics – poor facilities, many totally unqualified teachers, a concentration on the progress of older children to the detriment of the younger, and curricula which were usually stronger in their moral and religious influence than in their intellectual stimulation.

In spite of this, however, the Report asserted that universal compulsory education was **neither attainable nor desirable**, and its specific recommendations did little more than introduce a system by which the entitlement of a school to public money would be based on the attendance record of its pupils and their performance in a public system of examinations. It thus led naturally to the era of **'payment by results'** which was established by Robert Lowe through the Revised Code of 1862.

It is clear that this system did improve attendance and it also prolonged the attendance of many children. It resulted too in more attention being given to the less able pupil – sometimes at the cost of the more able. And it lasted until 1897. However, because of the unwillingness to make education compulsory, 50 per cent of children continued to have no education at all, particularly those living in the larger cities. Schools continued to be unevenly distributed across the country. Attendance, although improved, was still irregular. And the leaving age for most chil dren was still low.

These were the considerations which prompted W. E. Forster, Vice-President of the Education Department under Gladstone's Liberal government, to sponsor the **Elementary Education Act** in 1870, an Act whose express intention it was, as Forster himself said in Parliament, 'to bring English education within reach of every English home, aye, and within the reach of those children who have no homes', and to do this by 'covering the country with good schools'. To this end, **School Boards** were to be established in every area with the responsibility of either supporting existing schools or providing schools themselves from the rates or both. These Boards were also to have the power to establish bye-laws, requiring the **compulsory attendance** of all children between the ages of five and thirteen. These bye-laws would also permit the fining of parents for the non-attendance of children.

The Act thus created **a dual system** of voluntary and publicly established schools which, in most essential respects, is the system we still have. More importantly, it gave local Boards the powers to make education compulsory and thus marks the real beginning of the state system.

Major landmarks between 1870 and 1944

The Act of 1870 did not in itself make education compulsory; it merely gave that power to the local School Boards. Some Boards used this power; the London Board, for example, passed a bye-law compelling the attendance of all children between the ages of five and thirteen. Many Boards, however, did not avail themselves of this power, so that, although attendance again rose, the picture was still a far from satisfactory one.

Several further laws were passed which were designed to improve the situation. The employment of children under ten was forbidden and **half-time schooling** was made **compulsory** for children between ten and fourteen. However, the law permitted so many exemptions to this latter rule that it did not fully succeed in achieving its purpose. It was left to Mr Mundella's Act of 1880 to make it compulsory for all School Boards to frame appropriate bye-laws requiring attend-ance. A school-leaving age of eleven for all pupils was established in 1893 and this was raised to twelve in 1899.

Furthermore, although the 1870 Act had attempted to provide access to education for all children, it had done this not by abol-ishing fees but by making it possible for fees to be waived in the case of children whose parents could not meet them. In 1891, parents were granted the right to demand **free education** for their children so that a majority of schools at that point ceased to charge fees.

By the beginning of the present century, then, a system of **universal schooling**, albeit somewhat minimal, had been established and the ground thus prepared for further growth in the twentieth century. The most important single focus of that growth was the development of **secondary education for all**.

The establishment of secondary education in the public sector

Before the present century, the term 'secondary education' in England and Wales referred only to that education offered in the private (or 'public') schools. The extension of educational opportunities to all pupils had embraced only elementary education and this was one major reason why it had continued to be a somewhat low-level offering. By the end of the nineteenth century, however, there was a growing movement in favour of extending secondary education provision, in order to make it available to more pupils than those whose parents could afford it.

The first step in this direction had been the creation, towards the end of the nineteenth century, of a **'seventh standard'** for those pupils who were able to stay on at school after the age of thirteen and the establishment in many places of one **'central school'** to accommodate such pupils. These latter soon became the **higher grade schools**, which were schools offering a secondary education in everything but the name, and can thus be seen as the beginning of a movement towards opening up opportunities for secondary education to a wider group of pupils and as evidence of a desire on the part of some people in authority that this should be done.

In 1894, a Commission was set up under Mr (later Viscount) Bryce, in part to advise on the ways in which an increasingly complicated system of educational administration might be streamlined but also 'to consider what are the best methods of establishing a well-organized system of secondary education in England'. The Commission reported in 1895. Its view of secondary education is an interesting one. 'In every phase of secondary teaching, the first aim should be to educate the mind, and not merely to convey information. It is a fundamental fault, which pervades many parts of the secondary education now given in England, that the subject (literary, scientific, or technical) is too often taught in such a manner that it has little or no educational value. The largest of the problems which concern the future of secondary education is how to secure, as far as possible, that in all schools and in every branch of study the pupils shall be not only instructed but educated.'

However, in case that quotation should lead us to see this Report as an unambiguous statement of the philosophy of the 'public educators', it is worth noting the echoing voice of the 'industrial trainers' in its claim elsewhere that secondary education 'is a process of intellectual training and personal discipline conducted with special regard to the profession or trade to be followed'.

The Report recommended the establishment of **a central authority** to coordinate and supervise the provision of both elementary and secondary education – **an Education Department with a Minister of Education**. Local administration, it proposed, should be in the hands of **local education authorities** to be established by the county councils and county and other boroughs. These local authorities would be responsible for making adequate provison of secondary education in their regions and coordinating this with existing elementary schools. It suggested too that the higher grade schools should be treated as secondary schools.

The national body proposed was established in 1899 and the Education Act of 1902, largely as a result of the work of Mr (later Sir) Robert Morant, created the suggested local education authorities to set up 'an organized system of elementary, secondary, and technical education'. Thus the base was established on which could be built the provision of secondary education for all.

Secondary education for all

The next step towards the achievement of secondary education for all was not long in following this Act. The Education Act of 1907 introduced a number of requirements of local authorities, preeminent among which was the requirement that any fee-paying secondary school which was in receipt of a grant from public funds must make at least 25 per cent of its admission places each year available free to children from the elementary schools. This marks the beginning of that system of **scholarships** which was to develop and grow throughout the first half of the present century and which was to see some, if not ultimately a great many, children, especially boys, from relatively impoverished backgrounds reaching not only secondary/grammar schools but also the universities.

Further developments were somewhat retarded by the events of the Great War between 1914 and 1918, but, before that war was over, H. A. L. Fisher had been appointed President of the Board of Education and had begun planning that reorganization of the national system that was to be encapsulated in the Education Act of 1918. That Act's intention was to ensure that every local authority would make available a system and a level of educational provision **suitable for every child** capable of profiting from these. A school leaving age of fourteen was established and local authorities were empowered to make this fifteen in their own area if they so wished. Provision had also to be made for those children who wished to stay on beyond the minimum leaving age and those who did leave at this age were to be required to attend a continuation school for at least 320 hours each year until they were sixteen years of age. This was subsequently to be raised to eighteen. All fees in elementary schools were abolished. And, to make all of these proposals easier to achieve, the employment of children under twelve was forbidden and that of children between twelve and fourteen was to be carefully controlled.

The period between the two World Wars, between the Fisher Act of 1918 and the Butler Act of 1944, is notable, first, for the **economic difficulties** which delayed the implementation of the provisions of the 1918 Act; second, for **the rise to power of the Labour Party** whose ambitions clearly included a major expansion of educational provision; and, third, for a number of **official reports** whose combined effect was to generate much pressure for the creation of a system of schooling which would go beyond the offering of access to secondary education to those capable of achieving it and by making it a reality **for every pupil regardless of ability**. The existing system offered elementary education for all and secondary education for those who won places at higher grade schools of one kind or another – grammar, technical or central schools – the others remaining in the all-age elementary schools. The pressure now was towards the abolition of those all-age schools and towards the establishment of **secondary schools for all pupils** – and thus, by implication, the establishment of **primary schools** too.

Concrete proposals for achieving this came from three reports published between 1926 and 1933 as a result of the work of the Consultative Committee under the chairmanship of Sir W. H. Hadow – *The Education of the Adolescent* (1926), *The Primary School* (1931) and *Infant and Nursery Schools* (1933).

The first of these proposed the **'decapitation'** of the all-age elementary schools, a gruesome-sounding process by which it was hoped to ensure that every child, regardless of ability, would pass from primary school to some form of secondary or post-primary education at the age of eleven-plus. This new form of secondary education would mean for some the opportunity to enjoy a secondary education in the established sense of the term; for the others it would mean **a broader kind of secondary education** of a practical and realistic rather than an academic character in selective and non-selective schools or departments. In effect, this meant the existence of **two kinds of secondary education** in two kinds of school – in the **grammar** schools for pupils planning to remain at school until 16 years of age or later, and in the **'modern'** schools for those-intending to leave at the statutory leaving age of 14. The Committee was most anxious that these secondary modern schools should not be seen as inferior forms of grammar school and thus that they should not ape the grammar schools' academic curriculum. The Report also stressed that the leaving age should be raised to fifteen as soon as possible. This was to have been established with effect from September 1939, but the outbreak of the Second World War in that very month caused its postponement until 1947.

The appearance of the primary school

Two major developments followed from the proposals made in the first Hadow Report. The first of these was the creation not only of the primary school itself but of a climate in which **primary education** could develop along **quite distinctive lines**. Clearly, the old elementary tradition was a major factor in this development, as was the consciousness that the primary school must offer an education which would prepare the pupils for what they would go on to experience in their secondary schools. Both of these influences can still be identified in the primary school curriculum and in the practice of education at that level. However, the subsequent Hadow Reports, and especially that of 1931, ensured that a third factor would also play its part, that of **the developmental concept of education** which we saw in chapter 1 had grown from the work of theorists like Rousseau, Froebel, Montessori and Dewey and which we also saw was being given added force by the work both of practitioners such as Susan Isaacs and A. S. Neill and of developmental psychology. It is this that has led to the emergence of a philosophy and an ethos in primary education which is still fundamentally different from that to be found in most secondary schools.

The emergence of the tripartite system

The second major development which followed from the Hadow Report of 1926 was the emergence of a **tripartite**, or in most places a **bipartite**, system of secondary schools. By the time of the 1944 Education Act, many local authorities had established their secondary modern schools and some had even created technical schools to stand alongside the existing grammar school provision. Furthermore, two subsequent reports of major significance, those of the Committees chaired by Sir William Spens (1938) and Sir Cyril Norwood (1943), supported not only the idea of broadening and diversifying the curriculum of secondary education but also that of providing it by means of the establishment of **three different kinds** of secondary school, each offering a different form of education – the **grammar** school, the **junior technical** school and the **secondary modern** school. Indeed, the Norwood Report, perhaps in an attempt to offer a theoretical justification for what was already an existing state of affairs in many parts of the country, argued for this tripartite provision on the grounds that children can be divided naturally into the three types for which these schools seek to cater. The continuing influence of Plato is not difficult to discern in this.

Thus there arose the idea of an **eleven-plus examination**, an adaptation of the already existing examinations for scholarships and free places at grammar schools, through which it was intended to discover into which type each pupil fell and thus to which kind of school he or she should be sent. The Norwood Report acknowledged the difficulties of achieving this with any degree of real accuracy at eleven-plus and thus recommended that there should be a curriculum which was broadly common to each of the three kinds of school for the first three years of secondary schooling to facilitate subsequent transfer at thirteen-plus for those whose special interests might develop along lines not identified at eleven-plus.

Both of these reports also considered the idea of the **'multilateral'** secondary school, a development which was being actively explored by the Labour Party, but, for different reasons, each rejected this kind of solution. However, both were at pains to stress that there should be **parity of prestige and esteem** between the three kinds of secondary school they proposed, the Spens Report using this as an argument for the abolition of fees in all three forms of school and the Norwood Report having the good sense to recognize that 'parity of esteem . . . cannot be conferred by administrative decree nor by equality of cost per pupil; it can only be won by the school itself'. Indeed, the Hadow Report of 1926 had itself stressed that its 'modern' schools should not become inferior forms of grammar school but should offer their own distinctive curriculum.

Thus these reports set the scene for the reorganization of secondary education which was to be undertaken in the euphoria following victory in the Second World War.

The 1944 Act and subsequent developments

The 1944 Education Act, which was largely the work of R. A. Butler, was **the most comprehensive** of all the English Education Acts, but it was not revolutionary in so far as it was merely an attempt to give legal force to a number of developments which, certainly in some parts of the country, were already well advanced. It was, however, like the establishment of the free National Health Service, very much the product of the optimism of victory and reflected an attempt to build a fine new world in which the disillusionment of the 1930s would be forgotten, in which the privations of war would be shown to have led to the emergence of **a vastly improved social system**, in which all children would be given more generous opportunities to develop than most had hitherto even dreamed of, and in which the needs of a new age, both social and technological, would be met by **a new educational system** better adapted to those needs. Although the principles of the Act, then, were those which had emerged from the debate of the 1920s and 1930s, its scale was far grander than that debate had envisaged.

Its main provisions were, first, that the Board of Education should become **a Ministry** *under* **a Minister of Education with a seat in the Cabinet**; second, that **the school leaving age be raised** to fifteen – this came into effect in April 1947 – and again to sixteen 'when it became practicable' (in the event, not until 1972); and, third, that local authorities be required to provide **three successive stages of education** – primary, secondary and further – and to contribute 'towards the moral, mental and physical development of the community by securing that efficient education, throughout these stages, shall be available to meet the needs of the population of their area'.

Undoubtedly, the major feature of the Act was that it finally severed secondary from primary education, abolishing once and for all the all-age elementary schools. In doing so, however, it did not dictate to local authorities how they must organize secondary schooling.

In view of the strong preference for tripartism which we have just seen was expressed by the two reports which were most influential in the years immediately preceding the passing of the 1944 Education Act, it is surprising that that Act did not require local authorities to reorganize their provision of secondary schools on tripartite lines. There is no mention in the Act of grammar, technical or modern schools; it merely speaks of **education for all 'according to age, aptitude and ability'** and gives local authorities complete discretion as to how they will provide this. That it did not recommend tripartism can only be owing to the influence on the Act of the thinking of the Labour Party expressed by the Labour members of what in 1944 was still a wartime coalition government. That thinking continued to include the concept of a **multilateral** form of secondary schooling and the Act, by refraining from giving clear directions over the form that secondary education must take, left open the possibility of this kind of development.

The implementation of the 1944 Act

Some local authorities took immediate advantage of this to establish **comprehensive** forms of secondary schooling. All authorities were required to submit their plans to the newly established

Ministry of Education by 1 April 1946. (A three-month extension was later granted, and the London County Council – the forerunner of the Inner London Education Authority – was given an extension of twelve months, reflecting the fact that it faced the most difficult task of rebuilding after extensive bombing, including the more recent effects of the flying bombs.) Most of the country's authorities did, as one might have expected, submit plans for some form of **tripartite** organization of secondary education (albeit often without the technical strand), but almost one in eight had decided to introduce **bilateral** schools, schools containing under one roof two of the elements of tripartism, and about the same proportion were planning to build **comprehensive secondary** schools.

A major factor in this latter decision clearly was the existence of Labour-controlled local councils. Another factor, however, which must not be ignored was the extent of **rebuilding** which was necessary as a result of bomb damage. Where this was especially great and necessitated the building of many new schools, then sometimes, as, for example, in Coventry, the opportunity was taken to build these on comprehensive lines, an approach which was in any case more cost-effective in terms of both initial and recurrent expenditure. Conversely, where little rebuilding was necessary, and especially where progress had already been made before the war to create secondary modern schools, the obvious solution was to retain some form of tripartism.

It may be worth noting at this point some of the other problems which local authorities faced in the first years of the implementation of the 1944 Act. In addition to the rebuilding of schools which many of them had to attend to – not always because of bomb damage but often also because all building and rebuilding had been at a standstill since 1939 – they had to give priority to the building of **homes**. Second, they also had to cater for an **increased population** of schoolchildren, both as a result of the raising of the school leaving age to fifteen in 1947 – described by Ellen Wilkinson, as Minister of Education, as 'an act of faith rather than reason' – and as an effect of the enormous increase in the birth-rate immediately after the war, **the 'bulge'** as it came to be known. This latter development increased the school population by two million pupils between 1945 and 1958. Last, some were affected by a change in the **distribution** of the population as a result of the exigencies of war and the post-war establishment of new towns, a shift which resulted in the fact that such buildings as actually existed were not always in the places where they were needed.

The growth of the comprehensive ideal

In the period immediately following the Second World War, as we have just seen, about one local authority in eight was planning to establish comprehensive secondary schools. By 1965 this kind of reorganization was **required of all of them**. There were two main reasons for that rapid development. The first of these was the influence of the Labour Party at both national and local levels. The establishment of a universal system of comprehensive secondary education became a major plank in the Labour Party's platform, so that Labour-controlled local councils worked hard to introduce some form of comprehensive system at the regional level and eventually, in 1965, a Labour government established these at the national level.

There was another factor, however, one that clearly had also had its effect in hardening support for comprehensive education in the Labour Party itself, and that was the growing evidence of **the effects of tripartism**. The underlying philosophy of the 1944 Act had been egalitarian; its concern had been to establish an educational system which would ensure equality of educational opportunity for all children, whatever their background. Yet evidence of all kinds appeared in the years following that Act to suggest not only that we were still a long way from achieving this but also, and in particular, that the tripartite system was itself a major reason for this.

The problems of tripartism

Several features of tripartism have been identified as major barriers to the attainment of a fully egalitarian system of secondary education. First, the secondary modern schools did not develop their own distinctive curriculum but continued to ape that of the grammar school. Except for the fact that one would be unlikely to find the Classics there, it would be difficult to distinguish a typical secondary modern pupil's timetable in the 1950s and 1960s from that of his or her grammar school counterpart.

There were several good reasons for this. There was, for example, an enormous discrepancy in the **scale** of grammar school provison from one local authority to another, some offering this form of education to only 10 per cent of pupils, others to more than 40 per cent. In this kind of context, it is not surprising that secondary modern schools, especially in the areas where grammar school provison was lowest, felt they had to provide their pupils with comparable opportunities to those available to their contemporaries elsewhere. There were also the manifest **inaccuracies of the eleven-plus** which resulted in many pupils being misplaced, and this offered no encouragement to the establishment of different forms of curriculum. A further factor was the refusal of some authorities to provide separate junior technical schools. The secondary modern school, then, found itself attempting to compensate for all of these inadequacies and thus quite incapable of developing its own distinctive curriculum.

At first, such schools were not permitted to enter pupils for the newly established General Certificate of Education (GCE) examinations, although it was clear that many of their pupils were following comparable courses to those of the grammar schools and were capable of gaining passes at this level. Many schools got around this rule by persuading parents to enter their children privately and at their own expense or by entering pupils for other examinations, such as those provided by the College of Preceptors. All of this was most unsatisfactory and it led to the establishment of a committee of enquiry whose report, *Secondary School Examinations other than the GCE* (the Beloe Report) was published in 1960 and recommended the institution of **a new examination**, the Certificate of Secondary Education (CSE). This development we will consider in more detail in chapter 4.

The secondary modern school, then, for very good reasons, continued to offer a curriculum which was in most respects the same as that of the grammar school. It was **not different** nor distinctive; it thus was **watered down** and inferior. And so a second major flaw in the tripartite system was its **failure to achieve** that **parity of prestige and esteem** which we earlier saw all of the pre-war reports had stressed as essential. The claim which emanated from the Ministry of Education in 1947 that 'as the modern schools develop . . . it will become increasingly common for them [the parents] . . . to select the modern school as the one best suited to their children's requirements on grounds unhampered by consideration of prestige' seems in retrospect to have been based on an alarming under-estimation of the prestige of the grammar school in most parents' eyes. The secondary modern was never able to shake itself free of its senior elementary roots. The eleven-plus, supposedly diagnostic, continued to be seen as, and to be called by many, 'the scholarship', and selection for the secondary modern was regarded as 'failure' to 'pass' this test. Parents will always judge a school by the qualifications its pupils attain and, especially, the kinds of career it offers access to. Judged on these grounds, the secondary modern could never achieve parity of prestige or esteem.

A third major problem of tripartism was **the inaccuracy of the eleven-plus** selection procedures. These were very carefully planned and carried out, but for many reasons, most of them beyond anyone's control (such as variations in the rates at which children develop intellectually), the level of inaccuracy was such that one child in eight was wrongly placed at eleven-plus. Nor did the 'fail-safe' procedure of a second look at thirteen-plus succeed in correcting many of these errors. The idea itself that children be neatly allocated to one of three categories is highly simplistic, but the practice of attempting to do this at the age of eleven demonstrated that, even if the theory were sound, it could not be done to any acceptable level of accuracy, at least at that age.

Wastage of talent

Evidence of the failure of tripartism to achieve the ambitions encapsulated in the 1944 Act emerged from various sources and in many guises throughout the 1950s, and most of this highlighted the inadequacies of the selection procedure at eleven-plus. The most alarming feature of this was the evidence of a massive **wastage of talent** from the school system. A government report on *Early Leaving*, issued in 1954, offered statistical evidence that a very large proportion of the most able pupils was leaving school at fifteen with no formal qualification at all, and this evidence was soon confirmed by similar research recorded in the Crowther Report, *15 to 18*, published in 1959.

There were two disturbing aspects to this evidence. The Crowther Report itself stressed that the education system had two aims or purposes. First, it had to recognize that it represented **a national investment** made by the community 'to provide an adequate supply of brains and skill to sustain its economic productivity'. Second, however, it was 'one of **the social services** of the welfare state', a **'human right'** which 'exists regardless of whether, in each individual case, there will be any return'. On both of these counts, the evidence of wastage clearly indicated a major failure of the education system to fulfil its functions.

Clearly there were factors in **the home background** of many pupils which contributed to this failure and there was much research undertaken into these factors during the 1950s. It was also apparent however, that there were elements in **the education system** itself which were not only exacerbating these factors but also adding to them. Pre-eminent among these elements was the system of **selection** for a tripartite form of secondary schooling.

There thus emerged an overwhelming case for some kind of **non-selective**, comprehensive secondary education, which when added to the social and ideological case, resulted in the establishment in 1965 by a Labour government of a requirement that all local authorities organize, or if necessary reorganize, their secondary provision on comprehensive lines.

Comprehensive schools and comprehensive education

Several different versions of comprehensive secondary schooling have emerged not only in response to this requirement of central government but also in those areas which had already 'gone comprehensive'. In some places, **middle schools** have been established, along the lines discussed in the Plowden Report on primary education which was published in 1967. These are schools to which children move at the age of eight or nine and in which they stay until twelve or thirteen when they move on to secondary education. Other authorities have adapted this kind of arrangement by moving all pupils into comprehensive secondary schools at eleven and then moving them on into **selective schools** (in some cases the selection has been self-selection) at fourteen or fifteen. Some have kept all together until the statutory leaving age, which has been sixteen since 1972, or the first public examination at sixteen-plus, and opened **sixth form colleges** for those who wish to take their full-time education further. Others have establised large **'all-through'** comprehensive schools catering for all pupils in the area from eleven to eighteen.

The one thing they all have in common is that they **delay** any overt procedures of selection until an age later than eleven-plus, and sometimes to a time when the process of selection can be one in which children and parents are themselves involved rather than the largely impersonal and mechanical device which the eleven-plus test undoubtedly was. They also minimize the more overtly divisive effects of tripartism.

In practice, however, selection, even as early as eleven-plus goes on. This is often the effect of the organization of the comprehensive schools, which have sometimes been little more than a tripartite system under a single roof, with grammar, technical and modern **'streams'** or **'bands'** replacing the separate schools but nevertheless requiring the selection and the allocation of pupils to them at an early age. In some places too, the practices adopted by local authorities to ensure a full spread of ability in all comprehensive schools, while motivated by the good intentions of ensuring that all are fully comprehensive, have exacerbated this problem, not least by necessitating the retention of an eleven-plus testing procedure to make possible the allocation of pupils to the appropriate 'band'.

Thus the labelling of pupils at eleven plus, along with the taking of crucial decisions about their future at that age, has continued, if only now for purposes of **internal organization**. Even where the schools themselves have adopted a policy of unstreaming or de-streaming or mixed-ability grouping in the early years, this kind of categorization of pupils has sometimes had to continue in the interests of **local authority organization**.

A second major factor in the continuance of this process of early selection has been **the form of curriculum** offered and, in particular, the need to make crucial curricular choices at an early age. We will consider in some detail many of the issues relating to the school curriculum in chapter 4. We must note here, however, the importance of the kind of curriculum we adopt for the achievement, or non-achievement, of equality of educational opportunity. At a simple level, it is a matter of subject choices. If a pupil does not start to learn a second language, for example, in the first year or two of secondary schooling, it becomes very difficult to pick this up later, and certain avenues, both educational and vocational, can thus be closed at too early a stage. At a more complex level, the choice of 'options' at the beginning of the fourth secondary year can also be crucial for a pupil's future prospects.

More serious, however, are the effects of much of the **thinking** about the secondary school curriculum on this issue. It has been the practice, and often also the official policy, to devise two or three **quite different curricula** for pupils of secondary age, thus perpetuating tripartism in curricular form. The 'grammar' curriculum continues for those both sufficiently motivated and intellectually able to pursue it; often a 'technical' curriculum is available too; and for the rest a practical and vocational curriculum, too often not measuring up to those criteria of education we discussed in chapter 1 but falling more into our definitions of 'instruction' or 'training' or even, at worst, forms of 'indoctrination'.

This has been the explicit recommendation of some quite influential national documents. The **Newsom Report**, for example, in 1963 called itself *Half Our Future* and thus clearly divided the half it was concerned with, the less able, from the rest. For there it recommended a curriculum 'which is more "realistic" or more "practical"'. This, it was felt, would be, and would be recognized by the pupils as being, much more relevant to their needs than a watered-down grammar school curriculum. This suggestion was taken up by many secondary schools, especially in response to the problems of the 'extra year' created by the raising of the school leaving age to sixteen in 1972 which the Newsom Report also recommended. And this development has been more recently reinforced by the advent of such courses as those sponsored by the **Department of Trade and Industry** through the **Manpower Services Commission (MSC)**, especially those under the aegis of the **Technical and Vocational Education Initiative (TVEI)**.

We need to note three things about this kind of development. First, it necessitates the maintenance of those divisive procedures of **selection** which were a root problem of tripartism. Second, it represents a failure to achieve **a comprehensive curriculum**, in spite of the creation of comprehensive schools. Put into Raymond Williams's terms, it represents a failure of the case put by the 'public educators' for the development of a new curriculum, specially suited to the needs of mass education, and triumph for the 'industrial trainers' in some kind of alliance with the 'old humanists' – a curriculum framed in terms of the high culture of society for an intellectual élite and a vocational training in basic skills, along with some 'gentling of the masses', for the rest. Third, as a result of these developments, we are almost as far from attaining **the egalitarian ideals** of the 1944 Education Act as we were in 1944 itself. There is little evidence that access to educational opportunity has significantly increased for those pupils from materially and/or intellectually impoverished backgrounds, and the barriers to its improvement remain the same.

In part, it is a fundamental **curricular issue**. This we will consider in chapter 4. In part, it is a result of important recent developments in the realm of **political influences** on education. These we will examine in our next chapter. We must briefly note here, however, that it is also a result of the confusion which surrounds the notion of educational equality, and we will bring this chapter to a close with a brief exploration of that.

Equality of educational opportunity

A major reason why we have not achieved that educational equality to which the 1944 Education Act pledged us is that it is possible to interpret in at least **two ways** what the notion of equality of educational opportunity implies for educational practice. It is thus too imprecise a term to provide any clear indications of how the education system might be organized to achieve it. What is more, these different interpretations can be detected even in the pronouncements of those whose political ideology makes them the staunchest advocates of educational, and indeed social, equality.

What has been called the **'strong'** or the **'meritocratic'** interpretation of equality of educational opportunity commits us to no more than providing free **access** to education at all levels for those who can prove themselves to be capable of benefitting from what is provided there. On this interpretation, then, equality has been achieved if we ensure that every child who can cope with a grammar school education has access to such an education, and selection of pupils for this by the fairest tests we can devise is perfectly compatible with the notion of educational equality interpreted in this way. Indeed, it might be argued that we would have a fair and equal education system, on this definition, even if we operated a five-plus test to decide which children should be admitted to the school system.

It is worth noting here that this kind of view continues to be prevalent. Certainly, it is this view which lies behind the thinking of those whose main concern continues to be the provision of access to the academic curriculum of grammar schools and of institutions of higher education for all children regardless of their social or ethnic origins. It must also be mentioned, however, that this kind of view does not require of us that we make any provision for the rest. Thus to provide the rest with a practical, realistic and vocational curriculum is quite compatible with this interpretation. Indeed, it goes some way beyond what it demands.

The second kind of interpretation has been called the **'weak'** or **'democratic'** interpretation. This requires of us that we make **suitable provision for all pupils**. This commits us to that view offered by the Crowther Report, a view of education as a **human right**, as 'one of the social services of the welfare state'. Such a view cannot rest content with a system that offers full educational provision to the able, and thus inevitably the socially privileged, pupils, while offering the rest some kind of training combined with social 'gentling'. It lays on us the task of devising a curriculum which offers **genuinely educational experiences to all pupils**. Such experiences clearly need not be the same for all pupils (this is one of the inevitable confusions that follows from the use of a seemingly precise term like 'equal'); but they should be **of equal educational value and merit**.

It is this interpretation that the 1944 Act pointed us towards when it spoke of **'education for all according to age, aptitude and ability'**. And it is this form of equality we have palpably failed to achieve. For to achieve it requires the kind of rethinking of education provision and of the curriculum which the 'public educators' have long been calling for but which, as we saw just now, current developments are taking us further away from. Those current developments we will consider in our next chapter and the underlying curricular issues we will address in chapter 4.

Summary and conclusions

This chapter has outlined the slow development of the national system of education in England and Wales. It has done this against the background of three competing ideologies – that advocating the use of the public system to provide the masses with **basic**

training, both vocational and social; that pressing for access to the **high culture**, the academic curriculum; and that urging on us that we need to devise **a totally new educational curriculum** to meet the needs of the vast range of the school population.

We noted how the development of the system had progressed by way of, first, the provision of some **public funding** for schools, then the insistence on **compulsory attendance** and next the offering of **secondary education for all**, by progressive raising of the minimum leaving age, and finally by the introduction of **comprehensive secondary schooling**.

We concluded by claiming that, in spite of all these developments, we are still some way from the achievement of a fully equal and egalitarian system and it was suggested that, at least in part, this may be due to a lack of clarity over what that really implies.

We have seen that over the last 100 years or so there have been many assertions of a view of education not dissimilar from that we considered in chapter 1 and of the need to make this kind of education available to all. We have also seen that the realities of educational provision continue to make this improbable. Whether current official policy is likely to aggravate or to alleviate this situation may become clearer after we have explored some of the recent political influences on education in our next chapter.

Suggested further reading

Benn, C. and Simon, B., *Half Way There*, Penguin: Harmondsworth, 1972

Curtis, S. J., *History of Education in Great Britain*, University Tutorial Press: London, 1948.

Downey, M. E. and Kelly, A. V., *Theory and Practice of Education: An Introduction*, third edition, Harper & Row: London, 1986.

Gordon, P. and Lawton, D., *Curriculum Change in the Nineteenth and Twentieth Centuries*, Hodder & Stoughton: London, 1978.

Williams, R., *The Long Revolution*, Chatto & Windus: London, 1961, Pelican Books: London, 1965.

3
Politics and education

In tracing the growth of the educational system in England and Wales
in chapter 2, we were of course looking at a sequence of acts of
political intervention in education. Most of these acts, however, as we
saw, were directed at effecting changes in the **organization of schooling**
– the progressive raising of the school leaving age, for example, the
institution of secondary education for all, and the insistence that this
be achieved by some form of comprehensive schooling. We also
noted that too often the actualities of schooling, the form of curriculum offered, had not changed to match these organizational
developments; many of the changes proved to be cosmetic only.

Several important things follow from this and two in particular
we must note here since they will be the main concerns of this
chapter. First, this **lack of direct political intervention in the curriculum** itself has left development there open to influences of a
more indirect and subtle kind. And, second, because the effects of
these influences have not always been of a kind our political masters
or mistresses have approved of – especially at a time when rapid
technological development of a kind requiring curricular changes
has been accompanied by economic recession which has reduced
the budget available for education – **in more recent times** it has
become official government policy **to intervene more positively** in
the school curriculum.

This chapter, then, will set out to do three main things. First, it
will consider some of the sources of **indirect and informal influences**
on the curriculum and explore some of the effects of their impact.
Second, it will offer a theoretical analysis of **the interplay between
politics and education** and the implications of this for the processes
of education. And, finally, against the theoretical backcloth this
analysis will provide, it will trace and evaluate the **recent movement
towards more direct political control** of the school curriculum.

First, however, it may be worthwhile to note some more general
points about the interrelationship of politics and education.

Politics and education

At every level and from every perspective, education and politics are **closely interlinked**. Whatever form it takes, education must be some kind of preparation of the young for the social and political context in which their adult lives will be conducted. Nor can that social and political context be ignored in their upbringing. Whether the concern is merely to initiate them into the values and customs of their society, as is often the case in primitive societies, or to encourage them to challenge, question and possibly change those values and customs, the political dimension must be there. And even those who argue that the prime concern of education must be for the development of the individual rather than the needs of society must recognize that their stance is itself a political stance.

It is for this reason that educational theorists, from the time of Plato on, have also been political theorists and have offered us theories of education which have clearly derived from **their political positions and viewpoints**. Indeed, we saw in chapter 1 that for Plato education was not a central concern: rather his interest in it was an offshoot of his concern with the interrelated issues of moral and political philosophy. We saw there too that this connection was still to be recognized much more recently in the work of John Dewey, whose theory of education only has meaning when seen in the context of his commitment to a democratic political organization.

Chapter 2 revealed that at the level of **practical provision** too it is impossible to divorce education from politics. For all the events we listed there as contributing to the progressive development of the educational system in England and Wales were prompted by political motives – whether ideological, such as the pressure from the Labour party for comprehensive secondary education, or economic, such as the desire to ensure a properly skilled workforce. Indeed, one can make little sense of the history of education unless one views it against its political background, both ideological and economic.

Education is **a powerful political tool**. It is concerned to change people's attitudes and values. Clearly this is of great political significance. It is for this reason that control of the education system has been regarded by politicians as being so important. In most revolutionary situations, for example, control of schools and teachers has been seen as secondary only to control of systems of communications, even on some occasions important enough to warrant the execution of teachers unsympathetic to the ruling ideology. And it is for this reason that direct political control of the content of schooling is taken for granted in most countries, often to the extent of specifying most of the content of the curriculum of every school.

Where such direct control is not practised, as has been the case in England and Wales until quite recently, the development of the curriculum is to a much greater extent in the hands of the teachers themselves and is open to influences of a more indirect kind. It is to a consideration of what that implies that we now turn.

Informal political influences

The absence of direct political control of the actual content of the school curriculum has had several effects on the development of education in England and Wales. In the first place, it has led to teachers enjoying far **more professional freedom or autonomy** in relation to the development of the curriculum and the making of curricular decisions than their counterparts have had in most other societies. This we will consider more fully later in this chapter.

Second, this freedom has in turn created a climate in which the possibility exists for much **more rapid curriculum development** and for the development of the curriculum on **educational** rather than **economic** criteria. Thus, until recently, the primary school had been able to develop an approach to education far in advance of what is to be seen in most other places and much more akin to that 'progressive' view of education we discussed in chapter 1. In particular, as we shall see when we examine curricular questions in more detail in chapter 4, it has been able to get away from the idea that education is to be defined in terms of its **content**, a view that it is virtually impossible to avoid when curricular decisions are made centrally.

Third, however, this has also led to the possibility of much more **idiosyncratic** development. Many would argue that the latter is what is needed since education is a highly individual matter, but others have been concerned about the variations in level and quality that this might make possible. That too we must consider in more detail in chapter 4. It is worth noting here, however, that extreme kinds of idiosyncratic development are most unlikely in the context of all the **constraints** to which schools and teachers are exposed, constraints which derive from such sources as the organization of schools, the allocation of resources and, above all, the demands of the public examination system.

This last point brings us to the other major aspect of the absence of direct political control of the curriculum. That is the fact that it becomes a prey to these **indirect influences** and also to the attempts of various **interest groups** to influence it either through the manipulation of these indirect sources of influence or by attempts to persuade teachers of the importance of those things they wish to introduce into the curriculum or maintain there.

Interest groups

Many such interest groups can be identified not only in the history of the development of the educational system but also in the present educational scene. The most notable of such groups, and certainly the ones which have probably been in evidence longest, are the various **religious bodies** who were instrumental in first establishing many of our schools and colleges, who currently retain control of these and who still represent a powerful lobby in educational decision-making. It is worth noting that the only legal requirement laid on schools and local authorities in relation to their curricula by the 1944 Act was the inclusion of a daily act of worship and a regular exposure of all children (except those whose parents expressly withdraw them) to religious instruction. That requirement remains and offers the most convincing evidence possible of the continuing power of the churches in relation to the school curriculum.

Central and local government influences

A second source of influence is **the government** itself. Although hitherto it has done little to exercise direct control over the curriculum, it has from time to time, as we have seen, set up **Royal Commissions** to look into certain aspects of education and the reports of those Commissions have often been highly effective in persuading teachers to introduce changes, even if these have never been required by subsequent legislation. The impact of the Newsom Report on the curriculum of secondary schools, which we noted in chapter 2, is an especially good example of this. Increasingly too, what is offered in schools, and in colleges, is being governed by **the allocation of resources** and this is a powerful source of influence at both central and local government levels.

Parents and pupils

The consumers of education, parents, employers and even the pupils themselves, also represent a category of interest group whose influence on education is not to be ignored. Often that influence is exercised by quite formal and organized procedures. At the national level, such organizations as the Confederation of British Industry (CBI) and the National Association of Parent/Teacher Associations (NAPTA) offer regular comment on what is going on in schools and press their own views of what should be happening on teachers and others responsible for this. At the local level, the same groups will make their voices heard through local organizations, through Parent/Teacher Associations and/or through membership of the governing bodies of schools. Sometimes, too, parents in particular will express and urge their views as individuals in relation to the education of their own children.

Higher education

Another source of such influence is **the institutions of higher education**. These too have a vested interest in what schools are doing and the universities especially, through their **control of the public examination system** at GCE 'O' and 'A' levels and through their specification of their own entrance qualifications, have had the strongest possible means of making their views felt. The history of the last twenty years or so can offer numerous examples of proposed changes in the examination system, especially at sixth form level, mostly designed to broaden the curriculum for what seemed like good educational reasons which have come to nothing because of the opposition of universities to changes which might reduce the level of specialist knowledge reached by students prior to entering on their degree courses.

Teachers' associations

Last, the teachers themselves, particularly through the many national **subject associations** which exist, have created their own pressure groups to influence each other towards certain kinds of curricular provision. Again recent years can offer many examples of developments which have been halted because they seemed to offer some kind of threat to the status of certain well-established groups of teachers and others which have been promoted for the opposite kind of reason. A good example of the former is the opposition to the development of Integrated Studies in secondary schools, most of which was mounted by representatives of traditional subjects, such as history and geography, whose continued presence on the curriculum this kind of development might have put at risk. An example of the latter is the development of a subject such as Rural Studies, a development which can be shown to owe more to the skilful tactics of teachers of that subject, in, for example, establishing it as an accepted subject in the sixteen-plus examinations programme, than to any educational merits it may possess, and, indeed, even, some would say, at the cost of those educational merits.

Thus the curriculum has become a warring ground for many **conflicting ideologies** and many factors competing for control. Few decisions are made on grounds of purely educational considerations; most are made to forward particular intersts. It is this that has led some theorists in recent times to see all schooling as a form of **indoctrination**, as the imposition of the values of that ideology which is dominant and which has the power to influence the content of the curriculum. Some have even gone so far, as a result, to recommend **the abolition of schools**, a **'deschooling'** of society. This kind of thinking has led to the emergence of some interesting ideas within **the politics of knowledge** and we would not be doing justice to an exploration of the interrelationship of politics and education if we did not spend some time considering these ideas.

The politics of knowledge

We noticed earlier that there are numerous examples in history of the use by politicians of education as **a tool for achieving their ends**. This certainly is what explains Hitler's well-known interest in the upbringing of German youth and it is also a major reason why Lenin showed great concern for what schools should be doing. Nor is this merely something which can be identified in practice; it is also argued cogently at the theoretical level. Plato, for example, as we saw in chapter 1, had no qualms about urging that, for a majority of children in his ideal society, schooling should do little more than offer them a training in obedience. They were to learn how they should behave – not why they should behave in the prescribed ways – and to accept the dictates of their betters, the rulers, the philosopher-kings, those who had been fully educated and were thus able to offer them instructions based on superior knowledge.

It is this that has led some theorists in recent times, especially within the field which has come to be known as the sociology of knowledge, to claim that this is what education always is, that it can be no more than this, that it must always be the most powerful device the dominant factions in any society have for **controlling** the rest. Their argument goes something like this.

The sociology of knowledge

There is no objectively true knowledge, as Plato and others have claimed, and thus there is no objectively valid justification for offering any particular kind of knowledge to pupils. Knowledge is **socially constructed**; it is created not by God but by human beings;

in fact, it is created **by particular groups** within society; and values especially are the creation of such groups. A selection must be made of the knowledge to be transmitted in schools and, inevitably, that selection will be made according to **the values, the beliefs and the ideology** of those making that selection. What is more, those values and beliefs, that ideology, will be implicit in the knowledge selected for transmission and will thus be communicated to those young impressionable minds which are the recipients of it. Thus a form of **indoctrination** will occur as the values of the dominant group, that group which controls the curriculum, are communicated in this way to the next generation.

Education and the working class

It was this kind of thinking that led D. H. Lawrence a long time ago to oppose the introduction of compulsory state education for the working classes. For this, he felt, could only have the effect of ignoring and devaluing **the natural culture** of the working classes and distorting their lives by replacing it with an **alien culture**. Education stood for an intellectual understanding of existence; the understanding of the working class was based rather on the direct contact with the world of the craftsman. More recently, studies have confirmed that **a conflict of values** has often resulted when children from working-class families have been selected for highly academic forms of education in grammar schools and subsequently at universities.

D. H. Lawrence was not directly claiming that this was a form of social control; he was much more concerned with its cultural effects and dimensions. Others, more recently, have wished to impute more sinister motives and more overtly political effects to the institution of mass education. It is precisely this which lies behind the notion we considered in chapter 2 that the main purpose of the introduction of mass education in the United Kingdom was **a 'gentling of the masses'**.

The view of education as concerned to transmit and to ensure the acceptance of certain moral and social values is tenable, and even justifiable, if one can accept that the knowledge and values which are being transmitted and imposed are superior or even, as Plato argued, universally valid. If there is an inherently superior value in certain aspects of the culture of our society, if the **'high culture'** of society, which Matthew Arnold defined as 'the best that has been thought and said', is genuinely superior to the **'folk culture'** of the working classes, then to offer some or all of the children from these working classes access to such high culture is to be doing something of value for them, as we saw in chapter 2 the 'old humanists' have argued. And if the values inherent in that high culture are superior values, then, as Plato saw, we are doing no one a disservice in attempting to persuade them to accept those values.

Ethnic and cultural differences

It is, however, when one questions that initial premise that the difficulties arise. For if such culture and such values are merely different and not superior, then the justification for imposing them disappears and we find that what is happening is **indoctrination** rather than education. This has become particularly apparent in recent years in the context of **multi-ethnic education**. For a multi-ethnic society is a multicultural society; it is a **pluralist** society. And that implies that there are many different cultural backgrounds from which pupils come, backgrounds which cannot so readily be categorized as either culturally rich or impoverished. Many of them come from cultures which have longer traditions than the white Anglo-Saxon culture of the United Kingdom and which have every bit as much claim to richness. In short, these cultures are **different** rather than inferior. And once one has conceded that, then the imposition of a single culture and its values on all children loses its justification and does become a manifestation of **the dominance and control** of those who possess the political power to exercise such.

Knowledge as control

Thus a view has emerged which sees political values and attitudes residing in knowledge itself, or rather in the selection of knowledge which is made for inclusion in the school curriculum. At one level this is still seen as a device for gentling the masses – a notion which currently carries more force in certain Third World countries than it now has in the United Kingdon. At a second, and rather more sophisticated level, this is seen as the effect, even if it is not always the intention, of the selection of knowledge for transmission *via* schooling, and schooling is thus seen as a most powerful **mechanism** for maintaining and perpetuating the **culture, the values and the ideology** of those groups who are in a position to make such selection. The distribution of knowledge is thus seen as **a highly effective form of social control**.

It is an appreciation of this that has both led to attempts at increasing direct political control of the curriculum in the United Kingdom and has sparked off some of the major objections to that movement. This we will consider in a moment.

Deschooling society

First, however, it is worth noting that it has led to the emergence –
particularly in Third World countries – of powerful arguments for
the abolition of schools, for a **'deschooling'** of society, and, in practice, to the establishment of a number of 'free schools' in both the
United Kingdom and the USA in the early 1970s, schools in which
no set curriculum was imposed on pupils and to which they were
encouraged to go as and when it pleased them. Ivan Illich, for
example, an Austrian by birth who emigrated to the USA, where
he has worked extensively with ethnic minority groups, has described schools as representing **'the institutionalization of values'** and
claimed that universal education is 'intellectually emasculating' and
leads to 'social polarization and psychological impotence'. Paolo
Freire, a Brazilian, has criticized a system in which most people are
'dopes' whose curriculum is decided for them by others. Both have
suggested that one solution to the problem is to abolish such institutions and to abandon such practices.

Education as transaction

An alternative solution, however, as we shall see when we look at
issues of curriculum in chapter 4, is to view and to plan education
in a different manner, to adopt a different concept of both education and curriculum. The charges made by Illich, Freire and others
have some force but only when the curriculum is seen as planned in
terms of its **content** and only when education is conceived of as **the
transmission of such content**, the transmission of knowledge and its
inherent values. It has been suggested, for example, that we should
view and plan education not as transmission but rather as a form
of **transaction**, that we should accept the notion of curriculum
negotiation, acknowledging the right of the subjects of the educational process to have some say in the planning of their curricula.
The curriculum must be developed, it is argued, from the knowledge, the culture and the values which individual pupils bring with
them into the schools from whatever background they hail from,
rather than based on what is regarded as worthwhile knowledge,
approved culture or accepted values by those who control the
school system. In this way cultural differences whether they result
from social class or ethnic background, can be accommodated and
the charge of using the distribution of knowledge as a form of
social control might be avoided.

Education in a democratic society

What is being suggested is that it is the function of education in a democratic society to promote **diversity** rather than to attempt to impose uniformity, to encourage the development of different values and culture systems, indeed to recognize the richness which these can give to life and society, rather than to attempt to reduce all to one common system. Further, it is argued, for example by Paolo Freire himself, that education has the more positive function of **protecting individuals and minority groups** from the imposition of control by larger, dominant, more vociferous sectors of society, arming them against the many different forms of such imposition which exist, especially through the media, in modern, complex societies, and helping them to see their own problems in a proper perspective and to take constructive action to resolve those problems for themselves.

Thus recent developments in the sociology of education, and especially explorations of the politics of knowledge, have raised a number of crucial issues for educational planning, issues which need to be properly explored and taken full account of if we are to have a system of education which genuinely reflects those educational principles we discussed in chapter 1, and which require in particular a complete rethinking about and reappraisal of what we mean by curriculum.

It is the case, however, that at the very time when we are becoming more conscious of these needs, the realities of schooling in the United Kingdom are taking us in the opposite direction, towards **more direct and central political control** of the school curriculum, and towards a view, associated with this, of curriculum as the transmission of approved knowledge rather than as any kind of transaction or negotiation, and consequently, towards exactly those problems we have just been highlighting. This trend we must now trace.

The growth of direct political intervention in the school curriculum

Attention was drawn earlier to the fact that the lack of direct control of the school curriculum in the UK was in marked contrast to the practice in most other countries, where central planning of the content of the curriculum is the norm and where teachers have little discretion in deciding what they will teach. In the USSR, for example, the number of hours to be devoted to each subject each week throughout the period of compulsory schooling is laid down and all schools and teachers must adhere to what is required. Much the same can be seen in the USA and in most of the nations of Western Europe.

It was also suggested earlier that the relative **autonomy and freedom** enjoyed by teachers in the United Kingdom in curriculum matters gave no cause for concern when they were doing little with it, or at least when it was apparent that those other less direct constraints we discussed earlier were ensuring that nothing very idiosyncratic could happen. It did, however, come to be challenged when the curriculum came to be a major focus of debate and when dissatisfaction began to be expressed at the way it had been allowed to drift in most schools.

The advent of curriculum planning

A crucial event in this change was the launching of the first space satellite, **Sputnik I**, by the USSR in 1957. Up to that point, there had been, certainly since the 1944 Education Act, a relatively ready consensus over the school curriculum. There had been continuing debate, as we saw in chapter 2, over the organization of schooling, especially at secondary level, but there had been little questioning of the curriculum itself. Much the same had been true in the USA.

The launching of Sputnik I, however, threw the western block into a panic. For it seemed to suggest that Russian technology was more fully developed than that in the West and that as a result the USSR was considerably more advanced in the space race. Attention thus came to be focused immediately on **the school curriculum** and questions came to be asked about its suitability for **an advanced technological society** and its effectiveness in meeting the needs of such a society. These have been continuing themes since that time and it is as well that we become aware of them at the outset.

The challenge to teacher autonomy

What is important to note here, however, is that the response to this heightening of attention on the school curriculum in the United Kingdom was an immediate attempt to establish **more direct political control** over curricular decision-making. One of the earliest public declarations of this intent came from the Minister of Education, Sir David Eccles, in 1960 when he declared in the House of Commons his intention to 'make the Ministry's voice heard rather more often and positively, and no doubt controversially' on curriculum issues. He said that he regretted that parliamentary debates on education had been concerned with bricks and mortar and with issues of organization rather than of curriculum and he also at that time coined the famous phrase 'the secret garden of the curriculum', suggesting that it was to remain secret no longer.

Soon after this, in 1962, he set up the **Curriculum Study Group**. In doing so, he described it, somewhat unfortunately, as 'a commando-type unit', thus clearly indicating that its role was to breach the walls of the secret garden. The establishment of this group in this way attracted the hostility and opposition of the teachers, who rightly saw it as a threat to their autonomy in curricular matters, and of the local education authorities who also saw it as challenging their sphere of responsibility. This opposition led a new Minister of Education, Sir Edward Boyle, to replace this politically-controlled group in 1964 with the **Schools Council for Curriculum and Examinations** with a constitution which gave effective control of all aspects of its functioning, financial as well as educational, to the teachers.

Subsequent developments

Round 1 had thus gone to the teachers. Their autonomy had been challenged but that challenge had been resisted. The period that followed, however, was characterized by growing doubts about the **efficiency** of the school system and by a continuation of the struggle to establish more direct political control of it, a struggle which at first was slow and largely surreptitious but which, over the twenty years since 1964, has both gained in momentum and become more direct and overt. This is a road which is marked by many milestones and it will be helpful if we identify these in sequence.

The period following the establishment of the Schools Council in 1964 was a time of **considerable change** in education. We saw in chapter 2 that in 1965 a Labour government required all local education authorities to reorganize their secondary schooling provision on comprehensive lines. We also saw some of the effects of the proposals of the Newsom Report of 1963 on the curriculum of secondary schools, especially the proposal for the raising of the school leaving age to sixteen, which was to be implemented officially in 1972; and these effects were enhanced by the establishment of the new Certificate of Secondary Education examination at sixteen-plus in response to the recommendations of the Beloe Report of 1960. All of these changes also had an indirect effect on the work of primary schools, releasing them from some of the pressures of the eleven-plus and thus offering them the scope to introduce more informal approaches to teaching, a development which we have also seen was officially encouraged by the Plowden Report in 1967.

The 1960s, then, was a decade when much was happening in

education in the United Kingdom. The curriculum was changing significantly. The teachers were beginning to use their autonomy to move away from traditional forms of education. And not everyone was happy with the way in which things were going in the hands of the teachers. Nor was everyone content to leave control of the curriculum in the hands of the teachers, now that its importance had been recognized and the direction the teachers were taking it in had become clear. The struggle for control was thus rejoined or at least became public again.

The Black Papers

The first expression of this discontent and doubt came with the publication in 1969 of the first of a series of **Black Papers** on education, a collection of articles which were **severely critical** of many of the things which were happening both in schools and to schools. They attacked the notion of **comprehensive secondary education**, mainly on the grounds that it entailed 'the destruction' of the grammar school, in the eyes of the authors one of the greatest successes of the English (and Welsh) system. They inveighed against the growing tendency to match comprehensive schools with comprehensive or **mixed-ability classes**, a practice more common at that time in primary than in secondary schools. They criticized the **informal methods** of the primary schools, those approaches which the Plowden Report had just recommended, and the corresponding lack of attention to the teaching of the 'basic skills'. They expressed concern about the introduction of **new subjects** into the secondary curriculum, involving as this inevitably did the erosion of some traditional subjects. In general, they decided that developments of this kind were leading inexorably to a **lowering of standards** and would ultimately bring about a breakdown of the educational system. The gauntlet was thus now firmly thrown down.

The William Tyndale affair

Then, in 1974, the press made much of a series of events which occurred at the **William Tyndale Primary School** in the Inner London Education Authority, where some parents had become so concerned about the form of curriculum offered to their children there by the headteacher and his staff that they had first complained to them and asked for changes, and ultimately, when those changes did not happen, had refused to allow their children to attend the school. Inevitably, there were many complex features of this situation, as the subsequent public enquiry revealed in a report published in 1977, but, equally inevitably, it was on the simpler issues the press concentrated and thus encouraged the public to concentrate. Here was evidence, it was suggested, of the kind of **breakdown** which can occur when control of the curriculum is left entirely to the teachers, and, furthermore, we were encouraged not merely to recognize that this can happen but to infer that it is likely to happen soon in all schools. It was thus seen as concrete evidence of the worst forebodings of the contributors to the Black Papers and those who wished to made great play of this.

The establishment of the Assessment of Performance Unit (APU)

At about the same time, another significant event was occurring with far less publicity. In fact, it is true to say that most teachers did not know it had occurred until long afterwards. In 1975, the Department of Education and Science established its **Assessment of Performance Unit (APU)**, a governmental body whose task it was, and still is, **to monitor educational standards** in all the major areas of the school curriculum, a body, therefore, whose direct impact on the curriculum was potentially much greater than that of the Curriculum Study Group the teachers had fended off in the early 1960s. The APU, however, was established very quietly and with no opposition.

Its influence and importance in relation to the curriculum we will consider in rather greater detail in chapter 4 when we look at the curriculum specifically. What we must note here is that in 1975 it represented a significant step in the movement towards **increased public control** of the curriculum which we are here endeavouring to trace. It reflects a concern on the part of central government to respond to the complaints of those who were accusing the education system of a lowering of standards by establishing machinery to determine whether these criticisms were justified or not, and at the same time to produce evidence on the basis of which teachers might be, if not directed towards new ways, then at least discouraged from some of the developments which were giving cause for concern.

The Taylor Report

There was also a growing concern, not unconnected with the events at the William Tyndale school, that **parents' wishes** were not being permitted to play a sufficiently large part in educational decision-making. Teachers, it was claimed, were too ready to shelter behind their professional expertise, to refuse to inform parents of what they were doing and why, and even, sometimes, to refuse them reasonable access to the school. Too many signs announcing 'Parents must not go beyond this line' were still to be found in schools. There was thus established a committee under the chairmanship of Thomas Taylor to explore the issue of the government of schools and, especially, that of **greater parental**

involvement in this. The report of that committee, *A New Partnership for our Schools*, was published in 1977 and, as its title suggests, it did indeed recommend several devices for increasing the powers of governing bodies generally and for achieving much greater parental involvement at this level, some of which became legal requirements by their inclusion in the Education Act of 1980.

Economic recession

A further factor of great significance in the early 1970s was the **economic recession** which resulted from the oil crisis in 1974. Suddenly, money was in short supply, public money in particular was less readily available and, in all areas of public expenditure, a closer account of spending and increased justification were now being called for. Education was no exception to this general rule. There was to be less money available for it and such money as there was had to be spent sensibly and wisely. Again, it was felt that this could not be ensured if decisions were left largely to the teachers.

The 'Great Debate'

Finally, in the autumn of 1976, the Prime Minister, James Callaghan, in a speech at Ruskin College, Oxford, expressed a number of criticisms of the nation's schools. In particular, he criticized them for failing to provide an adequate training for most pupils in the basic subjects and for failing to meet **the economic needs of society** by not providing a sufficiently large workforce of suitable qualified technologists. Schools, he said, were concentrating too much of their attention on teaching the Humanities and too little on science and technology; they were permitting too many pupils, especially in the sixth form, to opt for Humanities subjects and not directing sufficient numbers of them towards the sciences. This, he claimed, is what happens when you leave matters to the teachers. Society must begin to have its say. Similar criticisms had also been mounted at about that time by the Confederation of British Industry (CBI).

He thus initiated the so-called **Great Debate** (which, as someone once said, whatever else it was, was not great) which was stage-managed by Shirley Williams, as the Minister for Education and Science in that government, and was conducted on radio and television and in the press. Its purpose was to bring education, and especially the curriculum, into an **open forum**, to open the gates of the 'secret garden' and to wrest from the teachers once and for all that monopoly they had enjoyed in educational decision-making. It is at about this time, therefore, that the term **'accountability'** enters the educational debate – accountability for **expenditure**, account-

ability for **curricular decisions**, accountability to **parents**, accountability to **society** generally. And this is the backdrop against which
to view a number of subsequent events which quite specifically have
established this kind of accountability.

Official publications

First there has been a series of **publications on curriculum issues**
emanating from the Department of Education and Science and Her
Majesty's Inspectorate. This began with the publication in July
1977, immediately following on the Great Debate, of a Green
Paper, *Education in Schools: a Consultative Document*. This was the
first of a flood of such documents – factual surveys, discussion
documents and proposals for change – which has followed. (A list
of the most significant of these is given in Appendix 2 on page 203.)
The main themes of these we will consider in rather more detail in
chapter 4. We must note here, however, that suddenly the view of
central government was being heard in a very positive sense in
relation to the school curriculum.

Further legislation

Second, and more positively, a number of concrete steps were
taken to change the government of schools and to shift the
balance of curriculum control away from the teachers. First, the
Green Paper of July 1977 was followed in November of that year
by the issue of **DES Circular 14/77**, a circular which required all
local authorities to make a review of the curriculum of their
schools and thus led to demands being made of schools and
teachers at the local level for **statements of their curricular provision**. It thus represents a major step towards **a reduction of teacher
control** and a recognition of what the Circular calls 'the legitimate
interest of others – parents, industry and commerce, for example
– in the work of the schools'.

Next came two **Education Acts** in 1980 and 1981. The second of
these was mainly concerned with giving effect to some of the recommendations of the Warnock Report (1980) on the education of
children with special educational needs. The former, however, was
concerned primarily to implement some, although not all, of the
recommendations of the **Taylor Report** and to give teeth to **Circular
14/77**. It laid down quite specific requirements for **the composition
and role of governing bodies** of schools, in particular **increasing
parental involvement** in the management of schools. It required
schools to **make public both their curriculum and their achievements**
(especially the examination results of secondary schools). And,
while it gave more powers to local educational authorities, it also
required them to provide **policy statements**, so that their con-

tribution to the curriculum of their schools might also become public.

Third, an increasing amount of money has been made available for curriculum initiatives not through the Department of Education and Science but through the **Department of Industry**, so that a shift has taken place with the curriculum of secondary schools towards a **more overtly vocational** and certainly a **more explicitly technological** flavour. Initiatives such as those of the **Manpower Services Commission** (MSC), the **Technical and Vocational Education Initiative** (TVEI), the establishment of the **Certificate of Pre-Vocational Education** (CPVE) and the allocation of resources to schools and colleges for an increased emphasis on **computer technology** have all contributed to this.

The demise of the Schools Council

Lastly, certainly the most symbolic, if not the most influential, of the changes that have occurred since the Great Debate has been the demise of the Schools Council. We will look in more detail at its work in chapter 4 and we will see there that one of its major weaknesses was its failure to produce direct changes in the curriculum on anything like the scale envisaged when it was established in 1964. Its recent demise, however, was only partly due to its record in this respect. Of much more direct significance was the growing movement towards **reducing the degree of control of the curriculum enjoyed by the teaching profession**. For, first, it was given **a new constitution and structure**, one which, while leaving a good deal of **academic control** in the hands of teachers, effectively placed **financial control** in the hands of others. And then, soon after, the government **withdrew its funding**, and, although attempts were made to finance it from other sources, this has effectively killed it off. It has been replaced by a new, politically controlled body, the **School Curriculum Development Committee**, a group very like that Curriculum Study Group which Sir David Eccles had failed to establish securely in 1962 and which the Schools Council had itself replaced. Thus within twenty years the wheel has come full circle and the kind of public control of the curriculum which was being sought in the early 1960s has now been established.

The major themes of the recent curriculum debate

The **major themes** of the developments we have just traced were clearly flagged in the 1977 Green Paper, where major sections were devoted to **'Standards and assessment'**, **'Teachers'**, **'School and working life'** and **'Schools and the community'**. All the major concerns are there and it will help us to become clearer about the issues if we try now to pick these out.

Education in a technological society

It will be apparent from our brief survey of events that two major concerns underlie these. The first of these is that which we saw sparked off the public concern over the curriculum in the late 1950s – the demands of **a rapidly developing technological society**. Those demands are, if anything, even more insistent and certainly more complex now than they were almost thirty years ago. For those thirty years have seen the most dramatic technological developments of any comparable period in history. It is not surprising then that society should be looking to schools to assist it to respond to these demands.

Nor is it surprising that, in a context of increasingly scarce financial resources, attempts should be made to ensure that teachers accept **technological and economic needs** as major priorities in educational planning. There are many reasons, however, why many teachers will not automatically share this view of educational priorities and there is no doubt that James Callaghan was right to claim in his speech at Ruskin College in 1976 that educational planning, as conducted by teachers, did not reflect this sense of priorities.

One reason for this is to be found in our discussion of the notion and concept of education in chapter 1. A great many teachers do see it as primarily concerned with **the development of individual children** rather than with the economic needs of society, as based on some notion of what is **intrinsically valuable** rather than what is instrumentally useful. Furthermore, most teachers have come into the profession from educational backgrounds dominated by studies in the Humanities. For a variety of reasons, the most significant of which is undoubtedly the low salaries teachers have always had in comparison to industry, few mathematicians and scientists have been tempted into teaching when they could earn far more elsewhere.

There is no doubt, then, not only that the need for schools to meet **the demands of industry** has been a major theme of recent developments but also that it is a concern which must inevitably lead to **clashes of interest** between teachers and their political masters. It is thus a concern which must also lead to attempts to wrest control away from teachers, since clearly, if left to themselves, most teachers will be inclined to develop their curriculum in rather different ways from those which technology and economic viability demand.

The concern over 'standards'

The second major theme has been equally important but is rather more difficult to unravel. We saw that first moves towards increased external control of the curriculum were prompted primarily by a concern over **educational standards**. This was the underlying concern of the Black Papers and it was to monitor standards nationally that the Assessment of Performance Unit was established. Educational standards are notoriously difficult to define and even more difficult to secure agreement over. We must again note, therefore, the **potential for conflict** between the teachers and their political masters. For again, and for the same reasons we have just noted, there is likely to be major disagreement between what each group sees as constituting educational merit. Thus, we have a ready explanation of why this concern too has led to demands for increased external control over the curriculum.

Specific proposals

These demands for increased external control have focused on four quite specific kinds of proposal.

A common curriculum

The first of these is the idea of a **common**, centrally determined curriculum, or at least a **common core to the curriculum**. We noted earlier that currently the only legal requirement bearing on the school curriculum is that for the inclusion of a daily act of worship and a weekly allocation of religious instruction. The concerns we have listed in this chapter have led some people to press for an extension of that requirement to ensure a basic educational diet for all pupils. We will consider more fully in chapter 4 some of the issues this kind of idea raises. Here we must merely note that it is one specific proposal that is being mooted as a device for introducing more direct control of the school curriculum.

The monitoring of standards

The second kind of proposal is for more detailed and extensive **monitoring** of the **standards of attainment** of pupils in schools. The work of the Assessment of Performance Unit continues. It has established procedures for the monitoring of standards in mathematics, language, modern languages and science, and is now extending its sphere of activity into the area of design and technology. Again we will consider the implications of this more fully in chapter 4. We must note here, however, that this kind of scrutiny of the work of schools is a second quite specific device for increasing external control of their work.

Accountability and appraisal

The third device which has been introduced to increase such scrutiny and thus to enhance this kind of external control consists of those procedures which have been introduced to make schools and teachers publicly **accountable** for their work and those which are currently being established for the **appraisal of individual teachers**. Again, we will consider the implications of these developments in greater detail in chapter 4. Here we must record that these too are major factors in the increased public control of the curriculum.

Parental involvement

The fourth major change which has been introduced as part of this process of increasing external control of schooling is the steps which have been taken to ensure an increase in **parental involvement** in the government of schools and of **parental choice** in the matter of which schools their children will attend.

The most obvious manifestation of this attempt to give parents more power, or at least 'say', in their children's education is the recent **change in the constitution of governing bodies of schools**, effected as part of the 1980 Education Act, which increased significantly the proportion of parent governors on the governing bodies of all state schools, both primary and secondary. And, although subsequent changes effected in the 1986 Education Act have been seen by some as a step backwards on this, it will still be the case that parents will be far more widely represented than they were prior to 1980. There will be equal numbers of parent governors and those representing the local education authority, and the number of teacher governors will be reduced.

Furthermore, it is not only through representation on the governing body that parents can exercise their greatest influence on the school and its curriculum. Schools have been required, again since the 1980 Act, to provide **public statements of their curricula and their achievements**. In the case of secondary schools, this has taken the concrete form of the publication of **results in public examinations**. In this way, schools and teachers have been made more directly **accountable** to parents as well as to the local education authority. The 1986 Act extends this by requiring the governing body of every school to prepare an annual report for its parents, and to hold an annual parents' meeting.

Last, a number of attempts have been made to increase the degree of **parental choice** over schools for their children. There is not much point in giving parents, as the 'consumers', detailed accounts of the achievements of schools if they have no subsequent choice in the matter of which of these their children will go to. Clearly, there are many difficulties in creating a completely acceptable scheme to achieve this. Logistical problems of sheer pupil numbers obviously make any absolutely free choice unworkable. Various other devices have, therefore, been explored.

One which has attracted particular attention, and indeed controversy, is that of giving parents and their children **'education vouchers'** which they could spend wherever they wished and however they wished on educational provision. The most controversial aspect of this scheme is that, as originally framed, it was to make possible the use of these vouchers in private, fee-paying schools, and was thus seen by some people as representing a state financial subsidy to the private sector of education. Even if it is restricted to the public state schools, however, some are seeing this as a device for destroying the comprehensive system and reintroducing forms of **selective secondary education** not dissimilar from the old tripartite system, except of course that selection will be based quite overtly on parental choice – and thus on the social status of the home – rather than on any attempt to measure or assess educational ability or potential.

Clearly, there will continue to be difficulties in providing parents with increased control over their children's schools and enhanced powers of choice of schools. Questions must also be asked about whether **the effects of this on the curriculum** will necessarily be advantageous, whether parents' expectations of schooling are always those which schools should concentrate on meeting or, more importantly, whether their expectations are so diverse that any increased powers for them in this area must lead to further confusion and uncertainty in curriculum matters. The suggestion has also been made that parent governors are often subjected to party political pressures from other governors, pressures with which they do not always find it easy to cope, since for the most part they lack the kinds of skill and command of political tactics which the 'professional' politicians on governing bodies can deploy, often to great effect. Nor is it likely that the opportunities for the training of school governors, which the 1986 Act will also give, will go far towards obviating this.

What is clear, however, is that, whatever the difficulties, attempts will continue to be made to involve parents more closely in the education of their children. And this is another major aspect of the recent proposals for change in the management of education.

Teacher education

We must note finally that, as part of this general movement, much has been occurring in the field of **teacher education**. This too we will consider in more detail later, in chapter 7. It must be recognized here, however, as part of the general scenario we have been describing. Institutions of teacher education have been under very **close and direct governmental control** in relation to the **numbers** of students they have been permitted to admit to their courses since the early 1970s when miscalculations by the Department of Education and Science led to a massive over-production of teachers and, consequently, teacher unemployment on a very disturbing scale. More recently procedures have been established to make possible the exercise of some **external control over the curriculum** of courses of teacher education. This reflects that concern we noted earlier over the quality of teachers as an important theme of these recent developments. It also, however, highlights their difficulties and the fundamental dilemma they raise. Such external control, while having as its prime object an improvement in the quality of the teaching force, is likely, as we shall hope to show in chapter 7, to have the effect of inhibiting developments at every level, mainly through the adoption of a greatly oversimplified view of what constitutes teaching quality.

A critique of these developments

This is in fact the central dilemma of what we have tried to describe in this chapter. As will become clear from our discussion of the school curriculum in the next chapter, the more you try to ensure the quality of schooling by devices for increasing external control of what goes on in schools, the more you put that quality at risk. In the last analysis, the quality of the education any child receives will depend on the quality of the **interaction** between that child and his or her teachers, and that interaction is not something that anyone can legislate for. Indeed, the more you try to legislate for and manipulate it from outside the more likely you are to destroy it altogether.

There is no doubt that the events we have described in this chapter have encouraged a deeper, a wider and **a better informed** discussion of curriculum issues. And it would be very difficult to argue that, at least in principle, that is anything but a very good thing. There is also no doubt that the idea of a wider form of **partnership** in education, in which parental, societal and even industrial/commercial interests are fully represented, is one that should have everyone's support. In practice, however, the **form** that these developments have taken, **the procedures and devices** adopted to implement them, have too often had the effect of inhibiting rather than promoting the very things which have prompted them.

Our discussion of the school curriculum in the next chapter will show that these procedures and devices, the forms adopted to implement these notions, have often been based on **an over-simplistic view of education**, which our discussion in chapter 1 will have shown to be a far from simple concept. They have made all kinds of unqestioned assumptions – about education, about curriculum, about knowledge, about values – of a kind that our discussion in chapter 1 also shows to be unwarranted. They quite often, therefore, can be seen to be based on a completely inadequate notion of what the curriculum is, again as chapter 4 will hope to show. And they reveal a total failure to recognize the true role that the teacher must play in the education of the child. He or she is not a mere instructor or trainer, not merely a possessor of knowledge with the skills to transmit that knowledge. Education is not merely the transmission of knowledge; the curriculum is not merely an inventory of that knowledge; and the teacher is not merely the purveyor of that knowledge. The process of education is far more complex than that; the notion of curriculum is far more sophisticated than that; and the role of the teacher is far more crucial in the development of the pupil than that.

Finally, we must note that this kind of view of education as the transmission of certain bodies of knowledge-content takes us right back to that debate about **the politics of knowledge** we outlined earlier. If the view of education and of curriculum which underpins those recent attempts to establish increased external control over what goes on in schools is framed in terms of the knowledge-content to be transmitted, then it must follow that it is also framed in terms of the values implicit in that knowledge-content and the values of those who have the power to select it. It thus becomes a clear-cut example of what we saw Illich, Freire and others warning us of – an attempt by those who control the curriculum and educational provision generally to maintain **their form of social order** by imposing **their values** on the next generation through the school system. The **distribution of knowledge** becomes **a major form of social control** when that knowledge is not seen, or at least when it is not presented, as problematic, as part of a continuing debate, as something to be questioned and challenged rather than merely accepted, and when neither teachers nor pupils are encouraged, or even permitted, to question and challenge it.

Summary and conclusions

This chapter has attempted to offer a summary of what may well be the most complex and intractable issue in the study of education – **the interplay of education and politics**. It first explained why the two must always be seen as inextricably interrelated and why few theorists have ever felt it made sense to discuss one without the other. It was also pointed out that the closeness of the link between the two has always been well appreciated in practice, especially by those political figures whose concern it has been to establish new political regimes.

We then turned to a consideration of the kinds of **indirect or informal influence** which the school curriculum becomes prey to when there is no direct control, as was the case in the United Kingdom until quite recent times. We noted that, while the lack of direct control leads to a good measure of autonomy for teachers, it cannot often lead to the emergence of totally idiosyncratic curricula because of the effects of those informal and indirect influences – the allocation of resources, for example, the demands of higher education, especially as expressed through the public examination system, the actions of teachers' associations and so on.

This led us in turn to consider, at a more general and theoretical level, the implications of this view of the curriculum as a battleground of competing views and ideologies. We noted some of the ideas about **the politics of knowledge** which have recently been advanced within the sociology of education. We noted too how these ideas have led some people to advocate a deschooling of society, the abolition of those devices through which the dominant groups in society can impose their ideology, and thus their control, on the rest. We also suggested, however, that schools might be viewed, and used, as a means of protecting individuals against this very process, but that, if we are to achieve this, a complete rethinking and reappraisal of education and of the curriculum becomes necessary. In particular, we must begin to explore the notion of education as **transaction** or **negotiation** rather than as **transmission**, as a process in which the recipient has some say as well as the provider.

It was then suggested that current trends in the United Kingdom towards **greater central control** over the curriculum were in fact taking us further away from that solution. And so we next traced the major events in those trends from the advent of the notion of curriculum planning in the wake of the launching of Sputnik I in 1957 to the recent legislation of the 1980, 1981 and 1986 Education Acts and the demise of the Schools Council. We also picked out the major themes of these trends, in particular the desire to create an education system to meet the economic and technological needs of present society and the concern to maintain educational standards, and showed that both of these seemed to point inexorably towards the idea of increased central control of the curriculum and a corresponding reduction in the freedom and professional autonomy of teachers.

We finally concluded that these developments raised a number of crucial dilemmas. In the first place, they certainly lay us open to all of the charges that we saw have emerged from explorations of the politics of knowledge. The more we aim at uniformity of educational provision, the more we are likely to achieve it only by ensuring that the **dominant ideology** prevails. And there is no doubt that current trends in education in the United Kingdom are taking us rapidly in that direction.

A second major dilemma is that which arises from any acceptance or recognition of the idea that true education comes from the **interaction** of the pupils and the teacher, or rather the interaction of the pupil with the knowledge and experience which are offered to or created for him or her by the teacher. It is not, as we saw in chapter 1, the knowledge itself which constitutes education, it is how it is received by the pupil, what he or she becomes as a result of exposure to that knowledge. This is a highly individual matter and something which is put at risk by attempts to plan education in terms of a uniformity of provision. It is also put at risk by the assumption that education is to be planned in terms only of the transmission of certain bodies of knowledge-content.

It thus raises important questions about the school curriculum to which we now turn in chapter 4.

Suggested further reading

Becher, T. and Maclure, S., *The Politics of Curriculum Change*, Hutchinson: London, 1975.

Kelly, A. V. (ed.), *Curriculum Context*, Harper & Row: London, Chs. 6 and 7, 1980.

Kelly, A. V., *The Curriculum: Theory and Practice*, second edition, Harper & Row: London, Ch. 8, 1982.

Kogan, M., *The Politics of Educational Change*, Fontana: Glasgow, 1978.

Lawton, D., *The Politics of the School Curriculum*, Routledge & Kegan Paul: London, 1980.

4
The school curriculum

It is with an examination of the school curriculum that we come to the core of education. For, whatever else the educational debate is about, it must concern itself centrally with **the actual experiences** of the pupils who are exposed to it. Indeed, the perceptive reader will already have noticed that in our earlier discussions the distinction between what we mean by the curriculum and what we mean by education itself has not always been an easy one to maintain. And in some contexts they have appeared to be almost synonymous and interchangeable.

This is because the term 'curriculum' has come to have a much broader connotation than it once had. Once it seemed to refer only to the **content** of educational provision and was thus barely distinguishable from terms like 'syllabus' or even timetable. One still finds it used in this way. Certainly, it was once the case that to ask a headteacher for details of his or her curriculum was to invite a list of the subjects on the timetable, and to press beyond that would almost certainly result in being given more detailed statements of the syllabuses being used in those subjects. One still finds the term used in this way. And, sadly, as we saw in the last chapter and will see again in this, it is that kind of view of curriculum that underlies many of the recent political statements and pronouncements on the school curriculum which we considered there. It is this that has led to a somewhat **piecemeal form of curriculum development**, especially in secondary schools, a development which has gone on independently within separate subjects and which has thus inhibited the emergence of any concept or overview of **the curriculum as a whole**. The need for planning the curriculum as a whole has regularly been asserted in some of the recent official pronouncements on the curriculum, but it has yet to be appreciated that to do this one has to get beyond subject-based planning in a way which most of the other demands of these pronouncements make very difficult.

It will also have been apparent from much which was said in our earlier chapters, and especially in chapter 3, that a more sophisticated view and interpretation of what is meant by the curriculum has been emerging both from the practice of teachers and the developments in our thinking about education which have gone hand in hand with that practice.

We noted in chapter 3 that the notion of deliberate curriculum planning is a relatively recent one. With that notion has come a growing awareness of the complexities of such planning, of the **several different interpretations** which can be placed on the term 'curriculum' and, consequently, of the **several different approaches** one can adopt to curriculum planning.

Any discussion of the school curriculum, then, must begin with an attempt to explicate some of the dimensions of that more sophisticated view, particularly because they have an important bearing on **educational planning** and **practice** and, as we shall see, significant implications for our thinking about **educational policy**, especially in so far as they help us towards a more closely analytical and thus more professionally acceptable approach to the framing of such policy. In short, any discussion of the school curriculum must begin from the question **'What is the curriculum?'**, and must, in the light of discussion of that, proceed to an analysis of the different approaches to, or models of curriculum planning which can be adopted.

What is the curriculum?

We must begin to answer this question by first making a number of important distinctions which recent discussions of curriculum have attempted to draw to our attention.

The formal and the informal curriculum

A distinction has often been drawn between the **formal** and the **informal** curriculum, between those activities and experiences which are **planned** to occur during normal school hours, and are thus included in statements of syllabuses or curriculum guidelines, and those many **informal activities** which go on outside this basic provision and outside normal school hours – at lunchtime, after school hours, at weekends and, sometimes even during school holidays. These activities – sports, clubs, societies, school journeys and the like – are more often than not voluntary activities and are often called **extracurricular**, a term which suggests that they are outside the curriculum and should be seen as separate from it.

This seems to some to be a very odd notion and certainly one which is based on a very **narrow definition** of what the curriculum is. For many would want to argue (indeed if this were not accepted one wonders what reasons there could be for creating these additional opportunities for pupils) that what is offered under this kind of heading has at least as much educational validity and point as most of the more formal arrangements of the school, and possibly, some would claim, more. Certainly, if one sees the point of education as being to attempt to attend to the **total upbringing** of the young and not merely to transmit to them certain bodies of useful or valuable knowledge, in other words if one's definition of curriculum goes beyond the idea of the mere transmission of knowledge, one would want to regard such activities as being a crucial part of both education and the curriculum.

It was for this reason that the Newsom Report (1963) recommended that they 'ought to be recognised as an integral part of the total educational programme' and that, in order to achieve this and to ensure that their advantages are enjoyed by all pupils and not merely those whose circumstances enabled them to take advantage of them, they be included in the formal timetable of an **extended day**. This idea has indeed been taken up in many places and has become a major feature of the philosophy of **community schools** and **community education**.

What lies behind this development, of course, is the view that there is more to the curriculum than lists of subjects or subject syllabuses, that education is concerned with the **full development** of the pupil and that any view of curriculum which ignores this is too narrow and perhaps also inhibiting. Certainly, in curriculum planning it would seem foolish to adopt a definition of the curriculum which excluded a whole range of activities planned by teachers in the conviction that they have a great deal to contribute to children's educational development. Thus, many have recently come to prefer a definition of curriculum as **all the activities planned** by teachers whether formal or informal, compulsory or voluntary, within school hours or outside them.

The planned curriculum and the received curriculum

This notion of the curriculum as embracing all that is explicitly planned by teachers for their pupils raises a second kind of distinction which it is important for us to consider and to be aware of, the distinction between the **planned** curriculum and the **received** curriculum, or the **official** curriculum and the **actual** currriculum.

There are several aspects of this distinction which we must note. First, it is a distinction that draws our attention to the possibility of a gap which might exist between what is stated in official documents as the curriculum of a school – in its prospectus, or in its syllabuses or in the curriculum guidelines which it submits to its governing body and/or its local authority – and the realities of the curriculum experienced by its pupils. In other words, this distinction alerts us to a potential **mismatch** between what teachers say they do or plan to do and what pupils actually experience. Teachers, like any other people, are entitled to package their wares as attractively as they can, but we must be aware that the curriculum actually received by the pupils may be very different from that officially described as the planned curriculum of the school.

Second, however, this is a distinction that takes us rather further than that. For it draws our attention yet again to the notion of education as being essentially founded on the **interaction** between pupil and teacher. Such interaction must be to a large extent peculiar to the individual pupil and may well turn out to be something different from what was originally planned or intended. Indeed, it is often better that it should be, some of the most educationally profitable experiences pupils have being those developed spontaneously by teachers who are sensitive to educational opportunities as they arise. We shall be suggesting soon, when we consider different curriculum planning models, that we would do well to adopt a model that permits this kind of spontaneity so as not to allow our planning to impose a rigid, and often inhibiting, structure on teachers.

This distinction, then, between the planned and the received curriculum alerts us to this problem, to the possibility not merely of a mismatch between our planning and the realities of our practice, but also to the dangers of adopting forms of planning which will make it **more difficult to be effective** in our practice. In fact, the major issue facing curriculum planners is to establish a base for a proper interrelationship between intention and reality, between theory and practice. We shall soon see some of the problems that can arise when this is not done.

The 'hidden' curriculum

A third aspect of this distinction between what is intended and what actually occurs is that which has come to be called the '**hidden**' curriculum. Many things are learnt by children at school as **by-products** of what is planned for them and often these by-products remain unrecognized and unappreciated. They are thus essentially unsatisfactory because they are usually random and accidental, and, indeed, often, when identified, they can be seen to be harmful.

There are many aspects of the ways in which schools are organized and run which make this kind of 'hidden' contribution to the actual learning of the pupils. **The organization and the procedures** used in a school will reflect the attitudes and the values of those responsible for them, and those attitudes and values will be communicated to the pupils through the procedures they are exposed to. This has been, for example, for many people a major argument against the practice of 'streaming' pupils into classes of A, B, C and D abilities, since that practice, in their view, reflects an élitist attitude to people and that élitist attitude will be communicated to all pupils. It is for this reason that some have even described this practice as 'unChristian'. Devices for maintaining order in the school, or even in the individual classroom, will also reflect the attitudes of those responsible for them, from on the one hand, the stern unbending discipline of Charles Dickens's Mr Gradgrind to the more relaxed and democratic forms of control employed in a school like A. S. Neill's Summerhill, on the other.

What is being claimed here, with some conviction, is that the organizational structure of a school **will reflect and communicate the values of those in control** of it in the same way in which, many claim, the selection of the knowledge to be transmitted does (see chapter 3). And that brings us to the second major aspect of this notion of a hidden curriculum.

There are many dimensions of what is offered to children in schools that are not always recognized or taken full account of by those who are responsible for curriculum planning, and thus there are many things that children learn which may not be the **intention** but are certainly the **reality** of the experiences offered them. Some good examples of this are to be found in the, seemingly harmless, materials selected for assisting children to learn to read. Too often it is forgotten that there is a content to these materials, that they consist not only of words to be read and verbal forms to be learned but of groups of words which actually say something and often imply a good deal more. Thus many of those well-known reading schemes that children have found themselves using in infant and first schools have on examination proved to be not only teaching them to read but also communicating to them a wealth of values and attitudes. To read about Janet helping mother in the kitchen while John helps father in the garage is not merely to learn to read, it is also to begin to learn a sex role, to acquire a set of values and attitudes which it is certainly not the intention of the authors of such schemes that children should learn. This, then, is the kind of **hidden learning** that goes on and it continues through schooling.

There are at least two aspects of this that we should note. The first of these is that one can find examples of this being used quite **deliberately** to foster certain values and attitudes. I have myself seen reading schemes for young children from other countries in

which the content of the schemes is overtly political and/or religious
and in which no attempt is made to conceal the fact that much
more is intended of such schemes than that the children should
learn to read through them. This is the worst kind of hidden curriculum, since it is hidden only from the pupil. The planners are
using it as a deliberate device **to implant certain values and attitudes**
within them and this is not education so much as the most insidious
form of **indoctrination**.

The second point we must note here is the need in general to
avoid such hidden learning as much as possible. For its effects are
indoctrinatory, whether this is intended or not. Some have wanted
to argue that because by definition this learning is hidden, it can –
logically – form no part of curriculum planning. It must be stressed,
however, that it would be very dangerous for curriculum planners
merely to ignore it. It is absolutely vital to the interests of education,
especially in the sense in which we attempted to define it in chapter 1, that teachers and other curriculum planners should be constantly aware of the **potential by-products** of what they plan and
should accept responsibility for what their pupils might be learning
in this unplanned way.

Not only must they take responsibility for the effects of their
planning and attempt to foresee as many of those effects as possible,
they must also recognize that many of those effects may be positively **counter-productive** to what they are fundamentally concerned
to achieve. For, if we are really concerned that education should be
helping pupils to develop the capacity to think critically about issues
and to make their own minds up about them, we must be greatly
concerned about experiences which may well be affecting their attitudes unconsciously, putting ideas into their heads without inviting
them to be critical about them, and in general making it more
difficult for them to reflect consciously about these issues. For this
is the effect on pupils of the learning that goes on as part of the
hidden curriculum. We shall see, when we come to examine personal, social and moral education in chapter 6, that it is this kind
of hidden learning that is the major barrier to the development of
anything one could describe as moral autonomy.

Some approaches we might adopt towards curriculum planning
make it easier for us to avoid these effects than others, just as some
of them, as we suggested just now, help us to bridge the gap between
the planned curriculum and the received curriculum better than
others. We must now turn to a detailed examination of these different approaches.

Curriculum planning models

Curriculum as product

It was suggested in chapter 3 that the main thrust towards deliberate curriculum planning came with the launching by the USSR of Sputnik I in 1957 and the consequent concern which that event raised about the quality and the content of what was being taught in schools. At the public and official levels that is undoubtedly true. However, a good deal earlier than this in the USA attempts had been made to encourage teachers to plan the curriculum more carefully and more scientifically, and, in particular, to plan it in terms of its **intended outcomes or its planned products**, and thus to begin such planning by statements of its **aims and objectives**.

This is a plea that we hear increasingly now in the United Kingdom, not least in some of those official pronouncements on the curriculum we have seen have emanated from governmental sources during the last decade. It is a sad reflection on the state of official and professional thinking about education in this country that this concept has only entered our thinking something like half a century after it was first advocated in the USA. It is an even sadder, and rather pathetic, reflection on the state of that thinking that this approach is being advocated as if it were **unproblematic** and even **self-evident** after almost two decades of curriculum theory have raised a number of **major criticisms** of this approach and highlighted several **major deficiencies** in it. Some of these we will consider when we have looked at what this approach entails.

The first thing to note about this approach to, or model of, curriculum planning is that it was originally advocated by people whose experience was largely **industrial or commercial** and who were impressed by the increased efficiency in industry which had resulted from the adoption of more scientific approaches to industrial planning. Thus the early advocates of this approach to curriculum planning in the USA were people who had seen the improvements that could be made in industrial processes by careful and detailed **job analysis** and who then attempted to apply this same technique to the school curriculum in order to increase educational efficiency. The concern was to make the approach to educational planning more efficient by making it more **scientific**, and they felt that, as in industry, the way to do this was to encourage those who were responsible for educational planning to begin from a statement of their **aims** and then to proceed by breaking these down into a series of **carefully sequenced and graded objectives**, so that a **step-by-step analysis** of educational progress could be made and a plan produced which, like those devised for industrial processes, would detail each stage of the journey from ignorance to knowledge, as that from pig to pork sausages. This, they argued, would increase not only clarity of planning but also efficiency of practice, and it would also lead to **ease of evaluation**, since, if you have a clear view of where you are going, you are in a good position to know whether and/or when you have arrived there.

In contrast to this, they declared themselves appalled at the inefficiency of the unscientific approaches to educational planning they could see in schools. Where could you find a headteacher capable of making as clear a statement about his or her aims and objectives as any factory manager? If education were to become as efficient as industry, such clear statements should be demanded of them. The links here with the pressure for increased political control of the curriculum which we explored in chapter 3 will not be hard to detect.

The people who took up this cause were not the teachers themselves but the educational theorists, and especially the **psychologists**. For they were the people whose 'scientific' knowledge was most appropriate to this kind of educational planning. Their 'scientific' exploration told them much about how children learn and thus about **how knowledge must be structured** to increase the efficiency of that learning, how it must be sequenced and the kinds of steps which are most appropriate for this form of graduated learning. Much of their knowledge in this field, as we shall see in chapter 5, was derived from studies of animal learning; and that in itself raises many doubts about its validity.

Then there appeared, again especially in the USA, a series of works suggesting that educational planning should begin with clear statements of its **objectives**, that selection of its content and the methods of teaching that content should be made in the light of those prespecified objectives and that the whole process should then be closely evaluated in order to establish whether those objectives had been attained. Furthermore, in order to help teachers and other curriculum planners with this process, they offered various **schemes** by which knowledge might be broken down into its constituent elements to assist in the creation of this step-by-step approach to teaching. The best known of these schemes is the *Taxonomy of Educatonal Objectives* offered in the mid-1960s by the American, Benjamin Bloom and his colleagues; a taxonomy which first divided educational experiences into three **domains** – the cognitive, the affective (i.e. the emotional) and the psycho-motor – and then proceeded to break down each of these three into a whole series, a hierarchy, of progressively more detailed and more immediate goals. To back this, others suggested that we should view and plan the educational process as consisting of **'ultimate'**, **'mediate'** and **'proximate'** objectives, the latter being the goals for individual lessons, the former the ultimate aims of education, so that the whole process could be planned in minute detail and step-by-step.

The major characteristics of this model of curriculum planning, then, are its central concern with the **products** of the educational process, its view of learning as a **linear step-by-step process** (the analogy of building a wall, brick by brick, is often used), its emphasis on education as the bringing about of certain **behavioural changes** (the objectives it offers us are behavioural objectives and their attainment can only be measured or evaluated by observation of pupil-behaviour) and its attempt to be **scientific** and thus **value-neutral**.

The difficulties of the objectives model

It is this last point that leads us into the first serious difficulty that some people have identified in this approach. Its emphasis on curriculum planning as a scientific activity leads it into an inevitable concentration on *how* to set about teaching. It assumes that *what* we set out to teach will be decided in the light of our ultimate aims or goals, but it can offer us no help with these ultimate goals; it cannot answer any questions directed at exploring *why* we should teach certain things. This, of course, is the inevitable consequence of adopting an overtly scientific approach. For science cannot offer us justification in any sphere; it can only offer us explanations. It cannot answer questions of values. It can tell us *how* to make a nuclear bomb; it cannot tell us *whether* we **ought** to use it or not, since this kind of question is beyond its scope. At a lesser level, it can tell us *how* to turn pigs into pork chops or sausages in the most efficient way; it cannot tell us *whether* pork chops or sausages **ought** to be made or eaten, *whether* they have any intrinsic value or worth; or *whether* they taste good. And in the sphere of education, it can tell us *how* we might most efficiently teach Latin or science or the art of torturing; it cannot tell us *whether* we **ought** to be teaching any or all of these things, or *whether* they have any ultimate value.

For this reason, the advocates of this approach have been at pains to inform us that their schemes, their taxonomies, are **value-neutral**, that they do not attempt to select or decide on the ultimate goals of education, merely to help us, once we have chosen these on other grounds, with the process of breaking them down into their component parts, for linear, step-by-step teaching. They thus, on their own admission, are not offering us **a basis** for educational planning, merely **a method** we can use when the essential, educational questions have been answered. This is, then, a model which by definition cannot of itself answer these essential questions. This is why its adoption, especially in those current official documents in the UK to which we are constantly referring, must lead to an ignoring of those essential questions and thus to **a very limited form** of curriculum planning.

Criticisms of the objectives model have gone further than this, however. For it has been claimed not merely that this approach is of limited value in educational planning but also that it is positively **counter-productive** to educational planning; that, if we plan our curriculum in this way, we will not merely fall short of certain essentials in education, we will actually put education in any real sense at risk.

It is here that we must refer back to the exploration of what education is that we undertook in chapter 1. We noted there, for example, the view which suggests that education in the full sense is concerned with what is **intrinsically worthwhile**, what is valuable in itself, rather than with something whose value and whose justification is to be found in what it leads to, in its **instrumental** or **utilitarian** functions. We have here, however, a model of curriculum planning in which all decisions are to be made in the light of certain **extrinsic goals**, certain **products**, certain considerations of a purely utilitarian or instrumental kind. The justification for teaching x is to be found in the fact that it leads on to y, and not in any merit it might in itself have. It has thus been argued that, while this might be a perfectly good model to use in planning forms of **training** or **instruction**, it can never be a satisfactory model for planning **education**. Its 'product' ideology, which leads it to take an instrumental view of knowledge, of science and of education, is in fact **inimical** to education as such. One can see, however, what its attractions are for those whose main concern is that the school curriculum should support industrial, economic and technological development, or even that its main purpose should be vocational preparation.

We also noted in chapter 1 the view that education must be concerned to promote **understanding** in the individual pupil and, ultimately, some form of **intellectual autonomy**, the ability to think critically for oneself. Again, it has been claimed that this systematized, step-by-step, process towards the achievement of certain prespecified goals is at odds with this aspect of education. It must regard the pupil essentially as the **passive recipient** of the curriculum that is offered, rather than as an **active participant** in his or her own education. It adopts what has been called a **'passive model of man'**, a view of the human being as a creature upon whom external forces work and upon whom it is quite justifiable for teachers and others to work towards goals which are theirs rather than his or hers. It is claimed, therefore, that this is a basis for the planning of forms of **indoctrination** rather than education.

This leads us in turn to recognize that such forms of planning must also lead to serious restrictions on the **autonomy** of both teachers and pupils in the educational process, and thus, indeed, to **constraints on the development of the curriculum**. They take us back to those views of education as the **transmission** of agreed bodies of knowledge, some of the problems of which we identified in chapter 3, and away from the ideas of education as **negotiation** and **transaction**. Again, therefore, we can see it as being in conflict with more developed views of what education is. If we have been right to claim that true education can only come about as a result of the **interaction** of teacher and taught, then we must recognize that anything which limits or inhibits the scope of such interaction must be inimical to education in the full sense.

A good teacher will be prepared to make many **adjustments** to what he or she has planned while actually in the process of implementing it. It would be a very poor and limited teacher of young children, for example, who was not able or prepared to make use of articles children might have brought with them to school or major events in their private lives, such as the birth of a sibling or even an interesting day out with their families, in order to promote the development of their understanding, their appreciation or whatever. Yet the approach to curriculum planning by prestated objectives does not permit this kind of **extemporization**. The detailed objectives are there to be followed and there is no basis in the model itself upon which we can decide when we are justified in deviating from them.

Several major projects developed by the Schools Council have found that, no matter how clearly they have prespecified the project's objectives, teachers will adapt them to their own purposes. Some of the project designers have thrown up their hands in horror at this, and have attempted to develop **teacher-proof** schemes. Such an approach would seem to be totally **self-defeating** in educational terms. Others, however, have accepted this, have described their objectives as **provisional** or **mutable** and have encouraged teachers to change them to suit their own needs and respond to what emerges as the work of the project develops. The major flaw in this approach, however, is that there is nothing in the project to help teachers with this kind of decision; they must go **beyond the objectives themselves**, and thus beyond what the project offers them, to find criteria by which to make such adaptations. It is a major inadequacy, indeed a fundamental contradiction, of such projects that they encourage such adaptations but do not recognize the need to adopt a planning model which assists in this process.

It is for these reasons that in more recent times there has come about a growing advocacy of and support for a very different approach to or model of curriculum planning, one whose main emphasis is on the **process of education** rather than on its content or its intended outcomes or products.

Curriculum as process

The view of curriculum as process, and the attempt to develop an approach to and a model for curriculum planning which adopts a view of education as a process of development, can perhaps best be seen and understood as a reaction to those aspects of the view of curriculum as product which we have just elaborated. It reflects the views that education is an **art** rather than a science; that its study is more akin to that of the **Humanities** than the sciences; and that, consequently, to attempt to plan it scientifically is to ignore, and thus lose, what is essential to it in the same way as would occur if one attempted to analyse 'Hamlet' scientifically or, worse, if Shakespeare had set about the writing of it as if it were an exercise in applied science.

This, then, is a model which has been developed to match the kind of view of education we explored in chapter 1. It begins from the view that education is not to be defined in terms of its **end-products**, in instrumental or utilitarian terms, but in terms of the **processes of development** of which it consists. It goes on to argue that educational planning must begin not from a statement of goals or aims, and certainly not from detailed linear lists of objectives, but with **an analysis of what those processes of development are**. It thus requires that planning should begin with a statement of the **basic principles** upon which the experiences we offer children will be based and selected.

This in turn means that we must begin with a statement of the **value positions** which are to underlie our practice, for that is what this statement of principles must make clear. These are statements of what we believe *ought* to be the essential elements of education and thus the basic principles of curriculum planning. Thus, this model attempts to get to grips with those value issues which we saw were beyond the scope of the objectives approach. It does not leave such issues to chance. It faces, as the prime issue of curriculum planning, the need to get to grips with those value questions which are central to education in the full sense. It accepts that the first question to be asked in curriculum planning is not *what* or *how* but *why*. It thus represents an attempt to plan education as education, not as a form of mere instruction or training. In short, it tries to get beyond the merely scientific concern of **means** and to cater also for those much more difficult decisions about **ends**.

It is sometimes argued in response to this approach that what it is calling **principles** are merely what the advocates of the other model call **aims** or **ultimate objectives**, that they too have those broader issues of what constitutes education in mind and that the distinction being presented here is purely semantic, a matter of definitions of terms. There is, however, significantly more to it than that. What the product model advises us to do is to break down these aims or ultimate objectives into a linear, hierarchical series of steps leading from the immediacy of this lesson here and now towards those ultimate goals. What the advocates of a process approach are claiming is that education is not like that, and that, not only can one not break the process down in this way, but that to do so will prove positively counter-productive to the attainment of those goals. To call these 'principles' is to imply that they must be **ever-present** and that they quite specifically are **not targets to be aimed at** sometime in the future.

One or two examples might help to make this clearer. If, for instance, we regard the development of **individual autonomy** as an important part of what it means to be educated, as we suggested in chapter 1, and if we then go on to call this our aim, we will be inclined, certainly in the early years of schooling, to concentrate on more immediate objectives on the assumption that this ultimate goal will be achieved much later – in the secondary school or in higher education. We are likely to find, however, that if we do not plan and implement our work with children at all stages in the light of this concern, our approach to their teaching may well ultimately prove counter-productive to this development. If, on the other hand, we regard this not as our aim, or ultimate goal, but as a principle, we will recognize that, as such, it must inform all that we do at every stage. We will be less likely to adopt, for example, the kind of authoritarian approach in the early stages of education which might well prove counter-productive to the ultimate development of autonomy.

A more concrete example, and certainly one that many will be able to relate more directly to, is to be found in the teaching of reading. Few would wish to argue against the idea that education has something to do with the development of some kind of **critical appreciation of literature**. Again, however, if we call this an 'aim' and, adopting the objectives model, break it down into its subordinate steps, we will be inclined to suggest, as one often hears being suggested, that the teachers in the infant, and even in the junior, school should be concerned only with the first steps in this process, with teaching the mechanics of reading, with what the popular press, and, unfortunately, much of the official literature, calls 'the basic skills'. It is, however, far from unusual for this kind of concentration on the **mechanics** of reading to lead ultimately to a rejection of literature and to make the task of developing any kind of critical appreciation of literature at a later stage doubly difficult. Much of the teaching of Latin in our grammar schools once had exactly the same kind of effect on the development, or non-development, of appreciation of classical literature.

Latin is a language as dead as dead can be.
It killed the ancient Romans, and now its killing me!

If, however, one accepts that the development of a critical appreciation of literature is a **principle** rather than an ultimate aim of education, one recognizes that, as such, it must be **present from the very beginning**, so that children in the infant schools must not merely be taught to read, to 'bark at print', but to **appreciate** what they are reading. Literature must be selected for them not only in terms of its effectiveness in developing the mechanical skills of reading but also in terms of its **literary merit** (and there is much children's literature about which has real merit) and, especially, in terms of its ability to foster **appreciation** and **enjoyment** of the process of reading.

It will be seen, then, that there is a fundamental difference between these approaches, and that this difference mainly consists in the attempt of the second to **analyse what the educational process is** and to produce a planning model which reflects that and attempts to help teachers to translate it into reality. A further major aspect of this is the concern to see education in terms of **transaction** and **negotiation** rather than of the transmission of knowledge. It does not set out to list *what* shall be taught and certainly attempts to offer very much more than advice on *how* it should be taught. It sets out to offer, or to help teachers to clarify, some basic principles of education, in order to provide them with the fundamental guidelines upon which they can themselves make judgments about **what kinds of experience** to offer to their pupils. It begins by seeing education essentially as a matter of the **developing experience of the individual** and not as the assimilation of knowledge pre-selected by others for his or her digestion.

In many ways, it may reflect a rather more **rational** approach to educational planning than the 'product' model. It has been argued in favour of that model that to plan anything, and certainly to practice it, without a clear idea of where one is going is to be engaged in an irrational activity, that what characterizes rational human activity is that it is **purposive**, it has clear goals and objectives. Reflection suggests, however, that that is not always the case and, in fact, that it is not often the case. For rational human activity may more often be characterized by being **based on certain principles** than directed at certain goals. When I resist the temptation, for example, to steal a purse or a wallet which I see lying around, I do so not because of certain goals or purposes I have but because of certain moral principles by which I conduct my life. Similarly, when

I suggest to a pupil that he or she might find it interesting to read 'Hamlet', I am not furthering goals or purposes which I have so much as acting according to certain principles of literary taste I have developed.

This latter example leads us on to the notion that this approach to curriculum planning might more clearly reflect the **realities** of the educational practice of teachers, most of whom are much more likely to plan their work in the light of their educational principles and beliefs than as steps towards certain extrinsic goals. To suggest to them that they should be planning in the latter way, then, is not to provide them with any positive help in their work. This was the problem we saw earlier with those projects which offered teachers sets of objectives and invited them to adapt and modify them but did not offer them any help in developing the criteria by which they were to do this. This model attempts to avoid such conflict by recognizing from the outset that it is with basic educational principles that all truly educational planning must start.

Finally, we must note that this approach to curriculum planning, whatever its educational merits and attractions, is fundamentally **incompatible with current trends towards increased external control** of the curriculum. It thus points up that conflict of interests and that dilemma with which we concluded our review of recent political intervention in the school curriculum at the end of chapter 3. Those developments we saw to be predicated on a view of curriculum as **content** or as **product** or as some amalgam of the two, and they are thus at odds with those developments within the profession which have taken teachers some way in recent years towards a greater appreciation of the notion of curriculum as **process**. What is most disturbing about them is their complete failure, or refusal, to acknowledge that this alternative approach exists or is possible.

We must return now, therefore, to some of the major aspects of those developments which we identified in chapter 3 and look at the major issues in the current curriculum debate against the backdrop of the discussion of curriculum planning models we have just examined.

Major current issues

In our discussion of curriculum models, we did not consider the notion of curriculum as content or the idea that curriculum planning should consist merely of statements of its content. There were several reasons for this. One is that to some extent this approach reflects not so much curriculum planning as an **avoidance** of curriculum planning; it is the model (if that is the right word) of the age when the curriculum was allowed to drift and no deliberate planning occurred at all. A second reason is that, to some extent, it can be **subsumed** within the product model, since, as we saw, that model assumes a content for the curriculum, selected in relation to its aims and objectives, and concentrates on the ways in which this content might be structured scientifically, for ease of assimilation and the most effective attainment of those aims and objectives. A third reason is that the notion of curriculum as content, or at least of education as the transmission of certain bodies of content (which is the same thing) has permeated much of our discussion of education so far, and especially what we said about the **politics of knowledge** in chapter 3. We saw there that it came to the fore most clearly in the issue of whether there ought to be a **common centrally determined curriculum**, or at least a **common core** to the curriculum, so that, since that is naturally the first of those current issues to which we now turn, we can more profitably consider the issue of curriculum as content in this context.

A common (core) curriculum

There are **three broad kinds of argument** which have been offered for the establishment of a curriculum, or at least a basic core to the curriculum, which would be common to all schools in the United Kingdom. The three arguments are very different from each other and each constitutes quite a different kind of justification for this measure and we must look at each of them in turn.

Before we do so, it may be worthwhile to remind ourselves of a point that was made in chapter 3 when we were discussing recent political intervention in the school curriculum. We noted there that the United Kingdom is quite exceptional in not having an agreed curriculum which all schools are obliged to offer (beyond that requirement for some kind of religious instruction which we saw was the only element of the 1944 Education Act in relation to the curriculum itself). In the USSR, in the USA and in most of the countries of Western Europe, the curriculum, or most of it, is decided by central fiat and not left to individual schools and teachers as it continues to be in the United Kingdom. We must also note here that the reasons for this are not the same in all of these other nations and it will be interesting to keep that in mind as we now consider the three major kinds of argument or justification for this kind of practice.

The philosophical argument or justification

The first of these is that derived from views which certain **philos-**

ophers have taken, and have urged upon us, concerning **knowledge** and, in particular, concerning that knowledge which, they have claimed, is valuable and superior. We saw in chapter 1 that some philosophers in looking at education have wished to argue that education should involve the initiation of the young into activities which are **intrinsically valuable and worthwhile**. We also saw that some of these theorists, such as Richard Peters, have gone further and listed for us those activities and/or bodies of knowledge which satisfy this criterion. Thus, on this kind of analysis, subjects or human activities such as science, history or English literature constitute intrinsically valuable activities of this kind, while subjects or activities such as physical education do not.

The arguments they have adduced to support this claim vary somewhat and need not concern us in detail here. It is argued, for example, that the former kinds of activity have a greater **cognitive content** and thus contribute more to intellectual development. It has also been argued that there are some activities, such as those of the former kind, which can only be understood through **full and active participation** in them, while others can be recognized for what they are without such direct and first-hand involvement.

What is worth noting here is the emphasis that all of these arguments place on the **intellectual or academic content** of subjects. We noted earlier that this kind of approach leads to the creation of a **hierarchy of subjects** with the highly academic ones at the top and those whose main thrust is towards physical or emotional development very much at the bottom. We also noted the implications of this view for the notion of **equality of educational opportunity** and we will see in chapter 5 that it has important implications too for children's emotional development. Here we must merely note that it is a popular, and a powerful, argument for the inclusion of certain kinds of subject in a compulsory common curriculum or in its core.

A supporting argument is one that takes this kind of case a little further. It has been claimed not just that there are certain bodies of knowledge which have this superior status but also that this knowledge can be, indeed must be, seen as divided into **several different kinds**. Rationality, it is claimed, takes a number of different **forms**; there are several quite different **modes of reasoning**; so that thinking, knowing, understanding must also be recognized as taking different forms. Different kinds of knowledge have different **logical structures**, different **ways of establishing truth**, even **different concepts** which are their central concern. For example, mathematical knowledge, and thus mathematical thinking, are quite different logically from scientific knowledge and thinking. In the same way, it is claimed, one can distinguish six or seven or eight different such forms. In addition to mathematics and science, it is suggested, we can identify also the human sciences, history, religion, literature and the fine arts, philosophy and so on as being logically different and discrete. If this is so, and if education is concerned with intellectual development, with the development of the individual's capacity to think or reason, then we must recognize that it will be necessary to develop that capacity **along several different dimensions**.

Thus to the claim that there is certain knowledge which is intrinsically worthwhile is added the view that such knowledge must be seen as coming in several different forms. So that, not only must the curriculum consist of worthwhile knowledge, it must also consist of adequate opportunities to experience that knowledge and to develop one's powers of rationality **in all of its forms**. We thus have a claim not only for the idea of a common curriculum but also for what major kinds of activity that common curriculum should consist of.

There is not time here to review critically the basis of this case, which is built on some quite abstruse arguments of a philosophical kind. We must note, however, that it is clearly in the tradition of that view of education we noted in chapter 1 which dates back to Plato, that it is **not the only view** one can take either of **knowledge** or of **education**, and that a quite different tradition has also emerged as a reaction to this view. While recognizing this as an argument that carries a good deal of force, then, even with those who have not thought the issues through very clearly at the philosophical level, we must also note that it is far from being conclusive, since its fundamental views of knowledge and of education are highly **problematic** and certainly not accepted by all.

The argument or justification from social justice

The **social justice** argument for a common curriculum claims that, whether knowledge actually has the value and the properties some of the philosophers claim for it or not, if certain kinds of knowledge are in fact valued by society and the possession of such knowledge leads to social advancement of one form or another, then social justice requires that this knowledge be made **available to all children**. Thus the main feature of this argument is its demands for a common curriculum so that all pupils may have the same opportunities.

It is this kind of thinking which, as we saw in chapters 2 and 3, has led many people to resist the proposals, such as those made by the Newsom Committee (1963), that we should develop different kinds of curriculum for different kinds of pupil, that there should be an academic curriculum for those who prove that they have academic abilities and inclinations and a practical, relevant and vocationally oriented curriculum for the rest. This kind of differentiation, as we saw in those earlier chapters, has led to criticisms of the latter kind of curriculum as merely an **education in obedience** and as a **curriculum for inequality**, and it has led to charges of **trapping children in the culture** into which they are born. Those who have levelled these criticisms have, therefore, wanted to argue for a common curriculum in order to ensure that this kind of differentiation could not be made and that all pupils, whatever their background, should receive **the same kind of educational provision**, so that their intellectual and cultural horizons might be extended and no limitations set on their potential development as people.

This is clearly a very powerful argument but we saw some of the difficulties it creates when we were exploring the politics of knowledge and especially the idea of equality of opportunity in chapter 3. It cannot accommodate the claim that in a **multicultural society** the many different cultures of that society must be catered for and permitted to develop; for this will not happen if one kind of knowledge, one form of culture, one set of values is imposed on all. It must lead to some notion of **cultural deprivation** or **inadequacy**; and this too we have seen to be a highly problematic notion. And it cannot cope with the obvious fact that when this kind of traditional curriculum is made available to or imposed on all, many pupils, usually because of their ethnic or social class background, find it not merely difficult to assimilate intellectually, but more often, and more importantly, difficult to relate to culturally. They thus become **alienated** and **disaffected**; they **reject education** altogether; so that what sets out as a genuine desire to do what is best for them ends up by preventing them deriving any real advantages from their schooling.

Nevertheless, the notion of **comprehensive education** would seem to imply some kind of **commonality** of educational provision, and we must not reject too readily the idea that all pupils should have equal access to that which is worthwhile. We have suggested before, and we will take up the issue again shortly when we look at some general difficulties of the idea of a common curriculum, that much of the difficulty and the source of this kind of dilemma are to be found in the view of curriculum as content and of education as the transmission of that content. As we saw in chapter 3, it is the attempt to provide all pupils, whatever their background with the same content to their education that leads to most of the problems. An attempt to develop a curriculum which would cater for cultural and other differences while being seen to be firmly based on **common educational principles**, on a common concept of the kind of process education is, might well be the device by which we may cut this particular Gordian knot.

The political/economic argument and justification

The **political and economic arguments** for a common core curriculum range from the relatively trivial to those which have recently been given sufficient force to make this the lively issue it undoubtedly is in the current curriculum debate.

The trivial argument is that which claims that, since we live in a society in which there is much **human mobility**, with families often having to move to different neighbourhoods and even different parts of the country in the wake of parental changes of job, we ought to ensure that in such cases children experience the minimum of educational upheaval by insisting that all schools follow the same basic common curriculum wherever they are situated. I have always felt this to be a very slender argument upon which to base such a major decision. To plan the curriculum for all pupils in order to minimize potential disruption of education for what must always be a minority seems to me to reflect some very strange reasoning. Only if one could be confident that such a course would have no disadvantages for the majority of pupils, could one give it any kind of weight.

A second kind of political argument which may appear to carry rather more force is the argument that the establishment of a common curriculum is the only way, or perhaps merely the easiest way, to establish **a closer control over the work of teachers**. Not only does it enable us to tell teachers what to teach; it also makes it easier for us to **evaluate** their work. As with the prespecification of objectives, if we know exactly what teachers are supposed to do, we can much more readily measure how efficient and successful they have been in doing it. It is for this reason that recent demands for a common curriculum have been part of the move towards more direct political intervention in curriculum planning which we outlined in chapter 3, and have been associated with parallel demands for greater **accountability** of schools and teachers. Again it is a highly simplistic view of education and of curriculum that this kind of argument is built on, but it is an important feature of the current debate and must, therefore, be recognized as such.

Much more serious, however, is the argument from **economic necessity**. This is the case which, as we saw in chapter 3, was put so forcibly by James Callaghan, as Prime Minister, at Ruskin College in 1976. Freedom of choice for schools, for teachers and for pupils, he claimed, was leading too many pupils into studying the Humanities and correspondingly too few into studying scientific and technological subjects. One way to put an end to this process, it has been claimed, is to establish a common curriculum with adequate elements of science and technology for all pupils.

Such an argument clearly makes no claim about the intrinsic merits of various subjects, although it is often to be seen dressed up in this kind of guise. It merely draws our attention to the **instrumental** and **utilitarian** advantages of certain kinds of knowledge, stressing that the economic health of society depends on its schools recognizing this and responding to it by producing adequate numbers of people skilled in these areas. Nor does it press its case on the basis of any kind of concern for social justice. Its concern is centrally with **society as a whole** and not with individual members of it. It is, however, an important argument and one which cannot be ignored, not only because it is currently the argument most commonly used in support of the idea of a common curriculum, but also because, whatever our views, we cannot ignore the social and political context in which education takes place, as we saw in chapter 3, nor its responsibilities to the society in which it is practised.

All of these arguments for a common curriculum, or a common core to the curriculum, then, seem to have some force; all equally can be seen to raise difficulties. It is to a consideration of some of the general difficulties of this kind of proposal that we now turn.

The difficulties of the concept of common curricular provision

Most of the difficulties which have been raised about this proposal to establish a common curriculum are those which derive from many of the points made in earlier chapters and, indeed, in the earlier sections of this chapter. They should thus come readily to the minds of those who have read diligently through the book to this point.

There are first of all those **political implications** we discussed in chapter 3 of the selection of knowledge to be transmitted, and thus the values to be imposed, by those who have the political power and authority to make such decisions. Perhaps the best example of this is to be found in the kind of debate which ensues as soon as agreement on the principle of a common curriculum has been reached. For, at the point when decisions have to be taken about what such a common curriculum should contain, the **dispute over values and preferences** begins in earnest. In particular, there have been notable participants in the present debate whose first decision has been to retain the present requirement that religious instruction should be an essential component of such a common core, while others, many of them of the same political stripe and persuasion, have been equally adamant that this should not be included.

Second, there are all of those difficulties we discussed earlier in this chapter when we were considering the proposal that we plan the curriculum by the **prespecification of its objectives**. Whether objectives or content are prespecified, the result is that we are forced to a view of education as **transmission** and of the curriculum as a body of content selected either for its own sake or as conducive to the attainment of certain extrinsic goals. Such a view does not, therefore, allow the notion of education as a **process** which is forwarded by the **interaction** of teacher and pupil, or even of the pupil with the content of that education, or of the curriculum as the subject of **negotiation**, as **transaction**. There is no scope for the teacher to exercise any kind of **professional judgment** or **autonomy** in relation to what he or she perceives as the educational needs of pupils. The scope of professional judgment is limited to the methods by which the predetermined content will be transmitted; it cannot go beyond that to considerations of what might be valid educational experiences for pupils.

In short, the establishment of a common curriculum or a common core, defined in terms of **subjects** or the **content of subjects**, must necessitate the adoption of **a view or model of the curriculum as content or as product**. The notion of curriculum as process is automatically ruled out. This creates particular difficulties for primary schools, because of the very different curricular traditions which have developed there, as we shall see in a moment when we consider in more detail the current debate about the primary school curriculum.

On the other hand, it must be noted that the lack of this kind of commonality, the lack of any consensus over what the curriculum must contain will lead, as we suggested just now, to problems for those who wish to establish some form of close check on the performance of teachers, some form of **evaluation** or **appraisal** as a basis for teacher accountability. Again this is a major current issue we must explore more fully shortly. It is perhaps sufficient to note here that it calls for **more sophisticated forms** of evaluation, appraisal and accountability, and, since it is predicated on a more sophisticated view of education and of schooling, we must not shy away from that.

As we suggested earlier, many of these difficulties derive from the view of the curriculum as **content**. The adoption of the view of curriculum as **process** would solve at a stroke many of these difficulties for us. There is far less difficulty in establishing **common curricular principles**, far less difficulty even in gaining some measure of agreement over what these might be. Once they had been established, their interpretation in relation to individual school situations and individual pupils might well be left to teachers. All we would then need would be those more sophisticated forms of evaluation, appraisal and accountability we referred to just now.

Finally, we must recognize that these difficulties over the establishment of a centrally determined common curriculum or core to the curriculum must raise important questions about the role of any **national agency** in curriculum planning and must thus raise issues related to the work of the Schools Council, the Curriculum Study Group and, indeed, the Assessment of Performance Unit. If there are intractable difficulties in central curriculum planning, then there must be major problems for the work of central curriculum agencies. These too we must consider shortly.

The curriculum of the primary school

It is worth our while spending a little time reminding ourselves about what was said about the curriculum of the primary school in chapter 1, because it is there that most progress has been made, in some schools although by no means in all, towards the establishment, at the level of practice as well as that of theory, of a model of curriculum based not on content nor on product but on **the processes of education**, and thus an approach to education which reflects a view of education as **development** rather than as the transmission of certain predetermined bodies of knowledge-content. In short, we can find, in some primary schools, more often nursery, infant or first schools than junior schools, an attempt to implement the kind of approach to and philosophy of education we described in chapter 1 as 'the alternative view'.

We noted there the main influences on this kind of development. First, we noted the **official support** which has been given to this approach by the **two major government reports** on primary education of this century – the Hadow Report of 1931 with its emphasis on education as 'activity and experience rather than knowledge to be acquired and facts to be stored' and the Plowden Report of 1967 with its view of the school as 'not merely a teaching shop'. Then we noted that a major factor which persuaded these two committees to take this kind of view was the influence of the work of the **developmental psychologists**. This we will explore in greater detail in chapter 5, but we must note here that its main thrust is towards viewing education as a process by which the child's development is promoted rather than as one by which he or she acquires certain bodies of information. And finally, we noted the more recent influence of those **'new directions' in the sociology of education**, which we explored more fully in chapter 3, and the emphasis there on the avoidance of the imposition of bodies of knowledge and thus of sets of values on children and thus on the idea of education as transaction rather than transmission, as negotiation rather than imposition.

There are two things we must add to this in the light of this chapter's discussion of the curriculum and especially the previous section's examination of the idea of a common curriculum. The first of these is that we can now see more clearly that what both the Hadow and Plowden Reports were advocating, and what many primary schools can still be seen to be operating, is what has more recently come to be called a **process model** of curriculum, that approach to, or model of, curriculum planning which we called 'curriculum as process'. The concern is with the development of the pupil according to certain agreed and established principles and not with the transmission of agreed and established knowledge-content nor the attainment of agreed and established aims and objectives. That many schools are still a long way from achieving this, in spite of the support of those two major reports, can be explained partly in terms of a lack of clarity over what this implies, at both the theoretical and the practical levels, and perhaps of the adoption in some places of the different, traditional view of education we also considered in chapter 1. Experience would suggest, however, that it is not so much the adoption of this alternative view as the **intrusion** of it into the thinking of teachers and others that inhibits the movement towards a process-based approach. The **rhetoric** of many schools, headteachers, teachers and others often reveals the latter kind of flavour, while their **practice** is confused by the intrusion of the former.

This brings us to the second point we must now note. The pressures for **increased political intervention** in the work of schools which we discussed in chapter 3, especially as these are exemplified by the demands for a common curriculum which we considered earlier, are of a kind which will have the effect of inhibiting even further the development of this kind of approach to the curriculum. The emphasis, as we have seen, is on product-based planning and on the idea of education as the transmission of content. And the effects of this which can already be seen at many levels of the education system, are not only to discourage the development of other approaches but, more seriously, to confuse and inhibit the work of those who find themselves attempting to adapt those other approaches to these new conflicting and incompatible demands.

A major reason why these external demands often tend to place the major emphasis on content and product is that this leads to greater ease of **evaluation** and **appraisal** and thus to simpler forms of **monitoring** and of teacher **accountability**. It is to this issue we now turn.

Monitoring the work of teachers and schools

There is no doubt that a major attraction of the content and product approaches to educational planning is that they both lead to **ease of assessment and evaluation** at all levels. If you state quite clearly in advance what knowledge a child should acquire or how he or she should be able to perform, you can readily assess the child's progress, appraise the teacher's professional skill and evaluate the school's standards and quality. The complex issues raised by the need to make assessments of children's progress we will consider in some detail in a later section. Here we must confine ourselves to considering some of the implications for the curriculum of attempts to evaluate the work of schools and to appraise the performance of teachers.

There is not the scope here to explore these issues in great detail, but some general points must be noted. First, those simplistic forms of evaluation and appraisal which it has been suggested are an inevitable accompaniment of approaches to curriculum planning in terms of content or product are essentially **summative** rather than **formative**, they come into play after a particular piece of work, syllabus, course or whatever has been completed rather than during the course of the work. They thus have no impact on that work itself, although they may of course influence how we set about the same project next time. They thus do not reflect the realities of the work of teachers and schools, since, as we have already noted, most teachers – quite properly – are making **constant modifications** to their work, in other words they are engaged in the continuous practice of a **formative** kind of evaluation. This kind of evaluation, then, does not help teachers to improve the work they have in hand, nor does it assist them in the task of continuously evaluating and improving their work. It measures **outcomes** not **processes**.

Second, it must be recognized that the use of these forms of evaluation, because they are predicated on particular views of education and models of curriculum, must have the effect of **imposing** those views and models on the subjects of the evaluation, in short, if they are applied universally as it is often suggested they should be, then they do not merely evaluate what schools and teachers are doing, they **determine** what they shall do. If, for example, evaluation procedures emphasize, as they often do, the more mechanical aspects of reading ability in say, seven or eight year olds, then teachers of these children will find themselves under a good deal of pressure to adopt the same kinds of emphasis in their planning and their teaching.

Thus evaluation becomes the **basis** of curriculum planning rather than an adjunct of it, in the way that we have for so long been conscious of the public examination system controlling the curriculum of the secondary school. It has often been claimed that examinations are the death of education since it is often felt that they fail to measure or even to take account of the things which many people feel really matter educationally, and concentrate merely on the less important things, on the regurgitation of facts or the performance of relatively simple tasks. It is this that it is being claimed is a major danger of these simplistic forms of monitoring and evaluation, since that kind of concentration on the mechanics of reading to which we referred just now can only lead to a corresponding loss of attention to the more complex and more important aspects of the child's becoming a reader.

Such simplistic forms of evaluation, then, must lead to **simplistic views** of education and curriculum and thus must put at risk those more sophisticated and subtle aspects of children's development which we have noted on several occasions are the essentials of education in the full sense. They also lead to the kind of **conflict** and **tension** for teachers we have noted elsewhere as the inevitable result of a mismatch between what is expected of them by such procedures introduced from outside and the perception they have of their own professional task.

The Assessment of Performance Unit (APU)

One kind of attempt to avoid this has been the approach adopted by the Assessment of Performance Unit (APU). This unit, from its establishment in 1975, has set about its task of monitoring standards in the nation's schools by adopting techniques of **light sampling** and **random and anonymous testing**. In the major areas it has explored, mathematics, language and science, it has tested a random sample of pupils across the schools of England, Wales and Northern Ireland in such a way that no one looking at the evidence can match it to individual schools, teachers, pupils or even local education authorities. A general picture has been gleaned not only of standards but also of the kinds of problem children experience in certain areas of learning, but no particular or specific judgments can or have been made. Thus the unit has genuinely attempted to monitor standards **without influencing curriculum planning**.

There are, however, one or two weaknesses here. The first is a question. What is the point of monitoring standards without influencing curriculum planning? Monitoring or evaluation are undertaken not only to find out what is the case but also to obtain evidence on the basis of which **changes and improvements** can be made. There can be no other point to these activities. If such changes and improvements are to be effected, however, as a result of the APU's work, then individual schools will have to measure their own performance against what emerges as the national picture.

It is thus at this point that the work of the unit begins to direct rather than merely to monitor the curriculum. And at this point its view of education and its model of curriculum begin, in the ways that we have noted earlier, to **impose** themselves on the planning undertaken by teachers, schools and local authorities. Clearly, what the unit feels is important enough to monitor is what they must accept as important enough to base their planning on. Thus where the unit's project teams have emphasized **content**, this has come to be – or continued to be – the focus of schools' planning; and where the stress has been on **objectives**, or **products**, these in turn have come to be the main planning concerns.

The most important message of this is that **forms of evaluation must be matched to models of curriculum**, since if they are not they will determine them. And further, if our curriculum model is a complex one, if our view of education is that more sophisticated view we attempted to outline in chapter 1, then we will need more complex and sophisticated mechanisms of evaluation to monitor all the essential elements in this multidimensional process.

Some of the APU project teams have recognized this and have attempted to develop instruments of evaluation which would allow for it. It is important for the development of education that such instruments be found. If they are not, the evaluation tail will continue to wag the curriculum dog, and to allow that is, if we may mix our animal metaphors, to place the cart before the horse.

The evaluation of processes

More sophisticated techniques of evaluation have been devised during that process of curriculum development which we have seen has been occurring over the last two decades and more. In particular, these have been developed within the context of those curriculum projects which have set out to be process-based or, to be more precise, which have set out to avoid being content- or product-based.

The first, and perhaps the most interesting, of these was the Humanities Curriculum Project (HCP). This project we will refer to in a little more detail when we look at personal, social and moral education in chapter 6. Its major concern was to assist pupils in the upper reaches of secondary schools to get to grips with some of the major controversial moral issues which they might need to understand not only generally as citizens but also more specifically in relation to their own personal lives – issues such as those concerning interpersonal relations, especially between the sexes, race relations, war and peace and so on. The prime concern was to help them to develop the abilities needed to handle such controversial issues. The project began from the conviction that a number of **different value stances** could be taken on this kind of issue and that for teachers to adopt any one of these would be an act of indoctrination rather than education. The concern was to encourage pupils to **develop** views rather than **adopt** them. In such a context, therefore, to have prespecified content or objectives would have been completely inappropriate. The concern was with processes.

The **evaluation** of this project, therefore, threw up some difficult problems and made it necessary to develop new and more sophisticated techniques of evaluation. The term which came to be used to describe the techniques which were developed was **holistic**. This term was used to indicate that the task of the evaluator was not to decide in advance what he or she was looking for and then move in to monitor or measure that. Such a procedure would imply a prespecification of content or objectives. Rather the evaluation was to **describe** the whole of what was to be seen, to attempt to offer as complete a picture as possible of what was happening, to provide the fullest possible **information** for those who needed it in order to make on-going or subsequent decisions concerning the work – the teachers, the headteacher, the local authority, even the governing body. The concern was thus not only to ensure that the evaluation process should actually promote continuous development of the curriculum but also, in order to do so, to make it possible for the evaluation criteria to evolve themselves in phase with the curriculum.

Others subsequently have developed similar techniques and have adopted different terms to highlight those aspects of these which they have felt to be appropriate. Thus one hears of **illuminative** evaluation which is concerned to describe and interpret what is seen rather than to measure it against some preconceived standards, of **portrayal** evaluation designed to portray a particular programme and reveal its **total substance**, or **responsive** evaluation which attempts to make possible a response to the very wide range of questions which might be asked about a particular programme or curriculum and is thus 'not trapped inside the intentions of the programme builders' or, worse, the evaluators.

We must, then, end this brief discussion of the monitoring of the curriculum with two final, general comments. The first of these is the observation that, in spite of the development of these more sophisticated techniques of evaluation designed to make possible the implementation, as well as the monitoring, of that more sophisticated, but much more satisfactory, view and form of education we outlined in chapter 1, those political pressures we discussed in chapter 3 are pushing us not only towards **more simplistic forms of** evaluation but also, and consequently, towards a concept of education which is not really education at all. There is thus a real danger that those pressures, in addition to creating dilemmas and conflicts of interest for teachers of a kind which must have a harmful effect on their work, will also lead to the loss of some of those fundamental and essential elements of education we identified earlier.

The second point we must make in concluding this section is one we have made already on several occasions, and that is the need to recognize that education in the full sense is an **individual** matter, that it cannot be implemented by remote control, whether this be attempted through the imposition of a common curriculum or through the use of common procedures for external evaluation. We are back to our notion of education as interaction and of the need for negotiation at the local level of individual local education authorities, individual schools and even individual teachers.

This in turn raises questions about the role of any kind of **national agency** in curriculum planning and it is to a discussion of that and, in particular, the work of the Schools Council, that we now turn.

The work of the Schools Council

Much can be, and has been, said and written about the work of the Schools Council. It is not the intention here to add very much to that. What we do need to note, however, in the context of our general discussion of the current issues in the curriculum debate, is what can be learnt from the experience of the Schools Council about **the role of central agencies** in curriculum planning and development. In fact, there are two general points to be made.

The first of these is that the record of the Schools Council in the twenty years from its establishment in 1964 to its demise in 1984 was a comparatively poor one if judged by its **direct and actual impact** on the school curriculum. The evidence of its own Impact and Take-Up Project suggested that even the best known and most successful of its projects had been adopted only by a relatively small proportion of schools.

Much can be learnt from this concerning the techniques by which one might **disseminate** curriculum innovations of this kind, and indeed the history of the Council's work reveals a good deal of progress and development in relation to models and forms of dissemination. Perhaps the most important lesson here, however, is that by far the most effective way of bringing about curriculum change is to tackle it on an individual basis at the local level. Many of the later projects which the Council sponsored attempted to adopt approaches of that kind, and, towards the end of its life, more and more of its efforts were being directed towards supporting

school-based curriculum development, innovations and initiatives at the level of the individual school.

This would seem to suggest that the planning and implementation of curriculum innovation at some central point is **not an effective way** of bringing about real change. We noted earlier how attempts to produce 'teacher-proof' innovations had failed and how natural it is for good teachers to adapt whatever is offered them to their own individual purposes. This would seem to support what we have suggested more than once, namely that education cannot be planned or practised by remote control.

It might of course be argued, indeed it has been, that what the Schools Council lacked was the **power** and the **authority** to insist on the adoption of its innovations, so that its failure to bring about more effective change may be attributed to its status and its lack of political and organizational 'clout', rather than being taken as evidence that central planning can never be effective.

However, experience elsewhere does not support such a view. There is some evidence already of schools and teachers being required to make certain changes, against their will and against what seems to be the dictates of their professional judgment. Some of the schemes for mixed-ability groupings in secondary schools were introduced in this way. The evidence there is that, whenever this kind of direct external control is attempted, it fails to work in one of two ways. Either the teachers **reject it outright** or, in some cases, even deliberately sabotage it; or, more significantly, they try to adopt it, but, because they do not believe in its value and are not committed to it, and may not even fully understand it, their practice, lacking understanding, commitment and thus all real conviction, is **neither effective nor successful**. Either way, the attempt at external control and direction fails to achieve its objects. There is even some evidence of this from the USA and other countries in which, as we saw earlier, a common curriculum has already been established. It is quite clear that in these situations the gap between the intentions of the planners and the realities of what goes on between teachers and taught is often a very wide one, so that the very purposes for which a common curriculum was introduced are lost.

Again, therefore, we find ourselves forced to acknowledge the individual nature of the educational process, as an **interaction between human beings** and thus not something that can be organized like a military or industrial exercise. And we must acknowledge that this necessitates that we develop procedures – for planning, for implementation and for evaluation – which take full account of this. Sadly, we must also recognize that many of the procedures currently being advocated or introduced reveal little or no understanding of this, and thus make no attempt at such acknowledgement let alone at the development of procedures which might match this view of education.

The second, and final, point it is worth noting about the work of the Schools Council is a far more positive one. In spite of its lack of direct effects on the curriculum (which, when viewed in the light of what has just been said, may be seen as a merit rather than a defect), it has had more influence than any other single factor on the development of **our understanding** of curriculum and of curriculum change, and has thus considerably enhanced the **quality** of the curriculum debate – at least within professional circles.

We have learnt a great deal over the last twenty years about **curriculum development**, as this chapter, which has touched on only some of it, will have revealed. We have learnt much about how **curriculum change** can, and how it cannot, be brought about effectively. We have learnt much about the impact of attempts at evaluation of the curriculum and, as we have just seen, how we might develop techniques of evaluation whose impact on the curriculum might be positive and supportive rather than negative and inhibiting. We have learnt much about **the role of the teacher** in curriculum development, and in education generally, and, conversely, about the kinds of contribution that curriculum development or support teams might make to this process. And we have learnt much in other related areas. It is no exaggeration to assert that most of this we have learnt from the work and the experience, the failures as well as the successes, of the Schools Council.

As a part, indeed a result, of this process, we have also seen a massive increase in the **level** and **quality** of discussions of curriculum, the introduction of **new dimensions** to the curriculum debate, such as many of those which this chapter has endeavoured to highlight, a much greater consciousness in teachers at all levels not only of curriculum issues but also of the need for them to keep constantly abreast of developments in curriculum. Most of this must also be attributed to the Schools Council, since it is for the most part the projects which it has sponsored which have raised the quality of discussion and the consciousness of teachers by introducing these new dimensions and offering ideas and suggestions in all areas of curriculum planning.

Both of these aspects of its work point clearly to the way things might, perhaps should, go in the future. While on the one hand its experience has shown the comparative **ineffectiveness of central planning** and innovation, its **influence on teacher's thinking**, on the other hand, has revealed that the only viable alternative is to help teachers to develop a level and quality of professionalism which will be such that we will be able confidently to place the major responsibility for the school curriculum in their hands. It is sad and unfortunate that, as both this chapter and chapter 3 have revealed, neither of these two lessons has been learnt by those currently concerned to adjust the balance of control in education.

The many publications which the Schools Council produced in its eighteen years of existence stimulated a good deal of discussion of curriculum issues at a level of sophistication which has not been matched by work emanating from any other single source. This source of publications on the curriculum has now been replaced by **official agencies**. Her Majesty's Inspectorate and the Department of Education and Science, whose documents on the school curriculum we noted in chapter 3 as a major feature of the recent move towards increased political intervention in schooling. (The most significant of these are listed in Appendix 2 on page 203.) One has to say, however, that the quality of these official documents is **far below** that of the output of the Schools Council and, in fact, reveals a sad failure to learn or to appreciate (or, worse, even to acknowledge) most of its work and most of what could, and should, have been learnt from that work. Some would even argue that, far from raising the quality of the curriculum debate, they have actually had the effect of lowering it. For their main thrust appears to be **political** rather than educational, since this, as we saw in chapter 3, is currently the flavour of the month, or the decade, in education.

The same might be said of current developments in **public examinations** to which we turn in this concluding section of this chapter.

Pupil assessment – the public examinations system

One of the difficulties which the Schools Council faced was that, throughout the period of its existence, it had responsibility not only for curriculum development but also for **the examinations system**. Its full title was in fact the Schools Council for Curriculum and Examinations. The difficulties stemmed from the fact that in both fields, as we noted just now, its powers were limited to the offering of **advice and comment**; they did not extend to the **implementation of proposals**, so that it had **no direct control** of policy. This proved particularly inhibiting in relation to the public examinations, since these have long been recognized as the most significant source of constraints on the curriculum.

Nevertheless, it did have responsibility for offering advice on the public examinations system, having taken this over from the Secondary Schools Examination Council (SSEC) which had been set up as long before as 1917 to coordinate and rationalize the many different examinations which had proliferated in response to demands from the universities, the professions and other bodies, especially employers, for clear, and standardized, information about pupils at the point at which they left the school.

The experience of the Schools Council revealed some of the problems of linking responsibility, especially when not backed by executive power, for both the development of the curriculum and the public examinations system. And, since its demise, these functions have again been separated, with the establishment of a new Schools Examination Council (SEC) as well as the School Curriculum Development Committee (SCDC) which we noted in chapter 3. However, these two functions are clearly interrelated. How we assess pupils according to nationally agreed and standardized criteria, must be matched to, and will unavoidably have an effect on, the school curriculum, so that no discussion of this would be complete without some reference to the impact on it of the public examinations system.

It is not the intention here to offer a directory of the public examinations available, but it is necessary to explore the implications of what has happened, and is happening, in this field for education in general and for the school curriculum in particular.

The background

Examinations of one form or another have been in use for a long time. Initially, they were used to determine suitability for entry to the Civil Service, the professions and university courses. The system of 'payment by results', to which we referred in chapter 2, led to their use to measure the efficiency of schools and teachers after the Revised Code of 1862. By the beginning of the present century, they were increasing rapidly both in their **range** and their **variety**, as more and more employers of school leavers looked for some trustworthy measure of their abilities. It was this, as we saw just now, which led to the establishment of the Secondary Schools Examination Council (SSEC) in 1917, and since that time a firm attempt has been made to keep the system under the kind of control which would ensure **comparability of standards** at a national level and thus justify and promote confidence in the system.

The first main task of this body was to coordinate the examinations at sixteen-plus and eighteen-plus and to achieve this it created a coordinate system of **School Certificate** (sixteen-plus) and **Higher School Certificate** (eighteen-plus) examinations, the first of which were held in 1919. Both of these were **group** examinations in that in order to achieve a certificate at either level a candidate had to pass in a number of subjects at the same sitting and those subjects had to be chosen according to certain fixed criteria, designed to ensure **a**

balance of interests up to sixteen-plus and a degree of specialism at eighteen-plus. The implications of this kind of scheme for the school curriculum are plain; it was intended to ensure a **broad curriculum** for all pupils who would be entered for this qualification up to the age of sixteen-plus.

This system was changed with effect from 1951, when, as a consequence of a report issued by the SSEC in 1947, the School Certificate Examination was replaced by the **General Certificate of Education (GCE)** at Ordinary (sixteen-plus) and Advanced (eighteen-plus) levels. The most significant features of this change were, first, that the standards for a pass were raised (a pass at GCE 'O' level was said to be the equivalent of a 'credit' in the School Certificate) and, second, that the 'group' requirement was removed, so that **single subjects** could be taken at both 'O' and 'A' levels, and a qualification could be obtained in only one subject and/or in one subject at a time.

Thus the requirement on schools to offer a broad and balanced curriculum up to sixteen-plus was removed and the effects of that were revealed in the recent survey of secondary schools undertaken by Her Majesty's Inspectorate who found that 'important areas of the curriculum were excluded, wholly or almost wholly', from the programmes of certain pupils, and they bewailed the lack of any view of the curriculum as a totality at this age and level, and the resultant **incoherence** of some pupils' educational experiences. Again, therefore, we can see the impact of the public examinations system on the school curriculum.

The next major landmark came in 1965 with the establishment of the **Certificate of Secondary Education** (CSE). The single subject base of the new GCE had made it possible for many pupils who were not felt to be capable of taking a range of examinations at sixteen plus to take one or two. And the problems and inadequacies of selection at eleven-plus, to which we referred in chapter 2, had encouraged teachers in secondary modern schools to adopt many different strategems in an attempt to enable some of their pupils to gain nationally recognized qualifications, often in practical areas such as building and commerce, even though pupils from secondary modern schools could not be entered, at least by the schools themselves at the public cost, to the GCE examinations without special permission. As we mentioned earlier, they were entered for examinations offered by bodies such as the Royal Society of Arts (RSA) and the College of Preceptors. Or, in some cases, their parents were advised and encouraged to enter them for the GCE as private candidates.

All was in something of a mess. And so the SSEC set up the **Beloe Committee** to look into the question of examinations in secondary schools other than the GCE. It reported in 1960, and recommended that **a new examination** be offered alongside the GCE, to provide for pupils of somewhat **lower ability**, and that this be called the Certificate of Secondary Education (CSE). This again is a **single subject** examination, and the first year of its operation was 1965.

There has thus existed since that time a **dual system** of examining at sixteen-plus, with many pupils taking a combination of examinations under both schemes, and, indeed, many being 'doubly entered' for the same subject under both schemes, the CSE being seen as a kind of 'fail-safe' device in the event of failure at GCE level. If one adds to this the fact that there are nine GCE Boards and fourteen CSE Boards, each offering their own syllabuses, one can see that the situation has continued to be a far from well coordinated one. As long ago as 1970, therefore, the Schools Council recommended that this be rationalized into **a single common system** of examining at sixteen-plus. We have seen, however, that the Schools Council had power only to recommend and advise, not to implement proposals for this kind, and this was one proposal which was not implemented, in spite of the fact that it was supported in 1978 by the report of the Waddell Committee which was set up to conduct an independent exploration of the issue.

Attempts were also made, again through recommendations emanating from the Schools Council, to modify the examinations offered at **sixth form level**, proposals such as those for the introduction of a Certificate of Extended Education (CEE), and for Normal (N) and Further (F) level examinations at eighteen. Here the intentions were both to cater for the wider range of pupils staying on at school beyond the statutory leaving age and to try to ensure a reasonable breadth of curriculum for sixth-formers. These attempts, however, also came to nothing, largely in this case because of the opposition of the universities who were concerned at the impact this kind of change would have on the eighteen year old's readiness for highly specialized degree courses.

The good sense of reorganizing the examinations system at sixteen-plus into a common system has now been recognized, partly, one suspects, because it is seen to be a more effective way of controlling the curriculum and of establishing some kind of common core to the curriculum, such as we discussed earlier in this chapter, than the more direct device of laying down such a common core by fiat of central government. It is currently intended that the first examination for the new common **General Certificate of Secondary Education** (GCSE) should be held in 1988, although the implementation of this is currently in some doubt because of the conflict between the Secretary of State for Education and Science and the teaching profession over levels of teacher's pay. The intention is that national criteria should be produced in all subject areas and that these should form the basis of this new common sixteen-plus examination.

It is further the intention that this examination should be devised in such a way as to make it **available to all**, or almost all, pupils. To this end it is planned that it should not grade pupils on a pass/fail basis, but according to the levels of ability they display. It can thus be seen as a positive attempt to overcome that **divisiveness** which has been the source of major criticisms of the present dual system.

Even as this attempt to establish a common sixteen-plus examination is getting under way, however, another development is threatening to reintroduce the very divisiveness it is the intention of the GCSE to abolish. For recent years have seen again a proliferation of examinations, sponsored and supported from another source. Those developments we referred to in the last chapter which have been promoted by the Manpower Services Commission (MSC), in particular those under the scheme known as the Technical and Vocational Education Initiative (TVEI), have attracted the attention of a number of bodies outside the orbit of the School Examination Boards, whether at GCE or CSE level, bodies such as the Royal Society of Arts (RSA) again and the College of Preceptors, along with other bodies such as the City and Guilds, The Business and Technician Education Council (BTEC). Much of this examining activity is now being coordinated under the title of the **Certificate of Pre-Vocational Education** (CPVE). The main focus of this development, as its name suggests, is on overtly **vocational** forms of schooling, and its effect on the curriculum for those pupils who are directed into, or themselves choose to take, this kind of course, must therefore be to encourage an emphasis on the **utilitarian** aspects of schooling and thus a loss of attention for education in its wider sense.

Implications for the school curriculum

It is probably not necessary to say very much more about the implications of what has been happening in the sphere of public examinations for the curriculum of the secondary school. Most of these have emerged in the brief survey of the major developments we have just offered. Two general points might perhaps be stressed, however.

The first of these is that examinations have always had a **divisive effect** on the curriculum. To say that is not to say that examinations should not do the very job that they exist to do, namely to indicate what strengths pupils have and to guide both the pupils themselves and others in relation to their future careers. Of course this must be done, and the public examinations system is the best device we have for doing it. It should be possible to do that job, however, without making it necessary to adopt the kinds of **divisive and differentiated curriculum** which now exist in most secondary schools.

While we have not only different examinations but also different **routes** to those examinations, schools will continue to find it necessary not only to offer two or three very different kinds of curriculum, but also to **divide their pupils**, sometimes from far too early an age, according to how they view their abilities and potential in relation to these different forms of provision. The public examination system has been a major barrier to the abolition of streaming and the creation of truly mixed-ability classes in secondary schools (just as the eleven-plus once was to similar developments in primary schools), and it has been a major barrier, therefore, to the attainment of comprehensive education in the full sense, as we saw in chapter 2.

The form this divisiveness is now taking is probably more a cause for concern than at any time in the recent past. To have children entered for two different levels of examination at sixteen-plus was messy, but it was not unduly divisive, or at least it did not have to be, as the schemes instituted by many schools showed. But to be required to decide whether they are to have some kind of education or what is basically a form of **vocational training** necessitates making more far-reaching and influential decisions that that. Not to put too fine a point on it, it amounts to having to decide, quite early in their lives, whether they are to have an education or not.

Many of the TVEI and CPVE schemes claim to have an element of **general education** in them, but this is too often a very low level offering, and even, on occasion, a form of mere tokenism. Effectively, these forms of curriculum are very far from those being offered to other, apparently more 'academic', pupils in respect of their educational content.

The second major feature we must note about the impact of examinations on the curriculum is their, perhaps inevitable, tendency to be **directive** of what goes on there. This was noted by the Clarendon Report as long ago as 1864; and it has been reiterated often since, perhaps most notably in the Beloe Report of 1960. Examinations were devised to test what pupils have learned, what they have gained from the educational experiences offered them; in reality they often **determine** what they will learn and what kinds of experience they will be given.

Furthermore, their effect is to push the curriculum towards that kind of **content-base**, or even **product-base**, which we suggested earlier in this chapter is counter-productive to education in the full sense. The tendency is for examinations to be concerned with what pupils know and can reproduce or regurgitate (to use the popular, if rather revolting, metaphor), and the approach to learning they invite is thus an **instrumental** approach, learning for the examination qualification rather than for its own sake, and an approach that takes us a long way from the notion of 'active learning' we shall explore in chapter 5. That this is not inevitable, however, will be clear if we remind ourselves of those forms of curriculum evaluation which have been developed especially to promote the view of curriculum as process. And we can find examples of similar kinds of development in the examination and assessment **procedures** adopted or devised by some schools and teachers. We must end our discussion of examination and the school curriculum by looking briefly at some of these.

Some recent developments in the forms of examination

Recent years have seen the development at all levels of education, including higher education, of **techniques of examining and assessing** pupils other than the traditional written examination paper. In some subjects, of course, such as modern languages and music, oral and practical examinations have long been the norm. To these have more recently been added, in every subject area, devices like **open-book** examinations, where candidates are permitted to bring books with them into the examination, **prior disclosure techniques**, where questions are made known to candidates in advance of the examination itself so that they can prepare for them, the use of **video material** as a basis for questioning, and many forms of **course-work assessment**, usually marked by the teachers themselves. There have even been experiments with **self-assessment** by pupils.

All these techniques make possible a **more effective** assessment of the candidate's abilities, especially when several are used together, since this can give a fuller picture. They all make possible too the development of the curriculum along lines other than those determined by content or product. They make it possible for the examination to follow the curriculum rather than leading it.

There have also been developments of other kinds. The CSE, for example, from the beginning made possible examination of pupils by three different **modes**. Mode 1 is the traditional form of examination, written papers on a syllabus set, published and marked by the Examination Board. Mode 2, however, permits the planning of syllabuses by individual schools or groups of schools, subject to the Board's approval, but requires that the examination papers themselves be set and marked by the Board. Mode 3 goes even further. Under this mode, an individual school can not only plan its own syllabuses, but can set and mark its own examination papers or individual assignments, subject only to moderation by the Board.

Again, therefore, we can see that the use of Mode 2, and perhaps particularly Mode 3, has enabled some shools and teachers to plan and develop their curricula in response to what they have felt to be the needs and requirements of **their own individual pupils**, to do this, if they wished, in terms of **processes** rather than content or products, and to do all of this without prejudicing their pupils' opportunities to achieve publicly recognized qualifications. It has thus made it possible to ensure that the role of the public examination in relation to the curriculum should be to assess what has been done by pupils rather than to determine what should be done. In this way it has been possible to avoid the charge of *dirigisme*, to assess and examine pupils without at the same time determining the content of their curriculum and thus inhibiting its development.

It has also proved possible by the use of these devices to avoid that **divisiveness** we referred to earlier as a serious effect of much public examining. The use of individual assignments makes possible a much greater variety of choice for pupils than the common written paper, and thus offers a greater range of topics, without in any sense leading to any falling off of standards. Indeed, most teachers who have used these devices are struck by the marked improvement in the quality of the pupils' work.

One final development must be mentioned. It has often been said, especially by potential employers, that examinations in traditional subjects, or even in those practical subjects which have more recently been added to many examination subject lists, do not give all the information about young people that one would like to have in deciding whether to offer them a job or a place in further or higher education. It tells us only about their abilities in particular subject areas, or even, some would add, only about their ability to perform in examinations. To meet this, there has recently appeared a number of different schemes for **profiling**. The idea of this is not new. It was suggested as long ago as the Hadow Report of 1926 as a device for creating clearer pictures of all aspects of pupils' abilities and qualities. It has only recently, however, been taken up to any significant extent.

It is not possible to consider the details of the several different schemes which can now be found. Their main feature, however, is that they attempt to gather together **all kinds of information** about individual pupils, not only marks in English or mathematics, but interests, hobbies, even personality traits. They thus attempt to produce a **composite picture** of all aspects of the individual. To do this, they include information from many different sources, not only from teachers or examiners; some of them even include comments by the individual pupils themselves; many of them certainly permit the pupil to decide what shall be included and, perhaps more significantly, what shall be left out of their profiles.

There are of course difficulties with these forms of assessment, but again we can see the potential for forms of assessment which will not be counter-productive to curriculum development or to planning curricula on a base other than the content or product base that traditional forms of assessment lead to.

We can conclude our discussion of examinations and the school curriculum, then, by saying that, while in reality their effect is often a damaging one, it is not necessary that this should be so. The use of **sensitive and sophisticated devices** for assessment can make possible not only the continuation of a curriculum we might wish to defend on educational grounds but also, almost certainly, a more worthwhile, and more revealing and informative, assessment of the individual pupil. It is foolish to suggest, as did the recent manifesto of one of the major political parties in the United Kingdom, that all public examinations should be abolished. It is necessary to assess educational growth, development and attainment. What is crucial is that we do this in ways which will not **inhibit** such growth, development and attainment.

It must finally be suggested, however, that there is little evidence that much of this has yet been assimilated by those whose political pressures and influences on the curriculum we discussed in chapter 3. It would be good to be able to believe that the new scheme which is about to be launched might reflect what has been learnt by those working in the field during the last two or three decades, but it would be unwarranted optimism to anticipate this. Like the lessons of the work of the Schools Council, which we considered earlier, those of the advances in modes and techniques of assessment have yet to be learned by those whose control of education and the curriculum is increasing. And again the major thrust is **political** rather than educational.

Summary and conclusions

This chapter has attempted the very difficult task of introducing the reader to some of the complexities of the current curriculum debate. It set about this task first of all by considering several of the different **meanings** which can be, and have been, given to the term 'curriculum', and then by considering the different **approaches** to curriculum planning, the different planning models, one might adopt according to where one's view of schooling encouraged one to place the major emphasis.

Thus we saw that it is possible to see the school curriculum primarily in terms of its **content**; or in terms of its **intended outcomes**, its planned products, its aims and objectives; or in terms of the **processes** of educational development it is concerned to promote. Perhaps the most important point to be made, however, is that there are three different approaches to, or models of, curriculum planning, that they are different from each other in highly significant ways, and that many of the major problems which education currently faces are a result of the failure to recognize this and the assumption, made either in ignorance or from malice aforethought, that all planning must begin from statements of its aims and objectives. It is one thing to recognize the significance of industry and commerce for educational planning; it is quite another to slip from that into the assumption that educational planning must be a kind of industrial or commercial process or exercise.

We found ourselves concluding, however, that, for whatever reasons, it is that kind of thinking which lies behind many of the proposals for the school curriculum which have resulted from that movement towards more **direct political intervention** in schooling which we had outlined in chapter 3.

It was for this reason that we turned to an examination of some of those proposals against the background of the more theoretical discussion of the earlier part of the chapter. We considered some of the arguments for the establishment of **a common curriculum** or a common core to the curriculum, and then some of the difficulties this raised. We considered some of the particular difficulties it raised for the curriculum of the primary school, which is in many cases built on quite different principles and assumptions from those underlying the demands for a commonality of curricular provision. We looked too at the similar impact and problems which are resulting from the attempts to introduce procedures for **monitoring and evaluating** the work of schools and teachers and for thus making them publicly acceptable. It was suggested that we need to develop far more sophisticated monitoring techniques than most of those currently being used or advocated if we are to ensure that education may continue to be that complex process we defined in chapter 1, and if its essential elements are not to be lost in the process of measuring only that which can be **prespecified** or, worse, **quantified**. We noted that more sophisticated techniques have been developed, but also that these have been such as to point us again towards the idea of education as an individual process depending to a larger extent than is often appreciated on the quality of the interaction between individual teachers and pupils.

This led us in turn to ask whether such **central planning** of the curriculum is possible, whether education can be planned and operated by remote control. In order to attempt to answer this, we looked briefly at the work of the Schools Council and suggested that, while its clearly documented lack of direct impact on the curriculum seemed to indicate that such external control is impracticable, its evident influence on the quality of our thinking about the curriculum encouraged the view that the role of such a central agency might be not to direct the curriculum so much as to promote in teachers the kind of understanding that would enable them to take greater professional control of it for themselves.

At this point, as indeed at several other points throughout the chapter, we noted the conflict between this view, based as it is on the experience of more than twenty years of attempts at supporting curriculum development, and the view that underpins the curriculum proposals emanating from current attempts to secure more direct political control over schools. And this was the conclusion we also reached when we went on to explore the impact of **the public examination system** on the school curriculum. There again, we saw that it is possible to use that system to support the kinds of development the experience of those working in the field have led to in many places; indeed, that these developments are likely to lead to better, more accurate and more useful forms of pupil assessment; but that the reality of current political pressures is likely to inhibit rather than to promote a positive move forward in this sphere, as much as in any other.

We thus conclude this chapter with the same dilemma with which we concluded the last. We saw from the political perspective the extent of the conflict between the demands for external control of the curriculum and the insistence of teachers that they must be free to make their own professional judgments. It was also made clear that this conflict creates or reflects a number of educational and curriculum problems. The present chapter has now highlighted some of these. It has also attempted to indicate some of the directions in which a solution might be sought.

A major aspect of this conflict, a major reason for this dilemma and a major source of the disagreement underlying both will be found in differences in the concept of education adopted. In particular, it is the view of education as **development**, rather than as merely the acquisition of skills or knowledge, which leads to the kinds of view which many teachers take and the kinds of practice they wish to be free to adopt. It is to a more detailed discussion of this notion of education as development that we must turn in our next chapter.

Suggested further reading

Blenkin, G. M. and Kelly, A. V., *The Primary Curriculum*, second edition, Harper & Row: London, 1987.

Downey, M. E. and Kelly, A. V., *Theory and Practice of Education: An Introduction*, third edition, Harper & Row: London, Ch. 7, 1986.

Holt, M., *Schools and Curriculum Change*, McGraw-Hill: London, 1980.

Kelly, A. V., *The Curriculum: Theory and Practice*, second edition, Harper & Row: London, 1982.

5
Education and the development of the child

Most of the issues we have explored in the earlier chapters of this book have suggested that there is a deep and fundamental conflict between the view of schooling as concerned with **the growth and development** of individual children and that which sees it in terms of the transmission of knowledge and skills or of the economic health of society. They have also suggested, however, that even those who stress the latter view still, albeit in a somewhat muddled way, hanker after the former. Most people do look to schools to bring children up 'proper', if only by making them one of the first targets for criticism when there is evidence of indiscipline in society, and thus implying that they regard schools and teachers as having a major responsibility for this aspect of the development of children. All teachers will be well aware that even those parents whose demands of the school seem to be confined to what it can offer their children in terms of examination successes, qualifications and career prospects are very quick to criticize if they feel the school is not attending adequately to their **character training**, their personal, social and moral upbringing, and even, in some cases I have known, their table manners. Yet there is a fundamental contradiction and inconsistency here, since concentration on the more academic or vocational aspects of schooling may not only lead to less emphasis being placed on other aspects of the development of pupils, it may also even be counterproductive to these forms of development.

The same inconsistency is to be seen also in those recent movements towards increased political intervention in schooling. The fact that these are framed, as we have seen, almost entirely in terms of the acquisition of knowledge and skills and of vocational and economic viability does not prevent the very people who are responsible for them from also expecting schools to attend to these other broader aspects of development. Again the potential incompatibility goes unrecognized and unchallenged.

Nor is the dilemma confined to the conflict between intellectual development and other forms of growth, such as the moral, the social or the personal. There is conflict too **within the notion of intellectual development**, since this too can be seen either as the acquisition of knowledge or as the development of understanding, and an emphasis on the former can be as detrimental to the latter as it is to any other kind of development. Again this is not always appreciated, and the emphasis on knowledge, especially as it manifests itself in most of the forms of pupil assessment used in our schools monitoring tests, public examinations and so on – not only leads to a loss of attention for the promotion of understanding, it is also too often inhibiting of and counter-productive to it.

Yet we noted in chapter 1 that even those major theorists who, from the time of Plato onwards, have been concerned to tell us what education should consist of, what kinds of knowledge pupils should be exposed to, have at the same time been concerned not so much with the knowledge itself as with what they believed it would contribute to **the development of the educated person**. Their prime concern has been with **qualities of mind**. None of them, as we saw, has been prepared to judge the educated person by reference to what he or she **knows** but rather by reference to the level and forms of that person's **understanding**, placing the emphasis not on bodies of knowledge acquired but on capacities of mind developed – powers of critical analysis, for example, breadth of understanding and the ability to think things through in order to come to one's own conclusions about them. Again, therefore, we see the inconsistency.

We also noted in chapter 1 that it was this as much as any other single factor which had led to the emergence of a quite different view of education, one which placed the emphasis on the processes of education rather than its content or its products, and which thus laid stress on the idea of education as development. We also saw that this view both encouraged and was itself stimulated by the advent of a new form of psychology, **the study of child development**. Rousseau himself, regarded, as we saw in chapter 1, as the founder of this new educational philosophy, stressed the need for its practice to be supported by research into the ways in which children think and the ways in which they develop. 'We know nothing of childhood; and with our mistaken notions the further we advance the further we go astray. The wisest writers devote themselves to what a man ought to know, without asking what a child is capable of learning. They are always looking for the man in the child, without considering what he is before he becomes a man.'

The concern to face squarely the implications of a view of education as development, then, has been there for a long time. And it is this that has stimulated the study of child development which has been a major feature of the development of psychology in this century. It is this, then, which will form the main focus of this chapter.

The inadequacies of behaviourist psychology as a basis for educational planning

Child psychology

There are two important points made in that quotation from Rousseau we have just noted. The first of these is the demand that we should attempt to learn more about **human psychology**. The second is perhaps less obvious but it is very important for an understanding of studies in child development and for the way in which we should set about our exploration of human psychology. For the second point that Rousseau is making is that we should begin by recognizing that **the psychology of the child is different from that of the adult**, so that, if education is to be planned as a proper form of development, then we must cease 'looking for the man in the child' and attempt to discover 'what he is before he becomes a man'; we must try to discover how children think and we must recognize that their thought processes may well be **qualitatively different** from those of the mature adult.

This, then, is not only a central feature of theories of cognitive development, as we shall see later in this chapter, it is also a major weakness in those forms of **behaviourist psychology** which have tended to dominate education theory. These have never acknowledged the possibility of such qualitative differences between child and adult psychology nor, therefore, between child and adult learning.

Animal learning

Indeed, not only have behaviourists been unwilling or unable to distinguish the learning of children from that of adults, they have also been unwilling to recognize the existence of qualitative differences between human learning and that of **animals**. Much of the experimental work which has been carried out in this sphere has taken the form of **studies of animal behaviour** – rats, dogs, cats, pigeons etc. – and, from what has been observed there, generalizations have been made about human behaviour and extrapolations made to human learning, so that teaching has been seen as the process by which we change human behaviour. Thus methods which have been shown to be successful in **changing or modifying the behaviour of animals**, in teaching them to perform certain tasks or tricks, have been offered to, recommended to, and even, one might say, pressed upon teachers and educationists for use in the teaching of children.

To this end, for example, the Russian psychologist, Pavlov, experimented with dogs. Dogs naturally salivate when faced by meat. In Pavlov's experiment, each time they were offered meat a bell was rung, so that they eventually came to **associate** the bell with meat. Finally, Pavlov was able to show that they would salivate at the sound of the bell even if the meat were not offered (although it is not irrelevant to note that they did not go on doing this for very long).

From this experiment emerged several notions which it was claimed were of great significance to the teaching of children. First the ideas of **association** and **associative learning**; we naturally associate things which we usually experience together, and this natural tendency, it is argued, can be used to promote learning. Second, the idea of learning as a **developed response to a stimulus**, the stimulus–response (S–R) approach to teaching; organisms respond to stimuli and this too can be used as a teaching device. This process of learning or teaching has been called **classical conditioning**.

Further studies, by psychologists such as E. L. Thorndike and B. F. Skinner, led to a development of this view of learning. Thorndike, for example, added to the notions we picked out in Pavlov's work, the idea of **trial and error learning**. His experiment involved hungry cats who were placed in a box with an escape mechanism and in full view of food outside the box. Once the cat had accidentally triggered the escape mechanism and thus obtained the food, it was likely to do so more quickly on subsequent occasions until eventually it had learnt how to operate the mechanism and was thus able to release itself immediately. Similar experiments were conducted by others who were able to show, for example, how animals can learn to find their way through mazes by the same kind of trial and error technique.

It was the American psychologist, B. F. Skinner, who did most to urge the transfer of this kind of knowledge of animal learning to the classroom. A major addition which he himself made to this kind of theory was the idea that, if learning is the result of this kind of reinforcement of trial and error behaviour, then **positive reinforcement**, in the form of reward, is more effective as a device for promoting such learning than **negative reinforcement**, in the form of punishment. Animals learn best when rewarded for correct responses, usually by the granting of food, than when punished for incorrect responses by some such device as an electric shock. Thus, if an animal is given food if it succeeds in pressing the correct button and activating a bell or a buzzer, it learns more quickly than if it is punished by the infliction of pain for incorrect behaviour.

This kind of knowledge of animal learning led Skinner to advocate the use of similar techniques in the teaching of children. He advocated the use of techniques of what he called **'operant conditioning'**, the giving of positive reinforcement each time the learner makes a correct response. It is not now a case of trial and error, of learning from one's own mistakes; it is a matter of receiving an immediate reward for the correct behaviour. Thus, in Skinner's view, the learning of anything, no matter how complex, could best be promoted by breaking it down into **very small component parts** and teaching children the correct response to each of these **in sequence**.

It was for this reason that Skinner expressed great contempt for teachers as inadequate operators of this kind of sequenced, reward-based learning, and suggested the development and the use of **teaching-machines** as likely to be far more efficient in providing children with access to knowledge.

Limited concept of education and curriculum

It is perhaps at this point that the inadequacies of this approach to education begin to emerge. The first of these is undoubtedly the very limited concept of education which lies behind this kind of learning theory. We have seen that the term **conditioning** is often used to denote such theories and our discussion of education in chapter 1 will have alerted us to some of the connotations of that term. Certainly it will have drawn our attention to important differences between conditioning and education.

The view of teaching which underpins such theories of learning is twofold. First, it is seen as concerned with **the transmission of knowledge**. And, second, it is seen as a form of **behaviour modification**. It is for this reason that it has been this kind of psychological theory to which educationists have appealed when they were concerned to press those views of education we have noted elsewhere as being framed confidently in terms of the knowledge-content or subjects to be transmitted. For, if we are certain about that, the only real question which remains is how we can transmit it most efficiently and economically. However, as we have also noted elsewhere, this kind of approach does not make it possible for us to ask questions about the value of what is to be transmitted nor about its impact on the child, except in narrow behaviourist terms. A major difference between this kind of theory and developmental approaches to psychology, as we shall see later, is that the latter have contributed much to our understanding of education itself, have promoted the development of a concept of education as different from **mere learning** and have thus adopted a role in education theory which goes well beyond considerations of mere methodology.

It is also not difficult to understand why it was from this behaviourist source that there emerged all that pressure to see education **instrumentally**, in **product-based** terms, to see it as a **step-by-step**, linear process towards the achievement of certain **aims and objectives**. We examined in chapter 4 some of the inadequacies and difficulties of that approach to educational planning. One can see now that the idea of careful sequencing of objectives is exactly what emerges from this kind of behaviourist psychology. One can see too how it offers no grounds upon which one might attempt to evaluate the aims and objectives themselves.

We come back to a recognition of the fact that the view of education which underpins this kind of approach and which lies behind the advocacy of the use of this kind of teaching technique is a view not of education as such but of some form of **conditioning**, or **behaviour modification**. And our discussion of education in chapter 1 raised some of the moral as well as the educational implications of that view, although we must note that there are still many people who do accept it, especially in relation to the schooling of handicapped children or, worse, those dubbed maladjusted or disruptive. The central inadequacies of this view are well illustrated in the story of the two rats in Skinner's laboratory, one of whom said to the other, 'I have this chap, Skinner, so well conditioned that every time I sound this buzzer he brings me something to eat'!

This implies in turn that there are inadequacies not only in the view of education but also in the **view of learning** which is adopted here and we must finally turn briefly to a consideration of that.

Unsophisticated view of learning

In addition to treating education as some form of conditioning or behaviour modification, indeed because they take that kind of view, these behaviourist theories also see learning as a **passive event** and the recipients of these forms of teaching, the children themselves, like the animals which have been the objects of their experiments, as having only a **passive role** to play in the process. They have thus failed to recognize any **qualitative differences** between kinds of learning.

Yet there clearly are such differences and they are, equally clearly, of great importance to education. A. N. Whitehead once drew an important distinction between the acquisition of **inert ideas**, pieces of knowledge passively received and remembered which at no stage become in any real sense a part of the individual's understanding or way of perceiving the world, and the **growth of understanding**, the assimilation of knowledge in such a manner that it becomes **genuine experience** and a significant part of the individual's armoury for coping with his or her environment. We can now see that behaviourist psychology cannot make this kind of distinction. It sees all learning as the making of **connections** between what is already known and the new information being presented; it regards the process as a linear, step-by-step building up of bodies of largely factual knowledge – the analogies most often used are those of bricks being added to bricks to build a wall or of links being added to a chain of learning; and it sees the learner as the **passive recipient** of what is offered.

However, it is clear that not all learning is the same, and, in particular, that **not all learning contributes to development**. It is clear that we need to be able to distinguish **cognitive or intellectual growth** or development from **mere learning**. It is thus clear that we need to be able to make **qualitative** judgments about the kinds of learning which teachers might promote and which children might be exposed to. And, finally, it might also be apparent that a crucial ingredient in the kind of learning which promotes, or even actually constitutes, cognitive or intellectual development will be the **active engagement** of the pupil with the material or the experiences which are offered him or her. Education is **an interactive process** and it is the one-way transmission model which is the fundamental weakness of behaviourist approaches to educational psychology.

All these last points are features of developmental psychology. The developmental approach to the study of human learning has endeavoured to avoid and to correct all the weaknesses of behaviourism. If, then, one's view of education goes beyond the mere transmission of agreed bodies of knowledge or the attainment of approved objectives, if one sees it as a form, or as many forms, of development, if one consequently recognizes it as a process in which the pupil must play an active part rather than adopt the passive role of recipient, then one needs **a different kind of educational psychology**. It is this that developmental psychology has attempted to offer. We must now look in some detail at what has emerged from work in this field.

Studies of cognitive development

We might begin our exploration of these newer forms of psychological study by looking at the work of the two major figures in this field, the Frenchman, **Jean Piaget**, and the American, **Jerome Bruner**. We should then be in a position to pick out what are the main features of this approach.

Jean Piaget

Jean Piaget was not a psychologist, and it may well have been that which enabled him to break the behaviourist mould. His concern was not to propose ways in which we might promote learning, or even development, nor to discover what makes learning or development possible. Rather he was concerned to describe development and, as a philosopher rather than a psychologist, to discover **what intellectual development is** and how human beings come to acquire knowledge. He calls this approach **genetic epistemology**.

He set out, by close observation of children, to attempt to discover how they develop certain **basic intellectual concepts**, such as space, time and the fundamental concepts of logic. His observations led him to the conclusion that the truth was to be found in neither of the two major current views of how understanding develops in children, neither that which explained this in terms of genetic inheritance nor that which regarded it as a result of environmental influences. In his view, both of these factors play a part and, more important, they do so only through a process of interaction in which the child must himself or herself be active. From the outset, therefore, he sees the child not as a passive object to be acted upon by external forces in the environment but as **an active participant** in his or her own development, **interacting** with the world outside first, in infancy, in a direct, overt and concrete form, and later, with maturity, in a covert and often largely abstract form.

We can thus see already two major characteristics of this approach. First, it sees learning, in the full sense of learning which is contributory to intellectual development, as **an active process** in which the learner must be directly engaged with the environment. And, second, it claims that the thinking of the child is **qualitatively different** from that of the adult, or at least of the mature adult.

Let us look a little more closely at what he says about both of these features.

Active learning

The notion of active learning implies that development, and thus real learning, will only take place if the child is actively involved in the process. Intellectual development comes about as we **structure and restructure our perceptions** of our environment through the manipulation of that environment.

He offers us several concepts which are of crucial importance to an understanding of what he is saying. The mind, or the intellect, is perpetually striving to achieve a balance between its current levels or modes of understanding and the new experiences which interaction with the environment provides. This balance Piaget calls **equilibration** and it is achieved by **assimilation** and **accommodation**, as the intellect assimilates new experiences and accommodates these to **existing cognitive structures** or 'schemata'. The analogy with the digestive system, which some people have offered, is quite helpful in understanding what he is suggesting here. Finally, this process is one by which the individual moves towards **maturation**. This point takes us on to a consideration of his second main claim, that the child's thinking is qualitatively different from that of the mature adult.

For 'maturation' is essentially a process by which intellectual development moves from a form in which it is immature and somewhat primitive towards one in which it has reached a level of sophistication associated with **full intellectual functioning**. Nor is this merely a matter of developing strengths; there are fundamental differences of **form**; and Piaget claims that there are several kinds of intellectual functioning, and that maturation is the process by which children pass through the **several stages of intellectual development** which he describes.

Stages of development

Piaget suggests that there are **four** main stages of intellectual development, each characterized by its own **qualitatively distinctive mode** of thinking and problem-solving.

The first of these he calls the **sensori-motor** stage, and it lasts, he believes, for about the first two years of the child's life. At this stage, the child's understanding of the world is limited to his or her own **physical interactions** with it. He or she makes purely **motor adjustments** to objects around him or her. There is no sense that these objects have any existence outside the child's perception and handling of them. Thus, if a toy is dropped by the baby or removed by someone, no attempt is made to recover it, and there is no evidence of any kind of sense that it still exists, of any understanding that objects have an existence outside of oneself, independently of one's own actions and perceptions. A major feature of this stage, then, is its **egocentrism**. Furthermore, the child is able only to **perform** actions, not to **represent** them; there is no basis for any kind of **symbolic representation**.

Several things occur during this period. Some kind of **concept of permanence** begins to emerge and the child begins to recognize the possibility of making some of the events in his or her world continue or endure. This in turn reveals the beginnings of what Piaget calls **intentionality**, a recognition that one can make things happen. Thus, at this stage, the child begins to look for the toy which has been dropped or taken away. Understanding of the world now goes beyond one's own physical interaction with it, and **the beginnings of some symbolic representation** become apparent.

The child is now entering the second stage of intellectual development, that of **pre-operational thought**, which Piaget suggests lasts from two until about seven years of age. This stage might also be described as **pre-logical**. For, although some kind of symbolic representation, through, for example, the rudiments of language or through games of 'pretending', begins to be possible, so that the child can go beyond the immediate environment in his or her thinking, the mechanisms of logical reasoning are not yet available to the functioning intellect. Piaget suggests that the most important characteristic of this stage is what he calls **irreversibility**, the inability to **retrace** thinking, to go back over things in order to sort them out. It is a period which is also still one of egocentrism; the child can only view things from his or her own perspective. Reasoning, if one can yet call it such, is still based on **perceptual appearances**.

Both of these features of this stage can be seen in the continued absence of what Piaget calls **conservation**, the ability to recognize that quantity of substance may remain the same even when put into different shapes. Thus, even after witnessing the pouring of water from a tall, thin container into a small, squat container, the child will confidently assert that there is less water there; and we can also see children at this stage converting tall towers of building bricks into squat 'houses' and then looking around for the 'missing' bricks.

It is the emerging ability to 'reverse', to 'retrace', to 'conserve' that is the major indication that a child has entered the third stage of development, that of **concrete operations**, which Piaget suggests lasts from seven to about twelve years of age. At this stage, the child can reason that his or her bricks have not been lost in the process of converting the tall tower into a squat house, because he or she can understand that simply by **reversing the process** the tall tower could be reproduced, or the water returned to the tall container. This is a major step forward and marks **the beginning of logical reasoning**.

A second important characteristic of this period, however, is that which distinguishes it from the following and final stage which Piaget posits. That characteristic is the continued dependence of the child on **concrete manifestations** or objects to aid the reasoning process. He or she can reason best when able to manipulate concrete objects in a practical situation. If and when the reasoning goes on in the mind, it is still necessary for the child to be able to relate this reasoning to **concrete experiences**. Margaret Donaldson, whose recent work may be seen as a development of that of Piaget, illustrates this very helpfully by suggesting that, whereas a child at this stage finds it very difficult to answer the question 'If Edith is fairer than Susan and darker than Lily, who is the darkest?', given three dolls to symbolize these three people, the same child seldom has difficulty in putting them into the correct sequence. The reasoning is dependent on the concrete.

The fourth and final stage of development is that which Piaget calls the stage of **formal operations**. This is the stage of the fully developed adult and is characterized by the ability to think and to reason in **abstract forms**, by the use of symbols rather than physical objects or their representations, and, in particular, by the use of that set of symbols we call 'language'.

Several things may now be clearer as a result of this brief survey of Piaget's stage theory of intellectual development. First, it should now be clear what is meant by suggesting that the thinking of children is **qualitatively different** from that of adults, along with the dangers of assuming that it is not and of 'always looking for the man in the child', as Rousseau put it. Second it should be apparent what is meant by **active learning**, what is implied by the claim that all learning which has significance for intellectual development involves a two-way process of interaction or engagement with the environment. Third, it should now be possible to see why some have claimed that the linear process of making connections in response to stimuli, whether rewards or punishments, and thus acquiring a chain-like collection of information, is far too unsophisticated a view of learning to be of any real value in promoting education in the sense of full intellectual growth.

Two further points must be made, however, both of which are forms of *caveat* and lead us quite naturally into a consideration of the work of the other major figure in this field, Jerome Bruner. The first of these is that the ages at which Piaget suggests children pass from one stage to the next are only **approximate**. They will vary greatly from child to child. What does not vary, Piaget claims, is their **sequence**; no one can reach the stage of formal operational thinking without passing through all of the earlier stages. (He also claims, incidentally, that they do not vary from culture to culture, that intellectual development follows the same sequence whatever the cultural environment.)

Second, it is very important to note that he is not claiming that everyone automatically reaches the stage of formal operations by a process of **simple maturation**. Intellectual development is not like physical development which happens more or less independently of the conditions created by the environment. Some adults, many in fact, never reach the stage of fully abstract thought but remain at the point where they are dependent on the concrete as a basis for their thinking. A moment's recollection of the amount of personal and anecdotal referencing that is to be found in many conversations between adults will confirm this. Many people can sort ideas out much better in terms of the concrete experiences of themselves or their friends and relatives than by reference to the ideas and concepts involved.

This last point leads us back to the significance of this theoretical perspective for education. For, if people do not automatically reach this final stage, clearly there is a **major role for education** to play in helping as many as possible to do so. We noted at the beginning of this section that it was Piaget's intention merely to describe the course of intellectual development and not to advise us on how we might promote it. This second task has been a major focus of the work of Jerome Bruner to which we now turn.

Jerome Bruner

Jerome Bruner developed this scheme of Piaget's in two major ways. First, as has just been indicated, he developed it positively and plainly into **a theory of instruction**, concerned not merely to describe intellectual development but also to suggest ways in which it might be promoted. Second, he modified Piaget's stage theory in such a way as to propose that what Piaget had described as stages, or something similar to them, are not merely points through which people pass on the road to intellectual maturity but also **modes of understanding and representation** which **persist into adulthood** and are used by people throughout their lives according to the particular contexts of the problems they face and their own favoured ways of approaching these.

Modes of representation

Bruner claims that the learner – not only in school but throughout life, since life is seen as a continuous process of intellectual reconstruction of experience – is constantly at work attempting to understand the world around him or her by **reducing its complexities** to bring it within the range of his or her **existing cognitive structures**. This the individual does by employing a number of different strategies or **modes** – ways of representing reality in a form in which it can be understood. He identifies three such modes by which the learner can represent the world.

The first way of representing the world is through **action**. This he calls the **enactive mode**. In this mode, children learn through action, through actually doing things. Clearly much of the small child's learning is of this kind, but it will not be difficult to see that in certain contexts much adult learning is of this kind too. If you want to teach someone to sail, for example, or, indeed, to learn to do so yourself, the only way to this is by doing it, by action, learning 'through the seat of one's pants', as it is often put.

The second mode of representation Bruner identifies is the **iconic mode**. This is somewhat like Piaget's stage of concrete operations. For in this mode, while it is not necessary to be doing anything, it is necessary to use **concrete representations** of the things one is attempting to understand or to teach, or at least to visualize these in concrete terms. Thus, in attempting to describe a particular move on the football field, for example, we might use counters or the cruets, sauce bottles etc. on the table in front of us, or draw diagrams on a blackboard or piece of paper. Or we might use models, as in the example of the dolls we referred to earlier. The point is that we understand and make sense of some things better when they are represented in this concrete form of examples, in an iconic mode. Again, it is not difficult to see that this is not merely a stage in cognitive growth or development, it is a **mode of representation** which we continue to use as and when it seems appropriate or suitable or congenial.

The third, and last, mode of representation Bruner identifies is what he calls the **symbolic mode**. Here our thinking is conducted and understanding achieved by the use of **symbols**, primarily those of **language**. Symbolic systems such as language greatly extend the potential range of our thinking and understanding. We are no longer tied to action or to concrete representations; we can go beyond the immediate and even into the realms of fantasy and hypothesis. And it is a much more economic system, offering great scope for the development of our understanding within a reasonably manageable frame.

Again, we can see that this is a stage in intellectual development, the final stage, the equivalent of Piaget's stage of formal operations. However, we can also see, first, that not all people automatically reach this stage, that it is not a matter of simple maturation, and, second, that it is not the case that those who have reached this stage use this mode only in the subsequent development of their understanding; **all three modes are now available to them**.

What he is suggesting, then, is that, although these three modes emerge in sequence, and thus at certain ages will be the most powerful and dominant influence on children's mental activity, they all **persist into adulthood**, continuing to function, and, indeed, interacting with each other, throughout all intellectual activity. As Bruner himself says, in his book *Towards a Theory of Instruction*, 'What is abidingly interesting about the nature of intellectual development is that it seems to run the course of these three systems of representation until the human being is able to command all three'.

Theories of instruction

Piaget, as we saw, was primarily concerned to describe the process of intellectual development; Bruner is concerned to go beyond that and to **prescribe** or recommend, in the light of our knowledge of how intellectual development proceeds, how we should be setting about the planning of educational provision. It is perhaps also worth noting that, in doing this, he offers us more than a mere teaching methodology, of the kind we saw to be the most that behaviourist psychology could offer. For this view of intellectual development leads us to a completely **different conception of education**, to a view of education as the process by which children's intellectual growth is promoted, not one by which certain bodies of knowledge-content are transmitted or acquired. **Knowing is a process rather than a product**, he tells us. If this is so, then the emphasis in education must be on the subject of that process, the child, and his or her growth and development, not on the knowledge or skills in which he or she is to be instructed or trained.

We are offered a view of education or a theory of instruction which begins from the notion that education is the **reconstruction of experience**, that it is the process by which children are assisted to make sense of their worlds, and helped to acquire the use of those different modes of representation which will enable them to do so with increasing effectiveness and competence. The prime concern is to **amplify** the individual's powers of understanding and thus his or her control over the environment.

An inevitable corollary of this is that education must be seen as an **interactive process**. If this kind of intellectual growth through the constant restructuring of experience is to take place, then the child must be **actively engaged** with the material of his or her learning; that material must represent **genuine experience** for the child. It must not, therefore, be 'disembodied', 'decontextualized', 'inert', as, one has to say, so much of school learning continues to be. It must be **meaningful** to the pupil; it must strike him or her as being worth understanding, worth making the effort to come to terms with, worth taking into and accommodating within his or her existing cognitive structures. Hence the notion of active learning, not in the sense of busy, gross, physical activity, as is sometimes naively assumed, but as full and active involvement in the process of learning, becomes supreme. Education is seen as concerned not with 'mere learning' but with **genuine intellectual development**. And the analogy for a curriculum which will promote this kind of process is not that of adding brick to brick, or links to a chain, or ascending a ladder step by step; it is that of a spiral staircase on which we constantly return to the same points but at higher levels of understanding.

Bruner's main contribution to this kind of thinking about education has been to direct our attention to **the role of the teacher** in this form of educational process. The teacher's role, as we have just suggested, is to promote the growth of the child by showing him or her how to recode his or her experiences through the development of increasingly powerful and effective systems of representation. As he himself says, again in *Towards a Theory of Instruction*, 'the heart of the educational process consists of providing aids and dialogues for translating experience into more powerful systems of notations and ordering'.

Thus not only has he modified that description of intellectual development which Piaget offered us, he has also, more importantly, begun the process of turning this into **teaching action**. Both of these dimensions are important to an understanding of subsequent developments in this field.

Subsequent developments

It would be a mistake to regard what has happened in developmental psychology since Bruner offered us the analysis which has just been outlined as developments *from* his work. Rather they are developments *of* his work and he himself has continued, and indeed continues, to be very much involved in them. In particular, much has come from his observations of **very young children** – not least the notion of the **'competent newborn'**, the claim that the newly born infant is not merely a physical presence with a body to be fed and attended to, but is also possessed of an intellect, which, from day one, begins to operate on all aspects of the environment, attempting to make sense of them and to develop those cognitive structures he speaks of. From day one, this is also an interactive process, the child attempting to manipulate the environment as well as to understand it.

Children are thus already **highly skilled when they enter school**. If the demands of the school are often beyond them, it is because those demands are wrongly framed and not properly matched to their levels of intellectual functioning. This is especially so when those demands are unduly 'academic'. There needs to be a proper level of **cognitive conflict** between the child's experience and his or her cognitive structures, a level at which any mismatch can be resolved and the new experience assimilated and accommodated. If the conflict is too extreme, if it exceeds the optimum level, the child will be faced with an impossible task and will thus not attempt it.

This highlights the importance of the **context** of the child's learning, and several points of major significance stem from that. The first is that it prompts some questioning of Piaget's claim that the young child's learning is egocentric. The evidence seems to suggest that, from the earliest age, children are highly sensitive to all aspects of the context of their development, including, most importantly, **the social aspect**. Even the very young baby is aware of significant adults, and his or her interaction is with the social as well as the material environment. Few parents are unaware of the attempts even of their very small babies to 'manipulate' them. And this is why we can also see older children becoming confused when dealing with what looks like a straightforward intellectual task by features of the social context of that task – being more interested, for example, in the nature of the relationship between the bus conductor and the passenger in a picture in a 'number' book than in the calculation of how much change he or she must give from a £1 coin for a 40p ticket.

Thus **the social aspects of learning** must be recognized as being highly significant not merely to the child's social development but also to his or her intellectual development. This has many important implications for the social context and climate of the classroom – for teacher–pupil relationships and for interpersonal relationships of all kinds. We have noted the claim that proper intellectual growth requires a genuine interaction with the environment. We must now note further that this implies a genuine interaction with the **social dimensions** of that environment too.

A second major development has been the emphasis which has come to be placed on **the development of language** as a major, indeed central, feature of the process of cognitive growth. It was noted long ago how successful children are in developing spoken language long before any formal attempt is made to teach them or to help them with its development. There is much to be learnt from that for the organization of education and the planning of the curriculum. It has also been noted that children do not merely learn language in the connectionist sense of the behaviourist. They actually seek out **the rules of language** for themselves, clear evidence of the process of intellectual structuring and restructuring in the attempt to make sense of experience. This is why children make those common 'mistakes' in English grammar – 'I taked' for 'I took', 'mouses' for 'mice' etc. They are seeking to identify rules of syntax and grammar and to apply them.

The development of language, then, can be seen as a paradigm of intellectual development. It is also, however, much more than that: it is the very stuff of that **symbolic mode of representation** we noted earlier as offering far more scope for understanding existence and experience than any other mode. Thus a major feature of the emphasis on education as development has been, and must inevitably be, a concern with language development as a crucial and essential part of that process.

A third aspect of the context of learning which has recently been stressed as being of great significance is the **cultural aspect**. Some writers have seen the role of the school in relation to culture to be that of responsibility for transmitting this culture. Thus many have argued that the culture of society should form the basis of the content of the curriculum – a very difficult position to maintain in a society which regards itself as multicultural. The view of developmental psychology is that the culture should be seen as influencing the child's cognitive growth by providing **cultural amplifiers** – amplifiers of action, amplifiers of the senses, amplifiers of thought processes – and thus facilitating both the understanding of experience through those modes of representation and their development within the individual child.

Thus education is seen as **the growth of competence**, as the development of powers of control over one's environment through increasingly sophisticated forms of intellectual interaction with it. The assumption is that all human beings naturally pursue **meaning**, that they automatically seek to make sense of their world of experience and that education offers us opportunities to help them to develop the powers of doing so. Meaning is seen as something human beings **construe** rather than **discover**, so that the role of the school is to help them to construe such meanings within their own experience, and not to offer them the experiences and the meanings of others, since these can only be understood if they are meaningful experiences to the child him- or herself.

Two further points need to be made. The first of these is that this is essentially an **individual** matter. To say that is not to say that the educational process must be individualized, that children will learn best on their own or with a one-to-one link to a teacher (or, better, a teaching machine). For the importance of the social context, as we saw just now, must not be ignored. It does mean, however, that we must view the development of each child, albeit within a supportive social context, as an individual matter. What is significant is not whether he or she has 'covered the syllabus' or 'developed the basic skills' as defined by someone else; it is whether his or her intellectual growth is being forwarded, whether there is evidence of the growth of competence, whether those general intellectual skills of handling experience, those modes of representation, are developing.

This takes us to the second further point. It is being claimed by many of those working in this field that the present school curriculum is far too narrowly conceived to make such development likely or even to encourage it. There is, it is claimed an **over-emphasis on discursive and numerical forms of representation**. The curriculum is predicated on a narrow view of the range of modes of representation available to human beings, the kinds of cultural amplifiers offered by the environment, and, indeed, a narrow conception of what language development itself is. The full development of our thought processes depends on our having access to a **range** of forms of representation and modes of expression. This range is notably absent from the curriculum of most schools. The effect of this is more likely to be a stunting of development than a forwarding of it. It is claimed, therefore, that the scope of the curriculum, even when defined only in terms of its content or the subjects it is to contain, must be expanded and, more than this, that the manner in which these subjects are taught or presented to pupils should also be modified to ensure that they are presented, and thus represented, in different ways.

In particular, the claim is that the school curriculum too often ignores the **expressive** and the **emotive** aspects of development, what has come to be called the **affective** dimension. This, it is argued, is an important part of human experience. We do not, as human beings, respond merely cognitively or intellectually to our environment; we respond emotively too. This, after all, is fundamentally the import of the social context of learning which, we noted earlier, is coming to be regarded as highly important. What we have come to, then, is the idea that the affective context of learning is also crucial for the achievement of properly skilled levels of cognitive functioning, so that, even if our concern is purely with that, we cannot ignore the need for simultaneous and harmonious development on the **affective** front.

To see education as development, then, is to see it as more than merely cognitive development. We must now turn to a consideration of some of the implications of that in the final major section of this chapter.

Affective development

The importance of this dimension

Few people would wish seriously to dispute the claim that a proper form of education should concern itself with the **emotional development** of children, their growth as persons, as much as with their intellectual development. Yet, in spite of this, a good deal of educational provision – too much, many would say – is planned and implemented as though education's sole concern was with knowledge and with learning of a purely intellectual kind. Far more attention is given, in discussions of education by the theorists, in the prescriptions offered by official groups, such as Her Majesty's Inspectorate, especially in their 'discussion documents', in the allocation of resources and, consequently, in the planning of school curricula, to **the acquisition of knowledge** and the development of intellectual abilities than to **the development of feeling** and the growth of capacities such as sensitivity to the needs and feelings of others, the ability to understand and cope with the emotional side of one's own nature and other features of what has been called the affective dimension or domain of education.

Furthermore, it is equally clear that, when attention is given to this dimension, the tendency is to see it as **separate** from the cognitive domain of education, and thus as something for which **separate provision** must be made. This is particularly true, as we shall see in the next chapter, in the area of personal, social and moral education, which is increasingly the subject of separate sets of prescriptions and thus of separate forms of provision.

Yet a moment's thought will reveal that there is – or should be – **an affective dimension to all areas** of learning and development of a kind we might, in the light of our discussion in chapter 1, be prepared to describe as educational. This is the case not only because of the claim we have just seen being made as a result of recent developments in psychology that the emotional context of children's learning is crucial even to their intellectual development; it is the case also because the view of education in the full sense which we outlined in chapter 1 requires that there be a proper emotional engagement with activities and experiences for them to be accepted as fully educational. Children's education will not be promoted unless, for example, they come to **enjoy** the activities and experiences they are engaged in, recognize them as **valuable**, see them as **sources of satisfaction**. All of these responses are, at least in part, emotional or affective responses, so that we must recognize that education does not merely have an affective domain or dimension, it is itself **essentially** an affective or emotional process.

For this reason, the importance of that emotional dimension has always been stressed in the works of the great educational theorists, even if it is has not always been fully understood or handled very productively. From Plato's time onwards, discussions of education have endeavoured to take account of the fact that human beings are creatures of feeling as well as of intellect. And all the major reports of the present century in the United Kingdom have, in one way or another, stressed the importance of this dimension of development, if only, for example, by pressing strongly for the inclusion in the curriculum of **the 'arts' subjects** as one way of attempting to ensure that this dimension would be adequately catered for.

Theoretical and practical inadequacies

Most of the major reports have felt the need to stress the importance of this area of education mainly because of an awareness of the inadequacy of much that was to be seen actually happening in schools. Furthermore, the inadequacies which they have identified have usually resulted in their recommendations in this area being largely ignored and seldom implemented. What is more disturbing is that the recent escalation of political interventionism in the school curriculum in the United Kingdom, which we noted in both chapters 3 and 4, has been characterized by **a reduction in the emphasis** placed on this aspect of education in favour of an increased stress on science and technology. It will be remembered that this was the theme of James Callaghan's speech at Ruskin College, Oxford, in which, as Prime Minister, he began the public debate on the school curriculum and set out its parameters, one of which was that, since teachers had been letting society down by placing too much emphasis on arts and Humanities subjects rather than ensuring a proper supply of scientists and technologists, the curriculum of the future should be planned in such a way as to redress that balance.

Thus the pressures on schools since that time have been in the opposite direction, and it has become increasingly difficult to attend adequately to this affective dimension of education. It has had little support in any of the official pronouncements which have emerged in support of new curricular initiatives, even the document on *English from 5 to 16*, for example, stressing the mechanistic rather than the literary aspects of that subject. And it is becoming increasingly difficult, at all levels of educational provision, including – and perhaps especially – that of higher education, to obtain adequate resources to support continued efforts and developments in this field. The implications of this kind of policy for society were well brought out by Enoch Powell in a recent article in *The Times Educational Supplement*, entitled 'A Modern Barbarism', in which he rightly drew attention to the fact that this represents an emphasis on **the mechanisms of existence** rather than its quality, and on questions of *how* we are to achieve certain goals rather than of *what* goals are worth achieving.

The same point needs to be made about the implications of this policy not only for society but also for the individuals who comprise that society. It is clear not only that education has always under-emphasized, and indeed undervalued, the emotional or affective development of children, but also that this tendency is rapidly increasing within our own present-day society. Its dangers, especially in respect of stunting the full growth of children into adult human beings, will be apparent from what has already been said. Some of the reasons for it, however, are interesting and worthy of fuller exploration.

Reasons for these inadequacies

One major factor which is of special significance in explaining the recent decline in the attention given to this area of the curriculum, and also that traditional attitude we mentioned just now, is the **lack of any utilitarian justification** for activities of this kind. At a time when there are increasing demands that the school system should be able to demonstrate its productivity, to show that the nation is receiving value for the money spent on the education system, there is an inevitable tendency to define productivity and value for money in terms of economic viability. That, after all, was the thrust of James Callaghan's Ruskin speech, as we have just seen. Evaluated in these terms, subjects or activities like art, drama, dance and even history are not likely to score highly, so it is not surprising to find the attention given to them diminishing and the resources allocated to them being reduced.

Allied to this is a second factor, **the difficulty of measurement and assessment** in these areas. It is much easier to examine and even to quantify a child's intellectual development – especially if one takes a narrow view of what this consists of – than it is his or her emotional or affective development. You can measure a child's mathematical abilities with some degree of accuracy, but how can one measure emotional maturity, sensitivity of feeling or even aesthetic awareness? Again, in a climate of increased school and teacher accountability, and thus of increased pressure for the measurement and assessment of educational achievement, those things which are difficult to measure are at risk. It is worth reminding ourselves in this context that the major agency established by the government for the monitoring of performance in schools, the Assessment of Performance Unit (APU), has given up, at least for the present, its attempts to monitor performance in the aesthetic field, having found this impossible to define, let alone measure. The main effect of this must be a loss of emphasis on this aspect of education in schools in favour of those areas of performance which can and will be monitored.

This last point highlights a fundamental difficulty which explains to a large degree the problems that always seem to have been experienced in this area of the curriculum, in both theory and practice, **the lack of any clear understanding** of it or of any really compelling theory of how it might be handled. Children's emotional development has never been fully understood, so that everyone, theorists and practitioners alike, have had the utmost difficulty in handling it.

Rationalist approaches

A major reason for this difficulty has been that emphasis on knowledge and, indeed, on a rationalist philosophical perspective on knowledge, which we noted when we were discussing theories of knowledge in chapter 1. From the time of Plato the human being has been regarded as a 'rational animal' and reason as his or her most important attribute. This kind of perspective must lead one to view education more in terms of **the knowledge to be transmitted**, or even of intellectual development, than of **the promotion of development of any other kind**. Furthermore, it must lead to major difficulties in handling, or even understanding, those other forms of development, since, by definition, it can only see the world in rational terms. It must, as a result, find it impossible to offer any explanation of those areas of human experience which are largely, if not totally, irrational; human feelings and emotions. In fact, it has devised only two ways of accommodating this aspect of human existence within its rationalist perspective, both of which are important not only for an understanding of why education has too often gone wrong in this area but also for the search for a more productive and satisfactory solution.

Reduction to the cognitive
The first device that has been used for explaining this dimension of human existence and for suggesting how education might be planned to take account of it is a device which we might call **reduction to the cognitive**. This is a device by which as much as possible of this area of experience is converted into a matter of **knowledge** rather than of **feeling**. Thus at the theoretical level, it is

claimed that aesthetic awareness or appreciation, for example, is the result of rational judgments made about a work of art rather than an emotive response to its impact. This in turn means that, at the practical level, we are advised to set about aesthetic education by teaching children what they need to know in order to be able to make such rational judgments; we are to plan their aesthetic education in the same way as we plan their scientific education, as a process of transmitting the appropriate knowledge and understanding. It is of course true that certain kinds of knowledge can and will enhance our aesthetic awareness and appreciation. To say that, however, is not to say that it can be taken as representing the whole story.

Similarly, those who have offered us taxonomies of objectives by which to plan our curricula in the cognitive domain have not been at all diffident in offering us the same kinds of taxonomy in the affective domain, so that they too have seen aesthetic education as a matter of developing certain kinds of **skilled performance** in relation to children's emotional responses. Teaching *in* the arts thus becomes teaching *about* the arts, and aesthetic education is seen as a training in appropriate responses to artistic experience.

It is also worth noting the extent to which teachers themselves have tended to adopt this kind of solution to the task of educating children in this sphere. Too often, for example, art has become art history, drama has become literary appreciation, music the study of notation and religious education a branch of history or sociology.

There are at least two reasons for this. First, one must recognize that this makes the area **more readily manageable** from the teachers' point of view. They know what they are teaching and they can assess and examine their effectiveness in doing so. Second, it is this which, especially in the current climate, gives a subject **status**, for it is this kind of emphasis that might give it the entrée to the high status area of the curriculum. The main characteristic of the subjects which are high in acceptance and esteem, and thus in levels of resourcing, are their cognitive content and their place in the public examinations structure. Subjects without this kind of cognitive base, and especially those which traditionally have not usually been included in public examinations, have become low status subjects also by being largely confined in their availability to less able pupils.

The effect of this process, however, whatever its explanation, is that those subjects which clearly have a major contribution to make to the emotional development of children come to **undervalue** or **underplay**, or even totally deny, their role in this respect, attempt to turn themselves into subjects exactly like many others on the traditional school curriculum, and thus fail to make that distinctive impact on both the curriculum and the pupils of which they are capable.

Repression or suppression

The second major approach to the emotional side of human life, and thus to this aspect of education, which has been encouraged by the rationalist perspective, again dating at least from the time of Plato, is the attempt to **repress** or **suppress** much of this natural feeling. All those philosophers and others who have seen rationality as the major feature of what it means to be human have, consequently, regarded the emotions, the feelings, the passions as being inimical to the development and to the full exercise of that rational faculty. Natural human inclinations have been regarded as leading away from reason and from rational behaviour towards forms of behaviour more appropriate to other, non-rational members of the animal kingdom.

Thus Plato was of the view that the passions could not be educated but only **tamed**, brought under the control of reason which would ensure that they were only given rein under properly controlled conditions. And the Christian doctrine of **original sin** reflects the same view and encourages the same approach to education in this dimension. The human being's passions are the domain of Satan, a result of Adam's fall from grace; it is reason that he or she shares with God, and those passions, that original sin, with which he or she comes into the world, get in the way of the full development and exercise of his or her God-like capacities for rationality. These passions must, therefore, be **suppressed** and **controlled**. 'Spare the rod and spoil the child.'

Again, therefore, there is no scope for a positive theory of the emotional dimension of human life nor for the generation of a positive theory of education in this domain. Education's prime concern is seen as being with cognitive development, and, if feeling, passion and emotion, cannot be reduced to some form of cognition, then they must be suppressed as harmful to that cognitive development.

The dangers of this approach will be apparent. While one must accept that our natural passions need to be controlled, and that education must concern itself with the development of the ability to exercise such control through what Freud, for example, called the **Superego**, the **Ego-Ideal**, a self-image consisting of certain standards we wish to live by, or what is perhaps more colloquially known as a **conscience**, it must be recognized that the development of this is a subtle process and that, if it is to be successful, it must be a largely conscious process; we must know why we do not feel it right to behave in certain ways. Repression, however, is a largely **unconscious** process; it is the process by which we internalize the taboos of others, not one by which we come to be in proper control of ourselves. And, taken to extremes, it is the source of psychopathic behaviour, the behaviour of those who, almost quite literally, do not know why they do certain things. It is very difficult, therefore, if we regard education as that conscious progression towards understanding, critical awareness and those other capacities which we identified in chapter 1 as the main characteristics of the educated person, to reconcile that with a view of the human passions as to be repressed, pushed below the level of conscious control and left to have whatever effect they will on our behaviour.

There are major inadequacies, then, in the approaches to emotional development which have emerged from this kind of rationalist perspective. The most serious problem, however, is that the dominance of that perspective has inhibited the emergence of a more positive approach to this aspect of education and development. We might do well, then, to end our discussion of affective development, and indeed of development generally, by considering what the main features of such **a positive theory** might be.

Towards a more positive theory

Such a theory would have to start from **a different concept of 'man'**, a different notion of what it means to be human. It would recognize that to be human is to be a creature of **feeling** and **sensitivity** as much as of reason and intellect. It is exactly this which, as we saw earlier, is emerging from recent developments in psychology, and it is that which makes those developments so important. As we noted, they offer us not merely useful aids to educational methodology, but a whole new concept of educational development. What is new and important about that concept is that it is endeavouring to embrace the affective dimensions of human existence and of human development as well as the cognitive.

From that base, a more positive theory would need to recognize that aesthetic education and affective development generally are as much matters of how people come to **feel** about certain things as of what they **know** *or* **learn** about them. How one responds emotively to a poem, a play, a painting is every bit as important, and in some contexts far more so, than what one knows about them. This, as we shall see in the next chapter, is also true in the realm of personal, social and moral issues, and the failure to recognize this has been a major weakness in approaches to education in that sphere. It is clear, as we noted earlier, that there has to be a knowledge component in all of these spheres, in the appreciation of a work of art as much as in the making of a moral decision or judgment, but to regard this as the only thing that is important is to take a distorted and distorting view and its result is that the very essence of affective education and development escapes through one's fingers. It is the interplay of knowledge and feeling that is crucial, and it is this that we need to know far more about.

We will also have to consider very carefully how we can **assess** this kind of development. We have noted the danger of ignoring it when assessment procedures focus their attention on other areas of education. And we have also commented on the mistake of trying to turn it into the kind of cognitive process which can and might be assessed by currently available and somewhat simplistic mechanisms of assessment. We need to recognize it for what it is, and endeavour to devise instruments which will test or measure it in its own terms. This will mean devising tests which will set out to evaluate affective development as a **process** and not merely in terms of its content or its products. We must learn to evaluate children's creations as works of **children** rather than as works of **art**.

We might even go further than this and look to a theory which acknowledges that, since it has often been the artists who have been first to make major advances in thinking, the affective might have to be seen as **taking precedence** over the cognitive in human development and thus in educational planning. It is usually the artists who see intuitively and express, albeit somewhat obliquely, through their art, ideas which philosophers only much later come to articulate rationally and explicitly. The Greek tragedians, for example, were wrestling with moral dilemmas long before Plato and Aristotle formulated any moral philosophy. And, in present-day society, we can see many examples of artists being the first to challenge beliefs, attitudes and conventions. A positive theory of the affective dimension of educational development must, at the very least, begin from an acknowledgement that this is the artist's role in society, to **challenge** rather than to **prettify**, to **express** rather than to **cover up**, to **urge us into thought** rather than to **do our thinking for us**.

Such a theory would also need to include **a genuine theory of the emotions**, one which did not see them as always in conflict with reason, one which did not see them as always bad and thus to be repressed, one which could distinguish between those feelings, such as love and benevolence, which might be encouraged, and those which might need to be controlled or even suppressed. One which will recognize that knowledge has a part to play but only a supporting part to play in this process, and which can help us towards an understanding of the proper **interplay** between knowledge and feeling.

This kind of theory would also need to take full account of the importance of **fantasy** and of the **imagination** in educational development, and indeed in human life. Too often these are allocated an inadequate role in education, as mere devices for self-expression in the sense of letting off steam, almost a form of therapy, or as methodological devices only. It is through fantasy and the free and full exercise of the imagination that children can best be helped to come to terms with their feelings, and there is far more to this process than most people appreciate or are prepared to concede.

And finally, a point which takes us back to a major feature of this whole view of education as development, a positive theory of education in the affective dimension would need to recognize that what it is primarily concerned with is a **process**, and the quality of that process can only be judged by reference to **the development of the child**. Here, least of all, can we plan or evaluate the work of schools or teachers in terms of the content of children's learning. It is the **quality** of growth and development that must be the concern, and this, as we have emphasised before, has to be seen as **an individual matter**.

That it is an individual matter is much more apparent when we recognize that it is the development of feeling we are concerned with than when we think of education in terms only of the development of the intellect. However, the interplay of the two is such that we are moving rapidly to the point where we can no longer ignore the fact that all dimensions of any development which is to be described as educational must evince this same concern for the individual child. It is precisely to that conclusion that recent advances in developmental psychology are drawing our attention.

Summary and conclusions

This chapter has set out to explore some of the implications of adopting a view of education as primarily concerned with the development of children. Inevitably, therefore, its focus has been largely psychological, and, in particular, it has been concerned to examine the contribution to thinking about education made by that branch or version of psychology known as child development.

First, however, it looked at **traditional psychology** and what that has had to say about children's learning and, consequently, the organization of that learning in schools. We noted that its approach was **connectionist**, in that it saw the major task as being one of making effective links between small pieces of knowledge, **as-**

sociationist, in that it claimed that learning is most effective when linked to associated experiences of either pleasure or pain – positive or negative reinforcement – and **behaviourist,** in that its view of education was as a device for bringing about certain behavioural changes or modifications in children.

It was suggested that this was an unsatisfactory form of educational psychology for several reasons, but mainly because it adopted a very **limited and limiting definition of education** as the acquisition of skills and knowledge, and because, having done so, it could find no significant difference between human learning and animal learning, and further, made no attempt to distinguish the learning or the thinking of children from that of adults.

It was the concern with this latter distinction that we indicated is a major characteristic of developmental approaches to the study of educational psychology. A major concern of this movement has been to stress that the child's thinking is **qualitatively different** from that of the mature adult, and to explore some of the ways in which this difference manifests itself. Thus we saw there had emerged the notion of **stages of intellectual development,** and later of these as not merely stages through which we pass but also as **modes of representation** which we continue to use, different strategies for handling new knowledge and new experience. This we saw has led to quite different conceptions of education and of learning, and, in particular, encourages us to the view of education as an **interactive process,** characterized primarily by what has been called **active learning,** a genuine involvement or engagement of the learner with the context or the environment of his or her learning. In short, we noted the claim that education's concern should be with cognitive development and that this must be seen as encompassing a good deal more than 'mere learning'.

We also noted that recent work in this field has identified the importance of both **the social context** in which learning takes place and its **affective or emotional dimension.** We thus turned in the last part of the chapter to an examination of this affective aspect of education. We recognized its importance but also the inadequacy of much of both the theory and the practice of education in this field. It was also suggested that those recent political initiatives we explored in some detail in chapter 3 were leading to even less satisfactory practice in this area, not least because of their emphasis on those aspects of schooling which can be shown to be productive in economic terms.

A major source of these problems is that this is an area of education which has proved difficult to handle both in theory and in practice. This, we claimed, has been largely owing to **the rationalist perspective** from which education has traditionally been viewed and planned. This perspective, we suggested, has led to two major ways of dealing with the affective dimension, both of them equally unsatisfactory. It has either attempted to reduce all, or as much as possible, in this area to **some form of cognition**, to render it a matter of knowledge rather than of feeling, or it has recommended that the emotional side of children's nature be **repressed**.

This led us finally to a consideration of what might be the major features of a more positive theory of the affective dimension of education. Such a theory, it was suggested, would, among other things, need to accept the importance of **the emotional side of human existence**, to recognize that aesthetic education and affective development are as much, or more, **matters of feeling** as of cognition, and acknowledge that the educational potential of **fantasy** and **imagination** must be explored more fully and more directly than has hitherto been the case.

This led us back to the idea that the main messages of work in developmental psychology are that education must be seen as a series of **processes**, and planned and evaluated in terms of these processes, rather than either its content or its end-products, and that this kind of education must be recognized as essentially an individual matter.

Throughout this chapter we have been touching on aspects of personal, social and moral education. For it is here that the points this chapter has made have perhaps their greatest impact. It is here that education must especially be seen as a form of development; it is here that the stages of that development have perhaps their greatest significance; it is here that the inability to handle our feelings and emotions is most serious; and it is here, consequently, that we most need a positive theory of emotional development.

It is to a more detailed and specific discussion of this aspect of education that we turn in chapter 6.

Suggested further reading

Bruner, J., *The Process of Education*, Vintage: New York, Ch. 3, 1960.

Bruner, J., *Towards a Theory of Instruction*, Norton: New York, 1968.

Donaldson, M., *Children's Minds*, Fontana, William Collins: Glasgow, 1978.

Donaldson, M., Grieve, R. and Pratt, C., *Early Childhood Development and Education*, Blackwell: Oxford, 1983.

Lansdown, R., *Child Development Made Simple*, Heinemann: London, 1984.

Piaget, J., *Science of Education and the Psychology of the Child*, Longman: London, 1969.

6
Personal, social and moral education

It is when we begin to look closely at the development of children in respect of their attitudes to and capacities for **interpersonal relationships** that we see much more clearly those difficulties over the affective dimension of education which we explored in the last section of chapter 5. It is here, as we shall see, more perhaps than in any other sphere, that the inability of many educational theories to accommodate the realities of human emotions has been not only most apparent but also most harmful and limiting.

An examination of these aspects of human development will also illustrate very clearly the problems and difficulties that arise when we view education and plan it in terms of **school subjects**. For personal, social and moral education cannot be viewed and planned as a subject, except in a very limited sense, and it is this, more than any other single factor, that explains why it is handled so ineffectually in many schools, especially those secondary schools where the subject base of the curriculum is dominant. The same difficulties and inadequacies will also be seen in most of the official policy statements on the school curriculum which we noted in chapter 3. These too begin from a concept of the school curriculum framed in terms of lists of subjects, and such a concept is seriously limiting when we come to plan education in the personal, social and moral sphere.

Yet clearly this is an area of the greatest importance, and it is seen as such not only by teachers but by parents and by the population in general. As was suggested in the previous chapter, most parents look to schools to 'bring their children up proper' as well as to provide them with access to qualifications and careers. It would in fact be difficult to say which the average parent sees as being the more important of these two expectations. It will almost certainly depend on individual circumstances. It has, however, emerged from a national survey, albeit conducted almost twenty years ago, that over half the population see this either as **the first or**

second most important task of the school, certainly at secondary level. As for the pupils themselves, several surveys have shown that a very large majority of them look to the school for moral guidance, especially during the difficult years of adolescence.

It might further be claimed that, however much emphasis has been placed on the acquisition of knowledge as a major concern of education, the main thrust of most theoretical discussions of education, from the time of Plato on, has been towards the development of the individual as a person. The prime concern, as we have seen on several occasions, has been with the sort of person the child was to become as a result of the educational experiences offered and received; and whether, as with Plato, there was to be a positive blue-print for this or, as with Rousseau, the advice was to protect the child from the corrupting influences of adult society, the fundamental concern has been the same, **the child's moral growth.** Indeed, it might be argued that education, however it is conceived, must embrace moral development, that all education in the full sense is moral education. It is this that makes this aspect of development not only all-important but also very difficult to plan and to carry through.

One final point must be made by way of introduction to this discussion of personal, social and moral education, and that is that this is seen as **a single concept.** The concern is with the child's developing ability to make judgments in relation to his or her own life and to the lives of others, and these are matters which are personal, social and moral **at the same time.** These three adjectives stress and draw our attention to different aspects of what is at root the same. Interpersonal relationships must always affect ourselves and those around us, and they must also be based on some set of moral attitudes or beliefs. Whether we use the term 'personal' or 'social' or 'moral' will depend on which aspect of a particular issue is to the fore in any given context; but all three aspects will always be there.

The concern in personal, social and moral education, then, is to assist children to develop all the many and diverse capacities they will need if they are to cope effectively, sensibly and, indeed, rationally with those personal interactions which are the very stuff of social living.

There is a further aspect of this same point which must be noted. It is very difficult to distinguish what we have just described from what is often called **political education.** One does find it so distinguished in many places, again most notably in those many official pronouncements on the school curriculum. And one does find some issues being distinguished from each other on the grounds that they are either moral or political – most often and most commonly in some of the debates which take place in the House of Commons, where it is quite usual for some issues to be described as 'moral issues' (as opposed, presumably, to 'political issues') and thus left to a free vote rather than being treated as matters on which the party-line is to be followed. Yet it is very difficult to discern precisely what the distinction is, exactly what it is that makes an issue such as abortion a moral issue and one such as the disposal of nuclear waste a political issue. Certainly in the context of education this is a difficult distinction to attempt to maintain. So we will also include some consideration of political education in our discussion in this chapter.

It will already be apparent to the discerning reader that personal, social and moral education is a complex issue. Perhaps some of its complexities have also begun to emerge. It is perhaps not an oversimplification to say that those complexities derive from two main sources. One of these we have already referred to, the need to include a proper consideration of the part **the emotions** play in our moral lives if we are to develop a worthwhile theory of education in this sphere. We will consider this in a little more detail later in this chapter. First, however, we must give some thought to the other major complicating factor, the lack of any conclusive theory about **the status and validity of moral values**.

Is there such a thing as 'moral knowledge'?

It would not be appropriate, and certainly not intellectually honest, to attempt to explore here the many facets of the debate which has raged over centuries in the arena of moral philosophy concerning what is good, bad, right, wrong, and what claims to truth any assertions in this field may or may not have. What we must do, however, is to take note of that debate, to appreciate its **inconclusiveness** and to recognize its **crucial implications** for anything that is to be called moral education.

It is clear that there are still many people, and some philosophers too, who believe that there are **absolute, universal moral values** which transcend individual, national and cultural differences; and there are many, on the other hand, who adopt the view that moral values are **relative** – to particular social or cultural groups, or even to individuals. There are thus those who still subscribe to the kind of view Plato offered, and believe in the existence of something like his 'form of beauty, truth and goodness', or something like Aristotle's 'right rule', or something like the Christian creed of ultimate moral principles, and regard these as transcending individual or cultural differences of interpretation or of practice. There are others, however, who regard all claims of that kind as metaphysical, mystical, not subject to any kind of proof or open to the production of any form of evidence, and thus as unproven and consequently unacceptable. Furthermore, the latter are inclined to worry when the former wish to impose their universal values on them or on others, especially through the education system, since they must believe that it is not universal or transcendent values which are being imposed, but merely different values which are no better, or worse, than their own.

There are several features to be discerned in modern societies which give added credence to the latter view, and certainly have led to some erosion of belief in the former. The first of these is the **reduction in the significance of organized religion**, or at least of the Christian religion, which has always been seen as offering the most credible base for any theory of moral absolutes. The second is the obvious fact of **social and cultural pluralism**. Every modern society can be seen to contain not one single value system but a plurality of value systems, and it has become increasingly difficult to argue that any one of those value systems has some objective right to be accepted as the overriding one. Third, all modern societies have witnessed in recent years changes on a scale never before envisaged, let alone experienced. **Technological development** has been bewilderingly rapid, and it is too seldom appreciated that such technological change leads to **social and moral changes** too. It is not possible to develop readily available and easy methods of contraception, for example, without creating new and complex personal, social and moral problems for everyone to face and resolve. It is not possible to develop the technology and skills to effect organ transplants without raising important questions about the conditions under which it is right and moral to carry out such transplants. Scientific exploration may increase our technological knowledge and understanding; it cannot answer for us the consequent moral questions it raises. In answering these moral questions, however, we do and must change the whole moral fabric of society.

What is more germane to our debate here, however, is that this process of moral and social change raises serious doubts about the existence of ultimate and universal moral values. It is clear that **moral values themselves change**. We cannot fail to be aware of quite significant changes of this kind which have occurred in our own lifetimes. And it becomes increasingly difficult to accept that what is changing is merely our interpretations of certain ultimate moral 'truths' which themselves remain eternally unchanged. The change we have all witnessed goes much deeper than that.

It will be apparent, therefore, that it is also increasingly difficult to conceive and plan moral education as if it were in some way a matter of providing pupils with access to these eternal and unchanging values, of transmitting to them something called 'moral knowledge'. The question of what personal, social and moral education is, then, can be seen as very much more complex than questions about mathematical or scientific education. It is a question we must now give some close attention to.

What is personal, social and moral education?

Moral behaviour

Doubts about the status and validity of 'moral knowledge' such as those we have just touched on are not the only reason why people are finding it increasingly difficult to view and plan moral education in terms of the transmission of such 'knowledge'. Another major factor is the very **notion of morality itself**. Even at the commonsense level, the view most people take about moral behaviour is that there should be clear evidence that it is behaviour which the individual has freely chosen and not the result of some kind of compulsion, or even of blind obedience. We do not usually regard a person as responsible for his or her actions if it is clear that these were not performed from choice but for some other, non-moral reason – out of obedience to some authority, for example, or under direct duress or as a result of some kind of indoctrination. It will be apparent too that this is the attitude we expect our courts of law to adopt in the administration of justice. It is not their task merely to establish whether a crime has actually been committed by the defendant but also to explore the conditions under which it was committed, to determine the degree of the defendant's responsibility, and in this second task the question of whether the crime was committed from deliberate choice or not looms very large. A judgment of this kind has to be made if justice is to be served; and it is for this reason that we call the person responsible for reaching such a decision a 'judge'.

It will be clear, then, that a major feature of any action that is to be properly described as moral, or immoral, is the **intention** of the individual who performs that act. Aristotle stressed this in an important distinction he drew between actions performed 'willingly' and those performed 'not unwillingly', the former, he claimed, being fully moral, or immoral, in a way that the latter are not. Kant too emphasized the importance of the will in moral behaviour, suggesting again that any act which is not directly willed by the individual does not qualify as a properly moral act, and thus is not open to discussions of its rightness or wrongness, of praise or blame.

If we accept this characterization of morality and of moral behaviour, then it becomes difficult, and perhaps impossible, to regard moral education as a device for implanting or inculcating values in pupils. Indeed, this looks more like a process of **conditioning** or **indoctrination**, and more likely to lead to actions performed out of **obedience** to rules which have been learned than from careful consideration and free personal choice. This was the kind of behaviour Plato expected from the ordinary citizens of his Republic and it has been succinctly described by Bertrand Russell as 'right behaviour with the wrong emotions'. Moral education, if it is to lead to the kind of freely chosen behaviour described above, must be concerned to help pupils develop the ability to make **their own moral judgments**, to choose **their own values** and to decide on **their own behaviour**.

The concept of education

We reach the same conclusion when we consider what might be implied in the use of the term **education** in this context, rather than speaking of personal, social and moral training, or conditioning, or indoctrination. All of these processes are possible. We can train people into certain ways of looking at the world (although there is some evidence that this is not very effective in leading them to the kinds of moral behaviour we want). We can condition or indoctrinate them into certain moral beliefs and attitudes. Our discussion of the concept of education in chapter 1, however, will perhaps suggest that to use the term 'education' in this context is to imply that these processes are not what we have in mind, but that, rather, our concern is to help pupils towards some kind of **autonomy**, **understanding** and **critical awareness** in this field, rather than the unquestioning acceptance of certain moral values we are attempting to inculcate. Again, therefore, it is plain that to see personal, social and moral education as the transmission of knowledge or values is to misconceive what is implied by the notion of education itself and to limit the process to something far less ambitious.

Indoctrination

Some would go further than this and claim not only that this approach leads to something less ambitious but also that it results in something which is actually sinister. The notion of indoctrination is not one that is usually regarded with favour in those modern societies which lay claims to being democratic societies. It is associated with such depressing visions of the future as those depicted in Huxley's *Brave New World* or in Orwell's *1984*, and it is also felt to be a reality in those societies the 'free world' would describe as **totalitarian**.

There has been lengthy debate among educationists about what constitutes indoctrination. It has been suggested, for example, that the definition is to be sought in the **methods** used for the transmission of beliefs or knowledge, methods such as those described in the two novels to which we have just referred. But, in response, it has been pointed out that, if these methods could be shown to be effective in teaching children the rudiments of Latin grammar or French irregular verbs or multiplication tables, we would not be likely to object to their use. Perhaps, then, it is argued, it is the **content** of what is transmitted which is crucial rather than the methods adopted for its transmission. This is clearly an important point, for it is the imposition or inculcation of values, attitudes and beliefs which worries us and causes us to describe this process as indoctrination rather than education.

A further point has been made which is very important to this discussion. In addition to **what** is transmitted, the **manner** in which it is transmitted is important, or, rather, the **intention** behind its transmission and whether that intention is to ensure uncritical acceptance or to invite reflection and challenge. Thus some people have argued that what is important is not merely, or not even, the content but, more crucially, the intention, that indoctrination is the deliberate attempt to bring about the **uncritical acceptance** of certain kinds of belief.

While this may be right in terms of the etymology of the word, however, and even of its current usage, it would be a mistake to allow that to lead us into thinking that any such uncritical acceptance of moral beliefs or values which occurred by **accident** or by the **negligence** of teachers and other adults was any less serious. If children come to accept moral values and to adopt moral attitudes uncritically, not because of the deliberate intentions of their teachers or others, but because no attempt has been made to help them to develop critical powers of understanding in this field, or even to protect them from the many insidious influences they are a prey to, then, while this may not be the kind of sinister process which Huxley and Orwell were describing, it is still as limiting, and indeed damaging, for the individuals themselves. They are just as effectively (and, indeed, perhaps more effectively) **indoctrinated** as they would be if someone had set out quite deliberately to bring about this state of affairs. We must return to this point later; for it is a central problem for personal, social and moral education.

Moral education, then, is not only to be seen as the polar opposite of deliberate indoctrination; it must also be seen as a positive counter to accidental indoctrination.

Personal, social and moral education and the emotions

A further, and rather different, point which must be made about personal, social and moral education is that which we referred to at the beginning of this chapter, namely that it is an aspect of education in which the **emotions** play a very important part. The main reason for this is that the emotions play a similarly important part in **moral behaviour**. It will be apparent to everyone that how we **feel** about a personal, social or moral issue or situation is every bit as important in determining our attitude towards that issue or situation as how we **think** about it. One can go further than this and consider what moral behaviour would look like, or, indeed, does look like, when performed without feeling or commitment. We are all familiar with the cold, clinical and 'heartless' carrying out of what is regarded as a moral duty, the performance of that which seems to be required by a rational appraisal of the circumstances of the situation with no positive engagement of the emotions, no real warmth or feeling. This is a form of behaviour which Dickens caricatured in many of his more austere and thus less lovable characters, and it is a form of behaviour which few of us feel completely happy to accept as moral behaviour in the full sense. The basic tenet of Christianity is that we should 'love our neighbour', and that implies a good deal more than the cold performance of our duty towards him or her.

Some have wished to argue further that it is not possible to **conceive** of anything we might call a moral existence without feelings or inclinations. We might interpret this claim negatively by defining moral behaviour as the overcoming of feelings or natural inclinations in the interests of a rational morality. Or we might see it more positively as requiring the **actual engagement** of the emotions in any truly moral decision or choice. Either way, it is claimed, the **centrality** of feeling must be acknowledged. To deny this dimension of morality, then, is to deny morality itself; and to deny this aspect of moral education is thus to deny moral education itself.

Yet this is what so many recommendations we are offered in this area do. Too often the emphasis is on the development of knowledge and understanding in this sphere, and the role of feeling is ignored or played down. The moral systems offered by many philosophers, from Plato's day on, have been systems for **rational** beings rather than for **human** beings, and this has been the case also when they have been translated into precepts for moral education.

In fact, we have here perhaps the best example of those two devices which we suggested in the last chapter are often used to

cope with this difficult affective dimension of education. Much of the emotional side of morality is reduced to some form of **cognition**, so that we are told, for example, that children must learn to understand their feelings and this is seen as all that is necessary to help them to come to terms with them. Or the advice is that they should be helped to **suppress**, or even **repress**, their feelings; the 'beast with many heads' must be tamed; 'original sin' must be stamped out: and again this is a device for taking the affective dimension out of the educational reckoning rather than including it in any programme positively devised to help pupils to come to terms with all aspects of their moral experience. Reason and feeling are too often seen as in perpetual **conflict**, a conflict in which it seems to be regarded as self-evident that reason must be victorious and feeling must be vanquished. This is not a very productive basis for a proper form of personal, social and moral education. Furthermore, as we shall see later, it is a potential source of much psychological harm.

In this sphere, then, more than in any other, we need the kind of positive theory of affective development we discussed at the end of chapter 5. This is among the most important of the many facets of personal, social and moral education which we will now attempt to identify.

The many facets of personal, social and moral education

Knowledge

In planning the personal, social and moral development of pupils, then, we need to be aware of the several dimensions which this must embrace. It is not one simple process but a complex of processes.

First of all, there is no doubt that some basic **knowledge** of a purely 'factual' kind is an essential part of the process. We cannot hope to make sensible moral decisions without the fullest possible knowledge of the situation, relevant background factors, the likely consequence of possible decisions and so on. If pupils are to make sound judgments on personal, social and moral matters, they cannot do so in ignorance. They cannot be expected to reach sensible conclusions on issues like sexual relationships, race relations or nuclear weaponry without a good deal of knowledge relevant to these issues.

Understanding

Furthermore, what is crucial to their moral development is that they should come to recognize that this is so. It is essential that they come to appreciate that knowledge is important and relevant in the making of moral judgments, for this is central to the development of a proper moral **understanding**. To claim that people must have the right to reach their own conclusions on moral matters is not to say that everyone's conclusion is as good as everyone else's. There clearly are important differences in the quality of people's opinions. And to a large extent those differences derive from the degree to which the opinions have been thought through and are based on a wide **knowledge** and **understanding**. This is true in every sphere; we do not take seriously views offered on anything – sports, plays, literature, art – if they are offered by people who patently have no knowledge of these things. And the same is true in relation to moral opinions; we do not give serious thought to the moral view of someone who clearly knows nothing about the issue on which he or she is expressing a view. In short, **informed opinions** are of much greater value, and indeed validity, than uninformed opinions. We only regard people's views as valuable, and perhaps only as fully moral, when we can see that those views are well informed and are the result of careful deliberation.

Moral education, then, must seek to provide pupils not only with appropriate knowledge but, more importantly, with the understanding of how important it is to be well informed before reaching a moral conclusion, at either a personal or a more generally social level.

Moral principles

Relevant knowledge and an understanding of its importance in decision-making are the bases upon which we must also help pupils to develop the ability to frame their own **moral principles**. Properly moral behaviour is behaviour based on settled moral principles. We are not acting morally if we act in one way today and in a totally inconsistent way tomorrow – not, at least, unless we have consciously and deliberately changed our principles in the meantime. So children must learn, first, that moral behaviour must be **consistent** behaviour, that it must be based on coherent and **consistent principles**. Second, they must develop the ability to reach sound principles, to decide what basic principles will govern their own conduct.

Making moral judgments

They must also learn to translate these principles into **particular judgments**, decisions about how they ought to behave in certain specific contexts and what their views will be on particular issues of a more general kind, what decisions and what views are consistent with the principles which form their basic moral stance.

It is at this point that the complexities begin to become apparent,

since it can now be seen that the making of these judgments involves all the other aspects we have identified – knowledge, understanding and principles – and that the making of particular judgments involves a highly sophisticated interaction of all three. It is also at this point that we begin to become conscious of the appearance of certain, quite specific, **emotional** factors.

Self-discipline

First, we must all be aware that feelings do often get in our way when we are attempting to make moral decisions or judgments of this kind, and especially at the stage when we are faced by the need to **implement** or act on them. It is this that has led many philosophers and educationists to see reason and feeling as in conflict, and to recommend the suppression of feeling. There are, as we have suggested, serious inadequacies, and indeed dangers, in such a blanket solution to the problem. However, it must not for that reason be forgotten that some **control** of feelings and emotions is necessary, nor must it be assumed that the alternative is to give the emotions full and free play. Emotions do need to be harnessed so that they do not oppose or inhibit the making of careful moral judgments, and, in particular, so that they do not prevent the translation of those judgments into appropriate action. St Paul reminded us a long time ago that 'the evil that we would not we do, and the good we would we do not'. The development of **self-control** or **self-discipline**, therefore, is another important part of the process of personal, social and moral education.

Understanding feelings

This in turn suggests that it is important that pupils learn to **understand their feelings** and, indeed, **those of others.** It is equally important, however, not to see this in purely cognitive terms, as some kind of intellectual appreciation that human beings have feelings and that they play their part in moral decision-making. It is necessary also, as we suggested above, to **come to terms with** those feelings, both in oneself and in others. It is important to see one's own feelings not as a hindrance to moral behaviour but as an essential component of it, to be expressed and given controlled rein rather than merely to be understood and held in check. And it is important to learn to see other people's feelings in the same light, to accept that they matter, to recognize that they are an essential part of their humanity, to acknowledge, therefore, that they must be taken fully into account in one's own decision-making, and to do all of this, not as a cold-hearted act of reason, but with full and proper sympathy for one's fellow humans.

It can be seen, then, that personal, social and moral education is a complex amalgam of a number of very different but clearly interrelated components. Its planning and implementation in schools, therefore, necessitates far more careful and sophisticated consideration than it has often been given. We must now turn to an examination of some of the factors which should be borne in mind as we plan this crucial dimension of the school curriculum.

Personal, social and moral education and the school curriculum

A subject in its own right

At the beginning of this chapter, it was suggested that one of the difficulties we face when planning for this dimension of education is that it cannot readily be regarded as a separate **subject** and thus does not fit well into a curriculum which is built on a subject base. We must begin our exploration of the place of personal, social and moral education in the school curriculum by elaborating a little on that point, and, in particular, by examining the two different kinds of attempt which have been made to see and plan it as a separate subject.

Religious education

The first of these is that traditional approach to education in the moral sphere which was, and in many places continues to be, to see and to treat it as a part of **religious education**, and thus as the province of the religious education specialist, or even, in some cases, of a visiting member of the local clergy. This certainly was once common practice, and the assumption underlying it clearly is that to be educated morally entails being initiated into a religious moral code, usually that of Christianity.

It is also the case that, in adapting to recent changes, most notably to the arrival in schools of many children from diverse ethnic, cultural and religious backgrounds, many teachers of religious education, recognizing the unacceptability, and, indeed, the impropriety, of teaching any one religion to this kind of diverse audience, have seen their role rather more in terms of assisting in the **moral development** rather than the religious development of their pupils. This can also be seen reflected in most of the official guidelines for the teaching of religious education produced by local education authorities.

It will be plain, however, in the light of much that has already been highlighted in this chapter, that to assume a moral consensus is no more **warranted** than to assume a religious consensus, and that, whatever the merits of linking morality to religion, the arguments against teaching any one form of religion to the children of a multicultural society also apply with equal force to the teaching of a single form of morality.

There are other difficulties in this approach too. The very assumption of this kind of **close connection** between religion and morality is not only questionable but also potentially harmful to that form of moral education we have just described. The assumption is made, at many levels, that religion and morality are connected. As evidence of this, we have only to note the regularity with which members of the clergy are called in as 'moral experts' to discussions of major moral matters in current affairs programmes on television. Yet, although it is clear that most religions do include a moral code as part of their total creed or their general set of religious beliefs, a moment's thought will reveal that it cannot be the link with religion which gives a moral code whatever validity it might be felt to have and that a number of problems must follow from the assumption that it is.

Two of those problems are of particular significance here. First, such an assumption would make any kind of **secular morality** impossible. If moral beliefs obtain their validity from the religion in which they are rooted, then there cannot be moral beliefs that are not so rooted – or, at least, any such moral beliefs will lack all validity. Not only does this seem to contradict most people's understanding; it is also an extremely unsatisfactory basis for moral education in a society in which religious conviction seems to be on the wane. If we encourage children to believe that the author of the moral law is God, then, if they come to reject God, they will feel no compunction not to reject all moral principles too. They will see no basis for such moral principles. The baby will go out with the bathwater.

Second, a moral system which is based on a religion, and which thus claims God as its author, will be essentially an **authoritarian** system. Our reason for accepting the system and for obeying the moral law will be the conviction that we must obey God, not the fact that we have thought the issue through and decided for ourselves that a certain course of action or a certain attitude is right. Our moral principles will not necessarily now be those we have come to accept through the exercise of our own **autonomous** thinking; they will be those which are part of the religious system of which we have become adherents. A major problem for any religious morality is whether it is a morality at all, in the sense we gave to morality in our earlier discussion. And a further major difficulty is the question of whether God is the author of the moral law, a view which renders human morality a matter of mere **obedience**, or whether he is himself subject to it, a view which raises doubts about his omnipotence.

A third difficulty which arises from too close a linking of moral education with religious education is that it encourages teachers in other areas of the curriculum, or at times when they are not consciously setting about the teaching of religion, to see it as **not their concern**, but as something which can be left to religious education lessons. This has certainly been the case for too long. It is a problem, however, not only for religious education but for any view of moral education or social education as separate curricular subjects.

Moral and social education as separate subjects

A number of attempts have been made in recent years to establish some form of moral or social education as **a separate subject** on the timetables of schools, especially secondary schools. In part, these attempts can be seen as a response to the problems we have just discussed of leaving it to the religious education teacher or lesson. They have also, however, been designed to ensure that something positive is done in this area, that children's personal, social and moral education should not be allowed to proceed by default, or, in effect, not proceed at all.

Most of the major curriculum projects in this area, especially those sponsored by the Schools Council, have made proposals for the establishment of lessons **specifically related** to moral and/or social education, and most of them have gone further than that and produced packs of materials for teachers to use in such lessons. The concern has been to ensure that pupils should have the opportunity to explore and discuss moral and social issues in situations where such exploration and discussion could be guided by their teachers.

The Schools Council's **Humanities Curriculum Project (HCP)**, for example, which we referred to briefly in chapter 4, offered resource materials to support the exploration of a number of controversial issues, such as 'War and Society', 'Relations between the Sexes' and 'The Family'. The purpose was to encourage pupils to recognize, to debate and to think about the many moral and social, and indeed sometimes personal, questions raised in these areas, and to help them towards the making of informed judgments on them. It was explicitly not the intention to tell them what judgments they ought to make, nor even to guide them towards certain kinds of attitude or belief. To avoid this, a major feature of the project was its emphasis on **'teacher neutrality'**; the teacher was not to take sides on any of the moral issues raised and was to protect all shades of opinion in the discussions. In this way, it was hoped, on the one hand, that some of those dangers of indoctrination which we noted earlier might be avoided, and, on the other, that pupils would learn to make sound moral judgments of their own.

The purpose of all these attempts to establish moral or social education as separate subjects in the school timetable has been to ensure that pupils should have quite **formal opportunities** for this kind of debate, and that a positive attempt would be made to support their moral development rather than leaving it to chance.

Such attempts, however, have not been without their own difficulties. One major problem has been that, for a variety of reasons, but perhaps most notably because moral and social education have not been regarded as suitable subjects for public examinations, wherever these have been established in the school timetable, they have been seen as **low-status** subjects. They have usually been offered only to the 'less able' pupils, and such opportunities for moral debate have been denied to the more academically gifted pupils. (The assumption presumably has been made that the latter would have ample opportunities of this kind elsewhere in the curriculum, but, as we shall see shortly, such an assumption is far from being well founded.) The question has also been raised of what kinds of teacher we need for these areas of specialism, and what kinds of initial teacher education they should be given.

The main danger, however, is that which we noted in our discussion of the role of religious education in this sphere. If moral or social education are seen to be separate subjects on the timetable, there will be a tendency for teachers of **other subjects** to fail to recognize their own responsibilities in this area, and thus a great potential for personal, social and moral education will be lost. For this reason, some have argued that these should only be separately timetabled subjects if the needs of pupils in this area are not being met elsewhere in the curriculum. And, even those who have argued most strongly for the explicit inclusion of these areas in the timetable in their own right have taken great pains to stress that this is to be seen only as **supplementing** what happens elsewhere not as a substitute for it.

There is much to be said in favour of the provision of such specific opportunities for moral debate and discussion, but in itself it will achieve little unless it is reinforced by what happens in all areas of the school curriculum, and indeed of the school life. It is to the implications of that assertion that we now turn.

Personal, social and moral education across the curriculum

There are several dimensions to the notion that personal, social and moral education should be a concern in all aspects of the planning of the work of any school and we must look at each of these in turn.

A major feature of all subjects

The first point we must note is that there is a moral dimension to **every school subject** and every branch of human knowledge. This dimension may be less easy to identify in branches such as mathematics and science, although we noted earlier the moral issues which every scientific discovery or development raises, but it is difficult to ignore it in all of those subjects which constitute the **Humanities**. Indeed, the reason why such subjects have come to be included in that category is precisely because it is recognized that their essential concern is with **interpersonal relations** of one kind or another, with the very stuff of human existence. There are also, again as we noted earlier, moral and social values implicit in our **choice** of subjects or activities for inclusion in the curriculum and of the content we offer or accept within each of these. This is especially true if we take that view of education as initiation into worthwhile activities which we discussed in chapter 1. For the notion of 'worthwhileness' is itself a moral notion. But no subject, however conceived, its value-free.

We must begin, then, by noting that every subject or area of knowledge has a moral dimension and that we will lose whatever educational point and purpose its study has if we ignore that dimension in our planning.

The specific contributions of certain subjects

We must note further, however, the **distinctive contribution** which different subjects can make to personal, social and moral education, and, especially, what each might contribute to those different facets of education in this sphere which we listed earlier in this chapter.

It will quickly be apparent that subjects like English and history have, among other things, a major contribution to make to the pupil's developing ability to reach established **moral principles** and to make **moral judgments**. While not wishing to deny or minimize the aesthetic dimension of poetry or other forms of literature, one has to recognize that the substance of such literature is the human condition, and the focus of most, if not all, great plays or novels is on some major aspect of the moral life. Thus, for example, major educational opportunities would be missed if, in introducing pupils to a play such as Shakespeare's 'Hamlet', one were to concentrate on the aesthetic merits of the play to the exclusion of any consideration of the important personal and moral issues it raises. In short, this area of the curriculum offers great scope for personal, social and moral education as well as for the development of literary appreciation. Much of history too is concerned with the making of moral judgments or with the evaluation of those made by great historical figures. Certainly it offers opportunities for such, and again these are opportunities which should not be missed if we are seriously concerned with the personal, social and moral development of pupils.

Dramatic activities in schools create similar opportunities, but they can also offer much more. It was suggested earlier that an important part of personal, social and moral education is learning to understand **one's own feelings** and, especially, **those of others**, in order to be able to empathize with them and to recognize them as important and relevant factors in the making of moral judgments. There can hardly be a better way to achieve this than by the kind of **role-play** that dramatic activities in school make possible. It is through activities of that kind that children can, sometimes quite literally, get into other people's shoes, adopt their perspective and thus see issues **from a different angle.** Playing the part of a parent, for example, in an exercise in free drama, can do more to help an adolescent to see the other side of those common parent–adolescent conflicts than many hours of debate and discussion. It is for this reason that one must deplore that process we have noted elsewhere on several occasions by which subjects like drama become increasingly 'academic', in order to acquire status and standing in schools, for it is a process by which the distinctive contribution of a subject like drama to education, and especially to personal, social and moral education, is put at risk.

The same is true of the area of physical education. Again, this has now become in many places 'sports studies', and thus a branch of sociology, or 'anatomy', and thus a kind of science. The other danger here is that it becomes no more than some kind of skills training – coaching rather than education. Again, we have to ask what it is that this area can contribute to education as such. The most obvious answer is to be found in what it can contribute to personal, social and moral education. And this goes far beyond the traditional view of 'rugby and cold showers' to dampen the ardour of the developing adolescent. There are many aspects of physical education, especially those activities known as **outdoor pursuits**, which have a unique contribution to make to the development in children of, for example, the kind of **self-discipline** we listed earlier as another important facet of personal, social and moral education. There is much scope for exercises in **collaboration**, involving the suppression of one's own immediate wishes in the interests of the group, and thus for learning to live with others. There is nothing quite like being in a sailing dinghy with two or three others when the wind begins to strengthen to promote a recognition of the importance both of self-control and of teamwork. This is often called 'character-training'. It is, or can be, much more than that, and we must acknowledge its value in order to ensure that it is not lost.

If it is the case, then, that every subject or area of the curriculum, every activity in which we engage our pupils, has a contribution to make to their personal, social and moral education, then it behoves every teacher to ask what that contribution is, and, the more highly specialized the teacher, the more necessary it is for him or her to face and answer that question. Education is not merely the transmission of knowledge; it is providing children with access to knowledge for certain quite specific purposes and reasons. Preeminent among these purposes and reasons must be the promotion of their personal, social and moral development.

Every teacher as a moral educator

This takes us on to a consideration of the next major aspect of the notion of personal, social and moral education as a concern in all areas of educational planning. It draws our attention to the fact that every teacher must recognize that he or she has a **responsibility for education in this sphere**. The Newsom Report (1963) put this very succinctly when it said that 'teachers can only escape from their influence over the moral and spiritual development of their pupils by closing their schools'. It is not just through the content of subjects and the kinds of experience they are offered by their teachers that children develop their moral attitudes and values; it is also, and perhaps more so, through the **attitudes** and **values** of their teachers, as displayed in the day-to-day management of their classrooms and their handling of all the many diverse situations which arise there. Every act of education, and indeed every kind of interaction between teacher and pupil, is a moral or social interaction, which will reflect the values of both parties. It is thus through every interaction of this kind that pupils will come to learn, and often to assimilate unconsciously, the values of their teachers.

Thus how a teacher responds to misdemeanours or disruptive behaviour, how he or she approaches the task of teaching or of promoting pupils' learning, whether he or she is relaxed and friendly or distant and austere, casual or punctilious, open to discussion or authoritarian, these and many other aspects of teacher–pupil interaction will all contribute to how children come to see the world, how they view personal relationships and thus how their personal, social and moral development will progress.

Several things follow from this. First, all teachers must recognize and accept this responsibility for moral development. Second, they must acknowledge the **impact** they will have on what children learn in the personal, social and moral sphere. Third, however, they must also appreciate that they will be responsible for *how* children come to view issues of this kind; for the **manner** of their moral development as well as the matter of it.

It is this which makes it such an important, but also such a delicate area. Whether pupils learn to approach moral issues in that open, enquiring, autonomous manner, which we suggested earlier is essential to moral behaviour in the full sense, or see such issues as precepts handed down from some higher authority, whether, in other words, they end up morally **educated** or morally **indoctrinated**, will be determined as much, if not more, by the **day-to-day experiences** of working with their teachers as by any formal provision which might be made. No amount of opportunities for moral debate and discussion in fixed, timetabled periods will have more than a minimal effect if such open debate and discussion is made to appear a sham, mere tokenism, by the kinds of experience they have at other times of the working week. In short, children have no more chance of becoming morally educated in the full sense if they work with teachers who are not themselves morally educated than they have of becoming, say, mathematically educated if their mathematics teachers are mere purveyors of mathematical 'facts'.

Moral education as a function of school organization

This takes us on to another major dimension of this view of personal, social and moral education as a concern of all aspects of school life. It is not only the individual teacher who has an all-embracing responsibility in this area. It is the **collective staff** of every school, and thus especially the **management**, those who are responsible for major and general aspects of school organization. The **'hidden' curriculum**, whose impact on the personal, social and moral development of children is greater than it is in any other sphere, is not only a feature of subjects and syllabuses and individual teachers' attitudes; it is also a major feature of the way the whole school is run, as was suggested in our discussion of this in chapter 4. We often call this the **ethos** of the school, and the use of that term clearly indicates its connection with ethical or moral development.

There are two major aspects of this – one negative, the other positive. In the first place, it has been suggested that children will learn much that may have a **detrimental** effect on their moral development from the way a school is organized and run. A highly authoritarian regime, for example, will have the same kind of effect as we were just now suggesting an authoritarian teacher may have, and the impact of this will clearly be stronger if it is part of the ethos of the whole school and not just an idiosyncrasy of one or two teachers. The official school policy on such things as punishment, as again was suggested in chapter 4, will clearly have the same kind of effect on the developing perceptions of its pupils.

The problem goes deeper than this, however, and it has been pointed out that **all aspects of the organizational structure** of the school will reflect the **values** and **attitudes** of those responsible for the creation of that structure, and that these will be **communicated** through that structure to the pupils. This we have seen has been a major source of criticism, for example, of the practice of 'streaming' in schools, since it has been suggested by many people that to divide children up according to what seems to be their intellectual capacity, and to make differential provision for them on that basis, is not only to take a narrow view of what constitutes human worth but also to convey that view to the pupils themselves. Much moral learning of a kind which may be positively inimical to moral education can go on through the organizational procedures and structures we choose for any school.

The positive aspect of this is reflected in the recommendations of those who have argued that, since the school structure must inevitably have this kind of impact on the personal, social and moral development of its pupils, we should **deliberately plan** that structure with this in mind. We should set out to create within the school a **social context** which is in every way **supportive** of what we understand moral education to be and what we are attempting to achieve under that heading. Indeed, it has even been suggested that, if we do not do this, we are wasting our time in making any other kind of provision for moral education. Thus it has been proposed that we interlink the theoretical elements of any course in moral or social education we may set up and the things we look to all teachers and all subjects to contribute in this area with the social context of living with others which the school unavoidably creates.

It has further been proposed that this implies creating some kind of **democratic organizational structure** for the school and encouraging some participation of the pupils themselves in school government. It must be admitted that it is difficult to envisage children developing a genuine ability to think for themselves and to make judgments and reach conclusions in relation to personal, social and moral issues in a context in which they are at every turn subject to rules created for them by others. Some have suggested that the traditional family should be seen as the model for grouping and for the organization of the school, although it must be acknowledged that few schools these days, especially secondary schools, are of a size which might make this easy or even possible. It is of course as some kind of gesture in this direction that many secondary schools have established 'house' systems or 'year groups'. The smaller primary schools have been much more successful in creating this kind of family atmosphere.

The pastoral curriculum

This takes us logically on to a consideration of the **pastoral dimension** of schooling and the implications for that of what has been said about personal, social and moral education. The first point to note here is that we have increasingly of late been hearing of the **pastoral curriculum**, and this suggests that our earlier message, that this aspect of schooling is the responsibility of all teachers and all subjects, may be going home.

There is a second important point to be made, however. Too often in the past – and too often in the present too – the pastoral function of the school has been defined in **remedial** terms; it has been seen as a device for sorting out problems, for helping children when they are in trouble, for picking up the pieces of one kind of personal, human disaster or another, whether in school itself or in the home or even in society at large, through involvement with the police, with courts of law or other agencies of law enforcement. One of the messages of what has been said so far about education in this area is that prevention is better than cure, and certainly better than the kind of patching up which is often all that schools can do once a child is in this kind of difficulty. The implication of that is that the pastoral function of the school should be seen not only negatively, as concerned to deal with problems which occur, but **positively**, as a device for attempting to **obviate** some of those problems. This in turn means that those who have particular responsibility for the pastoral side of schooling should see that responsibility not only in terms of advising, counselling, comforting children with problems, but in terms of **contributing to their moral education** in a more positive way and, perhaps particularly, influencing in a supportive direction all of those aspects of school life which add up to what is called its ethos.

Our conclusion must be, then, that personal, social and moral education requires careful and deliberate **planning** and **action**, that all teachers must recognize the need for this and the contribution they must make to it, but that those responsible for the organization of the school, and especially those holding pastoral responsibilities, must see it as one of their major concerns.

There is of course a strong temptation to dodge this responsibility. It involves us in highly **sensitive** and **controversial** issues –issues of race, sex, interpersonal relationships of all kinds – and it is easy to allow that fact to discourage us from facing up to our responsibilities in this area. It might be claimed that too many parents have abrogated their responsibilities in this area for precisely these reasons. The temptation is there for teachers to do the same, especially those who might claim that their prime role is to teach mathematics or physics or history or whatever. In this connection it is sad to see that the Assessment of Performance Unit (APU) has given up its attempt to monitor pupils' progress in this area, and has stated quite explicitly that it has done so because of the highly sensitive and controversial nature of the issues involved.

We must recognize that if we all, parents, teachers and others, abrogate our responsibilities here, we are handing them over to **other agencies**, we are leaving it to chance and to the random and vicarious experiences all pupils have from other, less organized and less responsible sources. In this case the moral development of most children is unlikely to satisfy those standards of moral education we set out earlier. The matter of it will be the values and attitudes which underlie the more popular television programmes and the offerings of the other media, and, what is more important, the **manner** of such moral learning will be **uncritical**, **unreflective** and largely **unconscious**. In short, they will acquire moral attitudes but these will be the moral attitudes of others; they will not learn to think about them and reach their own conclusions or considered moral principles. Thus not only will moral education not occur, it will actually be inhibited.

This process of uncritical and largely unconscious moral learning we must look at in more detail shortly, since it is of great consequence to those who would be moral educators. Before we do so, however, it may be as well if we complete our discussion of personal, social and moral education and the school curriculum by looking at a related area, which has recently come into prominence in the curriculum debate, that of **political education**.

Political education

There has been a good deal of controversy in recent times over the question of **whether** schools should be attempting to provide children with some form of political education or not. Clearly, this controversy arises mainly from the assumption (whether true or not is another matter) that it is in the sphere of politics that children are most susceptible to **indoctrination**, or that it is in this area that indoctrination is most likely to occur.

It is not the intention to rehearse here the arguments which have been exchanged on this matter. The nub of that debate will be clear from what we have said earlier about personal, social and moral education and especially about the dangers of indoctrination in that sphere. It would seem that the notion of political indoctrination is not in any real sense different from that of moral indoctrination, and, conversely, that the possibility of assisting pupils towards the development of the capacity for **autonomous thinking** in the moral sphere must extend to the political sphere too.

This last point, and indeed the whole debate, suggests that the distinction which is often drawn between the political, on the one hand, and the personal, social and moral, on the other, is a largely artificial one. And this is the main point that is to be made here. We defined personal, social and moral education earlier as being concerned to help children to acquire the capacity to make sensible judgments in the field of **interpersonal relations** and to act on them. It is difficult to know what politics is if it is not concerned with interpersonal relations, albeit on a large scale, and thus difficult to see how politics differs from morals in anything but scale. If I believe in treating people as ends in themselves in my private life, it would be inconsistent of me not to make my political judgments according to the same principle. If I believe that all people are equal in some sense, this must determine not only my political beliefs and behaviour but also my personal, social and moral beliefs and behaviour. This is why political and moral philosophy from the time of Plato have always been closely intertwined. And this is why it is difficult to understand, as it was suggested above, the logic of that practice of the House of Commons of declaring some issues moral issues, and thus open to a free vote, and others political issues, and thus subject to the party whip.

If political and moral issues cannot readily be distinguished, then, except possibly by their scale, then it is **equally difficult to distinguish** political and moral education, and especially difficult to argue that, while schools should be prepared to accept responsibility for the personal, social and moral education of their pupils, they should leave political education alone. Either they must leave both alone or they must accept responsibility for both. We saw above the consequences of abrogating responsibility for children's moral development, in the light of which it is impossible to recommend the former solution. The alternative, then, is to embrace both, not only as a responsibility but also as offering opportunities to forward children's education. We must help children to develop the capacities to live as responsible members of a civilized society, and that means that we must pay full attention to their political education side-by-side with their personal, social and moral education. Indeed, our case is that these are so **closely interwoven** that one cannot attend properly to the one without taking full account of the other.

It must finally be noted, however, that what we said earlier about the nature of personal, social and moral education and the importance of thinking very carefully about the **manner** in which we approach it, must also be seen as having the same kind of force in relation to political education. We must be very careful here too over how we approach it; our intention must be to help children to think about political issues and to reach their own **informed conclusions** on them, not to lead them to the uncritical acceptance of our conclusions; we must help children to become **politically autonomous** as well as morally autonomous. Indeed, our claim is that these are one and the same thing.

If that means that they **reject** our values in favour of others, or even if it means that they reject what may be regarded as the currently dominant values of society itself, then so be it. For the possibility of such rejection is of the very essence of democracy, and there can be no progress without disagreement. As A. J. P. Taylor said in a recent article in the *Guardian*, 'all advance comes from non-conformity. If there had been no troublemakers, no dissenters, we should still be living in caves.'

The danger in political education, as in moral education, is the **uncritical acceptance** of the views of others. This not only fails to forward moral education, it actually inhibits it and even prevents it altogether. The aim, in all areas of the curriculum, then, must be to encourage critical reflection, and it is this that is put at risk by all of the temptations in current society to the uncritical acceptance and even the unconscious assimilation of values, personal, social, moral and political. It is to this we turn as the next issue to be explored in the interests of education in this sphere.

Unreflective moral learning

It was suggested earlier that, if schools and teachers, and indeed parents, do not face up to their responsibility for the personal, social and moral education of children, then it will be left to other, **random and less responsible agencies**. The problem is even more complex than that, however. Even when teachers and parents do attempt to accept responsibility in this area, one of the difficulties they immediately face is the fact that this kind of unreflective, and largely unconscious, moral learning is going on all the time as a result of the **inevitable exposure** of children to other sources of moral influence. The French teacher can assume that his or her pupils for the most part know no French, and can plan his or her courses accordingly. The moral educator must recognize that pupils come to school, even at five years of age or earlier, with certain moral attitudes and values already acquired, and perhaps quite deeply rooted, and that they continue to be exposed to the sources of these attitudes and values all the time, both in school and out of it.

It is a consideration of what this implies for the practice of personal, social and moral education that we now turn.

The main sources of such learning

Parents and other significant adults

There can be no doubt that children learn, or pick up, many attitudes and values from their **parents**, and **other adults** with whom they come into contact, long before they go to school, and thus long before any formal attempt can be made to promote their personal, social and moral education. It is clear, for example, that this is a major source of those racist attitudes which even teachers of very young children often find well established at the time of entry to the infant, and even sometimes the nursery, school. Whether parents recognize their responsibility in this area and set about trying to meet it or not, they **cannot avoid** being major architects of their children's value systems.

There are several aspects of this which are of great importance. In the first place, we must recognize not only that parents will **differ widely** in the degree to which they acknowledge their responsibilities here, they will also differ enormously in how they respond to them, and in the kinds of attitude and value they demonstrate to their offspring. There are those at one extreme who are highly **authoritarian** in their approach to the upbringing of their children, and there are those at the other who are not merely **democratic** but even *laissez-faire*, if not positively **negligent**. The childrearing practices which children will have experienced before entering school will range from the quick slap, *via* the loud and angry reprimand, *via* the use of a 'dummy' or comforter, *via* the 'packet of sweets to keep them quiet' to the elaborate attempt at rational debate and persuasion. A visit to any shopping centre on a Saturday afternoon will quickly provide evidence of the truth of this in the form of examples of all these techniques and many more. Thus children's experiences in the area of personal, social and moral development will be of a wide variety, and this creates problems for teachers at all levels, not only in relation to the control of their pupils, but also, and more importantly, in relation to their moral education.

Second, it must be recognized that there will be a similar **diversity in the moral values** which parents deliberately embrace, often because of their religious convictions, and which they consequently, and very naturally, teach to their children and expect them to accept and live by. This is an especially important point in relation to the wide variations in religious, and thus moral, beliefs of children who come to school from a wide variety of ethnic backgrounds. It would not be proper of course for teachers to become involved in conflict with parents over the substance of their moral beliefs, not least because such conflict would be likely to be counter-productive to everything teachers might be hoping to do. It is a factor which must be recognized, however, by any teacher wishing to make proper provision for pupils' personal, social and moral education.

Third, it is important to be aware of the **inconsistencies** which may be found in the moral beliefs and attitudes of parents and especially of the divergence which is often to be found between what they preach and what they practice. 'Do as I say, not as I do' is not an uncommon principle in many families, and it is one which is not only confusing to children but also **counter-productive** to the development of the kind of ability to think moral issues through which we discussed earlier, and especially of the capacity for translating that thinking into action. We cannot blame adolescents, for example, for being confused by seeing their parents adopting a liberal attitude to sexual matters generally while attempting to insist on firm discipline in this area in relation to their own children. This, then, is another source of difficulty for the moral educator.

The peer group

Another source of the same kind of confused and confusing learning is the **peer group**. At certain ages and stages, children's attitudes are influenced by their peer group more than by any other single agency. This is particularly true of the highly impressionable years of **adolescence**, but we must not forget that younger children too pass through a 'gang stage', at which their friends are all-important and the influence of their peer group on their attitudes and behaviour is thus very strong.

The main point to be noted in relation to this source of influence, apart from the need to recognize its strength at certain points in the child's development, is that, in addition to reflecting all those inconsistencies we noted in the values of many parents, it is often, in fact usually, itself in **conflict** with what emerges from that other source. The main reason for those difficulties of adolescence with which all parents of teenagers are wearyingly familiar is the conflict between the pressures of the peer group and the demands and expectations of parents, a clash of values which again makes for difficulties in relation to personal, social and moral education. It is also of course what makes the kind of opportunity for reflection on these issues we have suggested schools can and should offer children particularly important at the adolescent stage.

The media

The other major source of moral influence is the **media**, perhaps especially television, although we must not lose sight of the impact of magazines, comics and other reading material, especially that aimed specifically at children and/or young people. It is a useful and informative, although usually depressing, exercise, in viewing any television programme, to attempt to identify the **moral values** which are **implicit** in it and which are thus likely to be communicated to all, both young and old, who watch it uncritically. The most obvious of these values are, of course, the attitudes to violence and death evinced by many of the more successful television series; it is also not difficult to identify the underlying sexual morality of many of the popular soap operas. Less obvious, but perhaps no less serious, are the encouragement to acquisitiveness and the emphasis on the importance of material possessions which underpin the many quiz programmes we are exposed to.

These last values are of course reinforced by all the **advertising** we are bombarded with, not only from television but from all the many other sources of such subtle persuasion. Advertising must be based on values many of us on reflection would wish to question and challenge. There is no point to it if it does not attempt to persuade us that we want this or that material acquisition, so that its prime concern must be to encourage **acquisitiveness**, **materialism** and even downright **greed**. Children are exposed to all of this pressure, and the values implicit in it, as much as any of the rest of us. They are also exposed to advertising addressed directly to them, and no attempt is made in such advertising to play down those values we have just suggested must be endemic to all advertising. Thus advertisements for sweets, chocolate and other such attractive foodstuffs are usually framed in terms which suggest that happiness consists in having the largest possible helping or supply of whatever it is they are being persuaded to buy – or to badger their parents into buying for them. The happy home is portrayed as that which offers a regular and lavish supply of such 'goodies'. For months before Christmas, children's attention is being drawn to the toys which they should persuade someone to buy for them as Christmas presents, possession being the most important factor. Acquisitiveness and materialism are all.

Again we must recognize that this is the reality of children's moral learning and we must acknowledge that no attempt is made to encourage them to be **critical** of these values or to give them any thought whatever. Indeed, this is the last thing the advertiser wants of anyone. His or her aim is to cajole and persuade us into purchasing the product; any thought or critical appraisal on our part is likely to prove **counter-productive** to that aim. We must take full account of this in planning children's personal, social and moral education, especially in schools.

The main features of this learning

It is worth pausing a moment to pick out the main features of the kind of learning which has just been described.

Its first and major characteristic is that it is largely **unreflective** and **uncritical**. Most of us, even as adults, are not constantly analysing the value positions implicit in what we are offered by the media or even in our contacts with other individuals. It is thus not only a very different kind of moral learning from that we described earlier as moral education; it is even likely to inhibit the achievement of moral education. It is, however, something we have to take on and overcome if moral education is to occur.

Second, it is by a process which is largely **unconscious** that we acquire values and attitudes from these sources. And this is perhaps an even greater barrier to moral education, for, it is not merely that we have not thought these values through; we are not even aware that we hold them. The best examples of this are to be found in people's attitudes to race and gender issues. There are many people who would hotly dispute accusations that they were racist or sexist, but whose behaviour, albeit in small ways, and whose language give the lie to all such disclaimers. They are in fact behaving in certain ways not only without thinking but also **without knowing**, and the problems and dangers of that will become clear shortly when we look at some of the psychological aspects of moral development.

Third, for both of the reasons just given, this kind of learning is totally **random** and thus is often completely **inconsistent**. People whose values derive from this kind of source will often say one thing but do another, will use one set of standards in judging the behaviour of others and another in relation to themselves, and will even behave according to different principles in different circumstances for no good reason. In short, they are the very reverse of morally educated.

Moral education, then, must be the process by which we encourage children and help them to learn to become **reflective** about these values, to hold them up to some kind of **rational scrutiny**, to decide whether they really wish to accept them and live by them or not, to establish whether they are consistent with one another. Personal, social and moral education cannot proceed in a vacuum; it has a very definite context and content. As was pointed out at the beginning, it is not something which, like, say, French, teachers can plan from scratch. Attitudes and values have been acquired long before children come to school, and they continue to be acquired throughout life from all the sources we have listed and many more. This, then, is the stuff of moral education, and the task of the moral educator is to provide children with the skills they need to **evaluate it critically** and to **go on doing so** long after they have left school.

A further factor which must be borne in mind when we are attempting to do this is that children will respond differently to different kinds of influence at different ages and stages. We have already suggested that the impact of the outside influences we have identified will vary in strength according to the age or the stage of development the child is at. This draws our attention to the importance of taking full account of the **psychological dimension** of moral development, and it is to that that we turn now.

Psychological factors

There are two main sources of useful advice for the would-be moral educator in psychological theory. The first of these is the work of **Sigmund Freud** (1856–1939) and those who have developed his **psycho-analytical** approach to the study of psychology. The second is the work of those **developmental psychologists** who have extended those explorations of child development which we outlined in chapter 5 into the sphere of moral development. We must look at each of these sources in turn.

Freudian psychology

It would not be appropriate nor even proper to embark here on a detailed examination or analysis of the major contribution made by Sigmund Freud to our understanding of human psychology. There are features of his work, however, which have a direct bearing on the problems of personal, social and moral education, and our exploration of that would be incomplete without some attempt to take account of these.

Freud's main contribution to the study of human psychology was his theory of the **unconscious**, the view that a good deal of human behaviour can only be explained in terms of **unconscious motivation**, actions undertaken for no conscious reason but because of attitudes deeply rooted in the **unconscious mind**. This is how he explained the experience familiar to everyone of strong feelings of duty, or perhaps revulsion from certain kinds of action, which we are hard put to it to explain, even to ourselves. Why do we 'take against' some people on sight? Why do we feel, sometimes unreasonably, that certain kinds of behaviour are totally unacceptable? Why do some people display what we might call an obsessive disapproval of, for example, strong drink or sexual relations outside marriage? Sometimes, says Freud, the explanation is to be found in the unconscious mind, in attitudes and values which have been **uncritically** and **unconsciously assimilated**, especially in the **early, formative years** of life, and which thus continue to influence our behaviour without our being conscious of their influence or able to explain our attitudes or behaviour.

The 'Id'

There are two main sources of such unconscious influences, he claims. The first of these is what he calls the **Id**. This is the term he uses for all those impulses, especially sexual impulses, which, as human beings, we all naturally have. It is not unlike what Plato had in mind when he spoke of 'the beast with many heads'. Clearly, many of these cannot be given full rein in a social context; we cannot behave as if other people were not there or as if their interests were of no account. Some **suppression** of these instincts, therefore, is necessary, as we have said before. Certain forms of suppression, however, result in these desires and impulses being thrust down into the unconscious, so that they are not recognized as even existing by the individual. Nevertheless, says Freud, they do exist and they **continue to influence our behaviour** in ways we are not conscious of and thus do not understand.

The 'Superego'

The second, and related, source of these unconscious influences is what he calls the **Superego** or the **Ego-Ideal**. This is the device by which we suppress those urges of the Id which our experience suggests to us are not to be allowed full rein; it is the device by which we **internalize** the **taboos** to which we are subjected by parents, teachers, society at large and other less deliberate and less organized influences during our formative years. It is by this means that we acquire what is more commonly known as a **conscience**, or what some have called a **self-image** or a **self-concept**. This is how we develop a sense of how we **ought** to behave, of what is proper for us.

Again, however, Freud was at pains to stress that much of this is often an **unconscious** process, and many of these taboos become internalized in a totally **unreflective** and **unperceived** manner, so that often our response to certain situations, even in mature adulthood, is of a kind which we would be hard pressed to give convincing reasons for.

The importance of early experiences

What Freud was drawing our attention to was not that this process is unsatisfactory and thus to be avoided. The suppression of some urges is clearly necessary – indeed, it might be argued that it is precisely this that constitutes moral behaviour. And the development of some idea of how we ought to behave – a conscience, a self-concept, a Superego, call it what we will – is also an important part of moral development; it is what we were referring to earlier when we spoke of the need to help children to develop their own moral principles. What Freud was concerned to demonstrate was that this is a very **delicate** process, that it is important from the point of view of a proper moral development that it should be as **conscious** a process as we can make it – proper moral behaviour, as we saw earlier, must be a result of consciously considered principles and action – and that there are serious and important dangers if we handle the process improperly, and especially if we permit too much of it to remain at the unconscious level. The more we suppress, the more we render unconscious, and the more we render unconscious, the less control we give to the individual over his or her behaviour.

There are two main kinds of danger to be avoided. The first of these is permitting too much of children's moral learning to remain at the unconscious level, to fail to encourage, **from the earliest age**, a proper level of reflection and consideration of the moral issues raised by their day-to-day experiences, even those of an apparently trivial kind, like the sharing of sweets or the taking of turns at playing with a particular toy. It is at this very early age and very basic level that moral education must start. If it does not, it may be inhibited for ever.

The second kind of danger to be avoided is the imposition of taboos so **emphatically expressed**, or perceived by the child, that those taboos become not only deeply rooted in the unconscious but so strongly rooted there that they are very difficult subsequently to bring to consciousness, and thus continue to influence the behaviour of the individual in an unduly emphatic way. In extreme cases, this is the source of **pathological behaviour**, behaviour which is not so much immoral as **amoral**, and necessitates psychiatric treatment, clinical assistance in the bringing to consciousness of what has been assimilated in this unconscious way. In less extreme cases, it results merely in the obsessions we referred to earlier, those unreasonable attitudes to certain things, especially those which are in themselves by any account trivial. This was well brought out in a study of young children's moral attitudes, which revealed that they believed that the worst crime a human being could commit was to kill another human being and the second worst crime was to run in the school corridors. Clearly, the taboos of the teachers of those pupils in relation to that form of behaviour had been **unreasonably strong**, so that the children's moral perceptions were, to say the least, somewhat distorted.

This kind of experience can have the effect of inhibiting moral education. It can result in children becoming, in respect of certain kinds of behaviour, **fixated**, stuck at an early stage in their moral development, and can thus make it difficult, and in some cases impossible, to assist that development further. Freud offered some very detailed ideas about the psychological stages through which children pass – or do not pass – in the early years, and about the effects these early experiences have on the development of their personalities. That is a rather more controversial aspect of Freudian theory, however, and it would be unproductive to explore it here. The notion of 'fixation', however, is an important one and becomes of particular significance in relation to the theories of moral development offered within the context of **developmental psychology**. It is to those that we now turn.

Moral development

We saw in chapter 5 the contribution that has been made in recent years to our understanding of child psychology by the work of the developmental psychologists, and, in particular, the impact that work has had on our understanding of the theory and practice of education. It will be obvious that it also has important implications for the education of children in the personal, social and moral sphere, and those implications have been explored by several workers in the field, notably by Jean Piaget himself and subsequently by Lawrence Kohlberg.

Stages of development

Both of these theorists looked at moral development in the light of that **stage theory** which we saw in chapter 5 was a major feature of the early theories of cognitive development, and it will be helpful if we look briefly at the stages they have suggested can be identified in moral growth.

Piaget saw the key factor in moral development as the child's **attitude towards rules** or moral principles. In the early years, he suggested, children respond to rules as emanating from **authority** figures, especially parents and teachers; they do not question them; they accept them; but they accept them as the precepts of authority. Later, at a second stage, they begin to see the **point** of them, especially in relation to social activities such as the playing of games, where, without an acceptance of the rules by all players, they come to recognize that the games could not proceed. At this stage, then, the rules begin to appear not merely as emanating from authority but as also having some **purpose** and **reason** to them, not the arbitrary pronouncements of superior beings but rules or precepts which make some kind of rational sense. This stage, Piaget claims, is an essential prerequisite of the final stage, which is that of **moral autonomy**, where the individual comes to see – if he or she ever reaches this stage – that morality really consists of making **one's own rules**, producing reasons for them and living one's life by them.

Lawrence Kohlberg developed and refined this broad scheme in a number of ways, and he suggested that we should recognize three main stages of moral development, which he called the stages of **heteronomy, socionomy** and **autonomy**.

The stage of heteronomy he described as a **premoral** stage. For at this stage the child is not in any sense acting according to his or her own moral values, decisions or choices, but out of **obedience** to others (the term 'heteronomy' is compiled from two ancient Greek words meaning 'other' and 'rule'). If a child is asked at this stage why something is wrong, he or she will reply by telling us that it is because his or her mother or father have said so, and, further, because **punishment** will follow disobedience – if he or she is caught out. A second level of this stage, Kohlberg suggests, is that where the child has moved to a consideration of what will satisfy his or her own needs, and will answer any question about why certain actions are right or wrong by reference to those needs. It is thus still a **personal**, even an **egocentric**, form of behaviour and thinking.

The stage of **socionomy** (a hybrid term formed from the Latin word for 'ally' or 'companion' and the Greek for 'rule') is that at which the child begins to recognize that rules come not from individual figures of authority but from **society** or at least from **social conventions**, that such rules are necessary for any kind of **social interaction**. This is the stage Kohlberg describes as that of **'conventional rule conformity'**, and again he sees it as subdivided into two levels. First there is what he calls the **good boy (or girl) orientation**, when actions are performed and judgments made in order to gain the **approval** of others. Second, there is a movement towards respect for the **social order**, an acceptance of rules as necessary for the preservation of that social order, at every level, and as reflecting some kind of rational scheme. It is now no longer a matter of avoiding punishment or censure, nor even of gaining approval; it is a matter of recognizing the point and purpose of rules and obeying them for that reason.

This is still, however, some way short of moral maturity. This is only reached, according to Kohlberg, at the next, and final, stage: that of **autonomy** (from the Greek words for 'self' and 'rule') or of

self-accepted moral principles. Again he suggests that there are two sub-levels here. First, the individual comes to recognize the importance of and to respect **the rights of other people**. The basic orientation at this point, however, is still largely a **contractual** one, based on mutual understanding and respect. It is only at the sixth and final level that **full moral maturity** is reached as the individual learns to act according to his or her own **freely chosen moral principles**.

Implications for moral education

There are several features of this scheme which we must now pick up as being of crucial importance if it is our concern to promote personal, social and moral education – at least as we defined it earlier in this chapter.

The first of these is that, as we saw in our discussion of cognitive development in chapter 5, it cannot be assumed that children will pass through these stages **unaided**. Psychological growth is not like physical growth; it is not a matter of mere maturation. Physical maturity of some kind occurs whether positive steps are taken to promote it or not; we may well be able to influence it, to accelerate or enhance it, but neglect will not prevent it happening. Intellectual growth, as we saw in chapter 5, will not occur without the right kind of assistance. And moral growth will not occur **without proper support and assistance** either.

It is quite clear that, just as many people have not reached the stage of 'formal operations' or acquired facility in the 'symbolic' mode of representation, even when they are drawing their old age pensions, so many people **never reach** the stage of 'self-accepted moral principles', but remain at the heteronomous stage of seeing all moral principles as emanating from authority (often that of God), or, perhaps more often, see their point in social, but not in moral, terms. Thus it is the role of the moral educator, parent or teacher, to assist in the process if children are to have any chance of becoming morally educated in the full sense.

Second, Kohlberg in particular has offered us some very useful advice about **how** we might set about promoting this kind of development. He has suggested that, just as in the intellectual sphere children will not be able to understand what is being offered them if it is framed in terms of a level of intellectual development well beyond that which they have already reached, so too they will have difficulty in understanding moral precepts if these are not expressed in a way which takes full account of their stage of moral development. A child at the heteronomous stage will find completely incomprehensible any appeal to his or her powers of reason and autonomous thinking in relation to a moral issue.

What Kohlberg has proposed is what has been called the **one stage above** theory. Children will be confused, as we have just noted, if presented with levels of reasoning which are well beyond them. They will also, however, remain for ever fixed, or fixated, at the same level if what is presented to them is always geared to that level. What is needed is what is known in other contexts (see chapter 5) as **cognitive conflict** or **mismatch** of a degree that the child can reasonably be expected to see as a challenge and to resolve. If we offer children arguments framed in terms of the next stage above that at which they are currently operating, then, this will challenge their thinking and their perceptions and encourage them to move on.

Thus, we are being warned of two possible ways of inhibiting development and causing children to become **fixated** at lower levels of moral functioning and development. First, if we approach them always in terms of rather primitive forms of moral response, for example by always adopting an **authoritarian** stance, then we will offer no inducement or help for them to move beyond these. This is a very common error of practice by both parents and teachers. Even at adolescence, there are many who continue to try to adopt an authoritarian approach to the control of young people's behaviour, and to do this is both to assume that they are still at the lowest level of moral development and to attempt to hold them there. Either way it is **counter-productive** to the process of helping them towards full moral maturity, which is what moral education should be essentially concerned to achieve.

Second, we can err by going too far in the other direction, by offering **reasoned arguments** of a kind which are **beyond the child's comprehension** and which bring no response other than bewilderment, an error which can often be seen in the treatment of children by well intentioned and liberal parents and teachers. We need to get the balance right and to challenge them to move, 'one stage above' that at which they are currently operating.

We must offer one word of caution on this, however. We saw, when we considered the development of children in a broader context in chapter 5, that recent work has suggested that, while we must recognize the invariant sequence of these stages, we should not tie them too closely to **chronological ages**. Thus, we must not assume that all children at the infant stage of schooling can or should be expected to respond to largely authoritarian forms of moral precept. Some quite small children can be seen and heard engaging in quite reflective discussion and exploration of moral issues. We must, as always, try to judge each child's needs **on his or her own merits**.

We must avoid, therefore, the adoption of an **authoritarian** stance even in the nursery or the infant school. Such a stance may not be right for many children, and it will certainly not help any of them to move forward in their moral development. The giving of reasons (as opposed to expecting the children themselves always to be 'reasonable') is important at every stage, since, even if the reasons themselves are not understood, **the idea that reasons are relevant** to moral decisions is one which we should be attempting to establish from the earliest of ages. We cannot assume that moral education can only begin in the secondary school. Like all other aspects of education, ultimate success depends on the vital experiences of the earliest years.

It will now perhaps be clear that the perspective on moral development which we have been offered by those working in developmental psychology complements very naturally the views on moral education which emerged from our earlier exploration of the more theoretical, or philosophical, analyses of morality and moral behaviour. For both lead to the conclusion that the ultimate goal of human morality must be some form of **individual autonomy**, and the explicit purpose and the underlying principles of any process of personal, social and moral education must be to lead pupils to this goal.

Summary and conclusions

Throughout our discussions of education in the earlier chapters of this book there has run one important theme, that, whatever else it is, education is fundamentally about the personal, social and moral growth of the individual, that no concept of education makes any sense or has any coherence unless this major dimension is acknowledged and that, consequently, no theory of educational practice can be satisfactory which has not taken full account of the implications of this basic element. This chapter has attempted to round off our exploration of education by concentrating its attention directly on this all-important theme.

The chapter began by attempting a **definition** of personal, social and moral education. It was suggested, first, that this could not be seen in terms of the transmission of 'moral knowledge', that anything which purported to qualify for that title must be spurious, and that, in any case, morality is a matter of **thinking** rather than knowing, of **making decisions** rather than merely carrying out moral precepts or obeying moral rules. It was suggested, secondly, that the **emotions** play an important part in any human morality, and that, if this is so, we must take full account of the role the emotions play when we are planning or practising anything which claims to be moral education. Third, as a consequence of both these points, it was proposed that we should see moral education as having a number of **distinct facets**, and that we should plan it accordingly. Certain kinds of knowledge are clearly relevant to the making of moral decisions, but so too is the ability to establish one's own moral principles, to interpret these in particular contexts by making appropriate moral judgments, to translate those judgments into action and to do all these things in a manner which takes full account of our own feelings and emotions and those of others, and which, indeed, ensures a proper engagement of those emotions and feelings in the process of behaving morally.

We next examined some of the implications of this analysis for the school and especially for the **school curriculum**. We considered the provision of **special lessons**, either through religious education or specific moral or social education courses. We suggested that there are important theoretical difficulties with the former, but that the latter could provide useful opportunities for pupils to explore moral issues. We decided, however, that these opportunities would only be useful if they were seen as supplementing what was going on **across the curriculum** and we proposed that all subjects and activities should be explored to establish what they might have to contribute in this sphere.

This led us to see that different subjects or areas of experience might have quite different, and even highly specific, contributions to make. It also led us on to a recognition of the crucial role that **every teacher** plays in personal, social and moral development, not only through the content of what is taught but also, and especially, by the very manner in which he or she sets about the many different tasks a teacher must perform. The moral education of pupils, it was suggested, is as much a matter of what they learn from the many different kinds of interaction they have with adults, and especially teachers, as of any formal provision schools might make for it within or across subjects. Finally, we were led from this to the conclusion that it is also a major function of the whole **organizational structure** of the school, and to the view that, if this is not positively supportive of the kind of development we are concerned to promote in this area, all other provisions may well be a waste of time.

The moral learning that goes on as a result of the child's perceptions of the hidden values of the school and its teachers is only one, albeit very important, aspect of the kind of **unreflective and unconscious learning** that goes on all the time. We turned next, therefore, to a review of some of the **sources** of such learning, in particular, parents and other adults, the peer group and the media. We concluded that, while this unreflective learning would have to be regarded as the substance of moral education, its very lack of conscious reflection made it potentially counter-productive to moral education, so that the moral educator must see it as his or her main task to encourage conscious reflection on it.

This took us finally to a consideration of some of the **psychological factors** of which account must be taken in planning education in the personal, social and moral sphere. We saw that one kind of contribution to the debate from this source, that of **Freudian psychology**, has been at great pains to warn us of the dangers of this kind of unconscious and unreflective moral learning, suggesting that in extreme cases it can even lead to psychological illness, and that, even when it falls well short of that extreme, it still acts as a barrier to the achievement of fully autonomous moral functioning.

Finally, therefore, we returned to the work of the **developmental psychologists** and to an examination of what light their theories of the stages of psychological growth could throw on the issue of development in the moral sphere. We saw that the two main messages which emerge from that source are again, first, that **moral autonomy** is the goal, the final stage of full moral development, and, second, that it is a goal that cannot be achieved without the right kind of support, in short, without a properly planned and conceived programme of personal, social and moral **education**.

If we have been right to claim that moral education is integral to all education, then there are clear implications here for all that we do in schools. It is thus highly disappointing to see this area of education so neglected, or, worse, badly handled and inadequately understood, in much recent discussion of the school curriculum, especially in those official pronouncements on the curriculum which we noted in chapters 3 and 4.

We must conclude here with the claim that there can be no education without personal, social and moral education, so that, if education in the full sense is our concern, this aspect of it must be given the fullest possible attention at every age and stage, and in both its planning and its implementation.

Suggested further reading

Downey, M. E. and Kelly, A. V., *Moral Education: Theory and Practice*, Harper & Row: London, 1978

Downey, M. E. and Kelly, A. V., *Theory and Practice of Education: An Introduction*, third edition, Harper & Row: London, Ch. 6, 1986.

Kay, W., *Moral Education*, Allen & Unwin: London, 1975.

Lansdown, Richard, *Child Development Made Simple*, Heinemann: London, Ch. 1, 1984.
Peters, R. S., *Reason and Compassion*, Routledge & Kegan Paul: London, 1973.

7
In conclusion

The earlier chapters of this book have explored the major issues raised by any discussion of education, they have offered a number of different perspectives on those issues and they have provided some of the background knowledge, albeit of a largely theoretical kind, which is needed before one can come to an informed and considered view of them.

The reader who has worked diligently through these chapters will be aware of several themes which run through them like threads, several underlying issues or questions which have been almost ever-present, certainly oft recurrent, but which may not have been fully explored in their own right. It is the intention of this final chapter to draw all these threads together by picking out for explicit discussion these major themes, attempting to put them into a clear and logical sequence and noting some of the further implications which they raise.

The major themes

These major themes are, first, that the study of education is an exploration of a series of **problematic and controversial issues**, not a scientific search for knowledge or certainty; second, that there are **many different forms of schooling** and many different approaches to teaching and that the form we usually call 'education' has a number of quite **distinctive characteristics**; third, that these characteristics are mainly concerned with the development of the individual's capacity for **autonomous thinking**; fourth, that they also, as a result of this, lead to a distinction between this form of schooling or teaching, focused as it is on **the development of the individual**, and those forms whose concern is with the transmission of knowledge, the development of skills or other forms of utilitarian, instrumental process; fifth, that this kind of educational development can only be fostered by **the right kinds of interaction** between teacher and taught; and, finally, that this distinction, while being crucial, has become somewhat lost in recent politically based forms of planning whose main thrust has been **economic and vocational**.

We must look at all these themes briefly in turn in order to round off our discussion and demonstrate its coherent sequence. We will then, finally, consider what they imply for the **quality**, and indeed the **qualities, of teachers**. So, appropriately, it will be with a short review of teacher education that our attempt at making education simple will conclude.

An exploration of controversial issues

The point was made in the Introduction, and developed at some length in chapter 1, that education is an extremely **controversial** subject and that its study consists in the exploration of a number of highly **problematic** issues, on every one of which a plurality of views is possible and legitimate. There is no one answer to any question that is concerned with education in its full sense. We have seen that even the question of what education itself is must be seen as one to which a number of different answers can be, and have been, given, all of them carrying a good deal of plausibility and conviction, and none of them having overriding and unchallengeable claims to our acceptance.

Subsequent chapters will have demonstrated the truth of that basic assertion. In tackling a range of educational issues, they have all revealed a **wide range of views** which have been offered and continue to be adopted on these issues, differences of opinion about the purposes of schooling; the meaning (as well as the validity) of equality of educational opportunity; the central concerns of schooling; the most appropriate approaches to curriculum planning; the forms of development schools and teachers should concern themselves with; what is meant by personal, social and moral education and so on. They have all been evidence for the claims made at the outset that education is an **art** rather than a science, and its study involves the **exploration of issues** rather than the acquisition of knowledge.

Some knowledge is of course needed, but its role in the study of education is to support the making of **informed judgments**. It is the judgments, the value positions from which each person makes them and the opinions upon which they are based which are central. Without these our study is not of education but of history, of psychology or of sociology. What makes it specifically educational is its focus on the controversial issues which comprise the continuing educational debate.

Education as a distinctive form of schooling

The most important of those issues, and that which is fundamental to all the others, is the question of **what education itself is**. We saw in chapter 1 that a number of different answers have been offered to that question. What is important to note is again that it is not a scientific question of fact; it is a question of **values and opinion**. When we – or Plato or Rousseau or the government or anyone else – face this question, it is what education *ought to be*, rather than what it *is*, that is the concern.

In answering that question, we have seen that it is necessary to recognize that there are many different forms of schooling, many different approaches to teaching and many different functions that schools can, do, and indeed should, perform. A good deal of what goes on in schools quite legitimately and largely uncontroversially can be described as **instruction** or **training**. Important as this often is, it is not especially interesting and does not offer much scope for elaborate study at any level beyond that of mere methodology. Its only two concerns are with *what* and *how* – *what* instruction is to be given or *what* forms of training offered, and *how* we can set about this most efficiently. Indeed, of such little interest is it that we suggested earlier that it might – and, one assumes, in the foreseeable future will – be undertaken by machines: robots or microcomputers or a combination of both.

There are two points at which questions about instruction and/or training become interesting. The first is when we ask *why* we are doing these things, what is their point or purpose. And the second is when we ask whether they should be undertaken **at the expense of**, or in the place of, other, more sophisticated forms of schooling and teaching. It is when we ask those questions that we have moved from the study of schooling to the study of **education**, since we have now opened up those issues of value and opinion of which that study consists.

We can, of course, answer the question of *why* we are offering certain forms of training or instruction in simple instrumental or vocational terms. We can justify them by reference to the qualifications, the skills, the career possibilities and so on which they are designed and intended to provide. This last kind of answer is of course perfectly acceptable. It does, however, take us on to our second question, 'Should we be doing these things at the expense of, or instead of, those other more sophisticated things that schools can and might be doing for children?', 'Is it acceptable that schools should only train and instruct in these basically instrumental ways?' And again, we find ourselves faced with those value issues which are central to the study of education. It has been claimed by many that the term 'education' specifically denotes these **more sophisti-**

cated forms of schooling, and thus that the study of education requires that we recognize them, attempt to analyse them and face the questions of whether and to what extent they should be our concern in planning the school curriculum.

Our concern, then, as students of education, should be to do exactly that, and we must undertake that task of analysing and evaluating those distinctive forms of schooling we call 'education'.

The distinctive characteristics of 'education'

When we face up to that task, as we did in chapter 1, and, less overtly, throughout all the other chapters, several points quickly emerge.

The first of these is that what this view of education suggests to us is that schooling can be more than an instrumental process whose justification is to be sought in what it leads to. It is possible to see educational activities as **justifiable in themselves**, in terms of their intrinsic qualities rather than what they are a means to. If this is so, our next question must be to ask whether schools ought not to be engaging in forms of teaching which can be justified in that way.

The second point which emerges is that, while it is possible to instruct and/or train children in ways which do not invite them to challenge or question the content of that instruction or training, this concept of education also draws our attention to the possibility of setting about their schooling in the opposite way, of seeing it as an opportunity to help them towards the achievement of a capacity for **mature and autonomous thinking**. Again, if this is so, we must face the further question of whether we should not be doing this and whether it is acceptable or justifiable to settle for less.

Third, this concept of education leads us to the view that there are forms of schooling whose main concern is with the **development of the individual pupil**, whose focus is not on the knowledge to be transmitted nor on the goals to be attained but on the subject of the educational process, the child, and on his or her growth and development. So again we must ask whether, if this is a possible function of schooling, it is not something we ought to pay a good deal of attention to, and, conversely, whether we are justified in permitting it to be left largely ignored as we concentrate on other approaches, justified in very different terms.

Finally, what we are describing here is a form of schooling which is far more **complex** than those simple forms of training and in-struction, one which, therefore, far from being something which can foreseeably be undertaken by robots, requires and is dependent upon **the most sensitive and delicate forms of human interaction** between teacher and taught. If children are to have access to education in this sense of the term, to forms of schooling which will help them to develop those capacities we have outlined, they will need the services of teachers who have far more than a mass of knowledge to transmit and some efficient methodological devices. This raises important implications for how we educate the teachers themselves which we will take up shortly.

Current political trends

First we must note one final major theme which has emerged from, and run through, earlier chapters, the current trend towards increased **political intervention** in schooling and towards more direct and overt forms of **external control**. There is no doubt that the major motivation behind this trend is **economic**, and thus **instrumental**, that its main concern is with the development of an education system which will meet the needs of society rather than one which will give priority to the needs of the individual child. In 1959, as we noted in chapter 2, the Crowther Report could not distinguish between the two functions of the education system which it identified – education as a national, economic investment and education as the right of every individual child regardless of any return society might expect from that. In the last decade, politicians and their advisers have experienced no such difficulty in deciding that the priority here must be the national economic interest. This is the basic theme of all those official documents we have noted before (see Appendix 2 on page 203).

No doubt the change in economic conditions is a prime factor in explaining this shift. Whatever the explanation, however, it would be wrong not to recognize that it has taken place. Clearly, it represents a move away from a concern with education as we have defined it towards those other **lesser forms of schooling**. It represents a decision not to pay too much heed to those things schools and teachers might attempt to do which go beyond mere instruction and training, beyond simple transmission of useful knowledge and skills. It thus represents the acceptance of a **limited concept of schooling** with the consequences that has not only for individual pupils but also for society itself and the **quality of the environment**, social and cultural as well as physical and material, in which we all must live. We live in an acquisitive and materialistic society. Schooling, as it is currently conceived at official levels, has the effect of reinforcing rather than questioning or challenging those major characteristics. The current emphasis on science and technology at the expense of the arts and the Humanities symbolizes this more than anything else, since it is based on, and must therefore encourage, a view that it is what we have and how we can get more that matters, rather than the quality of life and existence that might be possible for each individual, especially when that is conceived in social and cultural terms. We have noted before that people are inclined to blame schools and teachers for many of the ills of society. The responsibility would be more fairly lodged not with the schools and the teachers but with those who are exercising increasing control over what they can and cannot do.

Nowhere is this more apparent at present than in current policies for **the preparation of teachers**. It was suggested earlier that the teacher's role is crucial in creating the kinds of interactive process that are necessary for the educative development of the child. It follows from this that, if the emphasis in the preparation is not on assisting them to develop the abilities needed to meet that kind of professional demand, nor, indeed, even on helping them to recognize and understand education in those terms, then that form of education must be placed further at risk.

It is fitting, therefore, for both of these reasons, that we conclude our exploration of education with a brief examination of how we are currently setting about the preparation of those whose role in education is central, the teachers themselves.

The preparation of teachers

The two main entry routes

There are, and have been for many years, two main routes by which people may enter the teaching profession. One of these is *via* a **one-year course of postgraduate training** following a degree course; the other is *via* **a degree course specifically designed for the preparation of teachers**, that leading to the award of a **Bachelor of Education (BEd.)** degree. The most important thing for an understanding of teacher education in England and Wales is an appreciation of the differences and the interplay between these two routes.

First, it is necessary to clear up a common misunderstanding by stressing that these two routes are **not**, as in some countries, related to the age-range of pupils the individual teacher plans to work with. There are one-year postgraduate courses for both primary and secondary teachers, and the BEd. programmes also cater for both age-ranges.

It is important, however, to recognize the major differences in the emphases of these two kinds of course. Clearly, the one-year courses must by their nature suggest, and even give rise to, an emphasis on the **content** of education. For student-teachers following such courses will have spent a minimum of three years at a university or polytechnic or other degree-awarding institution, studying a subject, or perhaps two subjects, and only one year specifically preparing for teaching by a course whose very shortness encourages a stress on **teaching method**, and indeed on **classroom control**, and gives relatively little scope for a more reflective consideration of wider issues of the kind this book has explored and of a kind which might lead to that wider concept of education it has attempted to define.

This emphasis has recently been strengthened by the requirement that, for entry to this kind of one-year course, applicants must have obtained not just any degree but a degree in a subject **'cognate to the school curriculum'**, a clear indication that their role is seen as one of transmitting the knowledge-content of that subject and that the one-year course is viewed largely in terms of an opportunity to acquire an appropriate methodology – or 'pedagogy' as it is now fashionable to call it – for teaching that subject.

The BEd. degree programmes, on the other hand, almost all of which now extend over a full four years, have been planned **from the outset** with entry to the teaching profession in mind. Students who have chosen this route are **committed** for the full four years to a career in teaching, and thus can be assisted during that period to give a good deal of consideration to all aspects of education, and have the scope **to explore educational issues in some depth**. In some institutions, courses have been developed in which there is relatively little subject-content for those intending to teach in primary schools, and especially in nursery or infant schools or departments, so that far more of their attention can be directed towards exploring, in a deep and rigorous manner, the kinds of educational issue this book has raised. Many of these, therefore, on entry to the profession, have already come to recognize and appreciate that wider view of education we have identified, and have developed many of the skills and abilities needed to provide those delicate and sensitive interactions and, in general, to create those kinds of opportunity for their pupils' growth and development which it has been suggested are needed if education in the full sense is to become possible.

At the point of entry to the profession, then, those who have followed this latter route, in general, are much better equipped professionally for their task, and have a **much wider appreciation of the possibilities** which education offers, although often they will not have the breadth and depth of knowledge of any particular subject specialism that those graduates in other areas, who arrive *via* the one-year route, are likely to have.

Recent trends and developments

The shift of balance to one-year training

Several things have happened during the last few years, however, to affect this picture. The first of these is that there has been increasing encouragement, which has taken many forms, to **change the balance** of numbers entering the profession by these two routes in such a way that a higher proportion of new teachers are now to be found coming from the one-year courses. Although, as was indicated above, the distinction was never made on the basis of age-range, it was the case until quite recently that the vast majority of primary teachers qualified *via* the BEd. courses. The last few years have seen a significant, even dramatic, change in this.

The main reason for this change is **administrative**. We mentioned in chapter 3 the miscalculations which were made by the Department of Education and Science in the late 1960s concerning the number of teachers the schools would need and the consequent overproduction and massive teacher unemployment. In part, the move towards one-year courses is a consequence of that: such short courses make it much easier to control the output of teachers, the 'lead-in' time to any reduction, or increase, in numbers being less than two years.

A major consequence of this development, however, is that an **increased proportion** of teachers is entering the profession *via* this kind of **short course**, and, although these courses must now extend over at least thirty-six weeks, they are still too short to make possible that wider exploration of educational issues and the development of that degree of understanding of them that we are constantly referring to. Furthermore, if we are right to suggest that this route leads to an undue emphasis on curriculum as **content** and the teacher's prime role as the **transmission** of that content, then we can see that the effects of this change of balance go well beyond mere administrative convenience.

The emphasis on subject-content

That this is not merely a by-product of a purely administrative device but a result of deliberate policy can be seen from certain other recent developments. Mention has already been made of the fact that students wishing to enter teaching *via* the one-year post-graduate courses must now have a first degree in a subject **'cognate to the school curriculum'**, and that, as was suggested above, is a clear indication of the official preference for a **subject-based** curriculum.

Further attempts are now being made to introduce this same emphasis into the BEd. courses. A national body has recently been established to approve (or reject) all courses of teacher education. This body, the Council for the Accreditation (some say 'the Abolition') of Teacher Education (CATE), has been given very clear criteria to apply to all courses in this process of considering them for possible accreditation, and a major criterion to be used in the evaluation of all BEd. courses is that **at least two of the four years** of the course be devoted to **the study of a subject** at full first degree level.

It is clear from this that the official view is that the most important thing a teacher must possess, even for the education of nursery-age chidren, is **a body of subject-knowledge to transmit** and that it is only by this kind of study that the intending teacher's own intellectual development can be promoted. No acknowledgement is made either of the intellectual rigour of the study of education itself or of the professional need for teachers to have made such a study at the deepest possible level. And those courses we mentioned earlier which have been specifically developed to provide intending teachers with this kind of study will not be accredited and thus will not be able to continue.

We thus see again the same particular view of education which we saw underpins other examples of recent intervention in schooling, a view which neither recognizes nor acknowledges those **wider possibilities** we have identified and is thus at odds with the development of education in that form. The recent concern with the quality of educational provision has quite rightly included a concern for the **quality of teachers**, but in both cases that quality has been conceived and defined in terms which are far too **narrow and limiting**. What is more disturbing, no attempt is made anywhere to justify that definition; it is adopted and applied with no apparent reflection and without any obvious awareness of other possibilities.

In-service provision

Much is being made in the current debate of the importance of making appropriate provision for teachers' **continuing education**. The more teachers enter the profession *via* the short one-year route, the more necessary it becomes to create adequate opportunities for their further professional development. To this end, new machinery is being created, in accordance with the requirements of the 1986 Education Act, to extend provision in this area and, it is hoped, to make it more effective.

Again, however, we must look closely at the **form** this provision is likely to take. We must stress that what teachers need is not just an **updating** in the **knowledge-content** they need to be in command of in their teaching, nor even a regular **familiarization** with the **latest technological or methodological developments**. To offer them no more than this is, as we have said so often, to concentrate their attention on the *what* and the *how* of schooling. Beyond all of this, therefore, they need adequate opportunities to explore the *why* of education, to have access to those many **ideas and views of education**, both old and new, without a knowledge and appreciation of which their own thinking will remain half-formed. There are many such courses already available, diplomas, higher degrees and even research degrees. They must be maintained and, further, extended, if teachers are to have the opportunities they need to develop their **thinking** about education to a properly professional level, well beyond the narrow concerns and confines of their own specialist subject.

Summary and conclusions

This final chapter has attempted briefly to draw together the major themes of the book in order to indicate its overall coherence. It has first restated the fundamental claim that the study of education is the exploration of a number of highly **controversial and problematic issues** to which no single, final, 'scientific' answers are to be found. It then went on to show that a major reason for this is that education itself is **a highly sophisticated process** which goes far beyond mere teaching, instruction or training. In particular, as the chapter went on to say, education is the process by which the individual's **development** is promoted **towards fully mature and autonomous thinking**. Its concern is with the **quality** of the individual's life and its intention is to **enrich** that quality by opening up **new possibilities and potentialities** and developing **new capacities**. It was further stressed that such a process requires **the most sensitive and delicate interaction of teacher and taught**, and that, if this is so, it requires teachers with qualities and abilities which go far **beyond the mere possession of subject-knowledge** and the ability to communicate that to others.

This led to a brief survey of some of the current trends in the preparation of teachers. It emerges from that that these can be seen as reflecting the same **narrowness and limitations of thinking** we have identified in recent political intervention elsewhere in education. The concept of education which underpins all these political initiatives is, perhaps understandably, that of the **outsider** asking only what education is *for* rather than that of the **insider** whose concern is also, and primarily, with what it *is*.

We cannot study education adequately unless we can adopt that **inside perspective**. It is only when we adopt that stance that we can recognize its complexities and acknowledge its problematic nature. As this chapter has tried to show, any other approach to its study will be the study of something else – history, psychology, sociology or even methodology. It is that inside view we must take first, then, if the study of education is ever to be made simple.

Appendix 1
Landmarks in the development of the educational system in England and Wales

Date	Event	Major figure	Most significant impact
1833	First public money spent on education		
1861	Newcastle Report	Duke of Newcastle	Compulsory education neither attainable nor desirable
1862	Revised Code		'Payment by results'
1870	Elementary Education Act	W. E. Forster	'Covering the country with good schools' The beginning of the state system
1880	Education Act	Mr Mundella	Compulsory attendance
1893	School leaving age of eleven established		
1895	Bryce Report	Mr (later Viscount) Bryce	'The best method of establishing a well-organized system of secondary education',
1899	School leaving age raised to twelve		
1899	Board of Education established		National coordination and supervision of education
1902	Education Act	Sir Robert Morant	Local education authorities created

Year	Event	Person	Description
1907	Education Act		All grant-aided secondary schools to offer at least 25 per cent free places
1917	Secondary Schools Examinations Council (SSEC) established		Coordination of school examinations
1918	Education Act	H. A. L. Fisher	School leaving age to be raised to fourteen. Continuation schools till age sixteen
1919	First examinations for the School Certificate and Higher School Certificate		
1926	Hadow Report on Secondary Education	Sir Henry Hadow	'Decapitation' of all-age elementary schools
1931	Hadow Report on Primary Education	Sir Henry Hadow	A new philosophy for primary education
1938	Spens Report	Sir William Spens	Support for tripartite secondary system
1943	Norwood Report	Sir Cyril Norwood	Further support for tripartism
1944	Education Act	R. A. Butler (later Lord)	'Education for all according to age, aptitude and ability'. A Minister of Education with a seat in the Cabinet
1947	School leaving age raised to fifteen		
1951	First General Certificate of Education (GCE) examinations		
1954	Early Leaving Report		Evidence of wastage of talent
1957	The Crowther Report	Sir Geoffrey Crowther	Main concern with education from fifteen to eighteen. Further evidence of wastage of talent
1960	The Beloe Report	Robert Beloe	Extension of examinations system at sixteen-plus
1963	The Newsom Report	Sir John Newsom	Concern with the curriculum of the 'less able' pupils in secondary schools
1964	Schools Council established		
1965	Circular 10/65		Comprehensive organization of secondary education required

Appendix 1 – *contd.*

Date	Event	Major figure	Most significant impact
1965	First Certificate of Secondary Education (CSE) examinations		
1967	The Plowden Report	Lady Bridgit Plowden	The Hadow philosophy of primary education reaffirmed
1972	School leaving age raised to sixteen		
1975	Assessment of Performance Unit (APU) established		
1978	Schools Council reconstituted		
1980	Education Act	Sir Keith Joseph	Reduction of teacher control Changes to the composition of governing bodies of schools Public statements of school curricula and achievements required
1981	Education Act	Sir Keith Joseph	The assimilation of children with special educational needs into the ordinary school Re-establishment of political control
1984	Demise of the Schools Council Establishment of the Schools Examinations Council (SEC) and School Curriculum Development Committee (SCDC)		
1986	Education Act	Kenneth Baker	Reconstitution of governing bodies of schools New arrangements for the in-service education of teachers Powers for Secretary of State in relation to teacher appraisal
1988	First examinations for the General Certificate of Secondary Education (GCSE)		

Appendix 2
Major official publications on education issued 1977–86

Date	Title	Source	Status
1977	Education in Schools: A Consultative Document (Cmnd 6869)	Secretary of State for Education and Science and the Secretary of State for Wales	A green paper
1977	Curriculum 11–16	Her Majesty's Inspectorate	Working papers
1977	A New Partnership for Our Schools (The Taylor Report)	The Taylor Committee	Official report
1978	Primary Education in England	Her Majesty's Inspectorate	A factual survey
1979	Aspects of Secondary Education in England	Her Majesty's Inspectorate	A factual survey
1980	A View of the Curriculum	Her Majesty's Inspectorate	A discussion document
1980	A Framework for the School Curriculum	Department of Education and Science and the Welsh Office	Proposals for change
1981	The School Curriculum	Department of Education and Science and the Welsh Office	Proposals for change
1982	The New Teacher in School	Her Majesty's Inspectorate	A discussion document

Appendix 2 – *contd.*

Date	Title	Source	Status
1983	*Teaching Quality* (Cmnd 8836)	Secretary of State for Education and Science and the Secretary of State for Wales	A white paper
1984	*English from 5–16. Curriculum Matters 1*	Her Majesty's Inspectorate	A discussion document
1985	*The Curriculum from 5–16. Curriculum Matters 2*	Her Majesty's Inspectorate	A discussion document
1985	*Mathematics from 5–16. Curriculum Matters 3*	Her Majesty's Inspectorate	A discussion document
1985	*Music from 5–16. Curriculum Matters 4*	Her Majesty's Inspectorate	A discussion document
1985	*Home Economics from 5–16. Curriculum Matters 5*	Her Majesty's Inspectorate	A discussion document
1985	*Better Schools* (Cmnd 8469)	Secretary of State for Education and Science and the Secretary of State for Wales	A white paper

Appendix 3
An alphabetical list of the further reading suggested

Becher, T. and Maclure, S., *The Politics of Curriculum Change*, Hutchinson: London, 1975.

Benn, C. and Simon, B., *Half Way There*, Penguin: Harmondsworth, 1972.

Blenkin, G. M. and Kelly, A. V., *The Primary Curriculum*, second edition, Harper & Row: London, 1981.

Bruner, J., *The Process of Education*, Vintage: New York, 1960.

Bruner, J., *Towards a Theory of Instruction*, Norton: New York, 1968.

Curtis, S. J., *History of Education in Great Britain*, University Tutorial Press: London, 1943.

Curtis, S. J. and Boultwood, M. E. A., *A Short History of Educational Ideas*, University Tutorial Press: London, 1953.

Donaldson, M., *Children's Minds*, Fontana, William Collins: Glasgow, 1978.

Donaldson, M., Grieve, R. and Pratt, C., *Early Childhood Development and Education*, Blackwell: Oxford, 1983.

Downey, M. E. and Kelly, A. V., *Moral Education: Theory and Practice*, Harper & Row: London, 1978.

Downey, M. E. and Kelly, A. V., *Theory and Practice of Education: An Introduction*, third edition, Harper & Row: London, 1986.

Gordon, P. and Lawton, D., *Curriculum Change in the Nineteenth and Twentieth Centuries*, Hodder & Stoughton: London, 1978.

Holt, M., *Schools and Curriculum Change*, McGraw-Hill: London, 1980.

Kay, W., *Moral Education*, Allen & Unwin: London, 1975.

Kelly, A. V. (ed.), *Curriculum Context*, Harper & Row: London, 1980.

Kelly, A. V., *The Curriculum: Theory and Practice*, second edition, Harper & Row: London, 1982.

Kogan, M., *The Politics of Educational Change*, Fontana: Glasgow, 1978.

Lansdown, R., *Child Development Made Simple*, Heinemann: London, 1984.

Lawton, D., *The Politics of the School Curriculum*, Routledge & Kegan Paul: London, 1980.

Peters, R. S., *Ethics and Education*, Allen & Unwin: London, 1966.

Peters, R. S., *Reason and Compassion*, Routledge & Kegan Paul: London, 1973.

Piaget, J., *Science of Education and the Psychology of the Child*, Longman: London, 1969.

Rusk, R. R., *Doctrines of the Great Educators*, Macmillan: London, 1957.

Thompson, K., *Education and Philosophy: A Practical Approach*, Blackwell: Oxford, 1972.

Whitehead, A. N., *The Aims of Education*, Williams and Norgate: London, 1932.

Williams, R., *The Long Revolution*, Chatto & Windus, Pelican Books: London, 1961, 1965.

Index of proper names

Index of subjects

abortion, 153

access, 7, 32, 33, 37, 50, 51, 52, 59, 97

accommodation, 130, 136, 137

accountability, 8, 67–8, 72, 98, 100, 102, 142

active learning, 88, 116, 128, 129, 130, 132, 135, 136

adolescence, x, 167, 176, 185

advertising, 177

aesthetics, 3, 5, 7, 11, 13, 14, 142, 143, 144, 146, 150, 166

affective domain, 86

'aims and objectives', 85–9, 90, 91, 92, 94, 98, 100, 102, 105, 106, 119, 127, 128, 144

alienation, 97

appraisal, 72, 100, 102, 103

arithmetic, 5, 6

art, 10, 12, 42, 144, 147
  history, 144

arts, the, 4, 5, 6, 9, 13, 32, 96, 141, 144, 194
  see also Humanities

assessment, 69, 103, 110–18, 120, 123, 142, 144, 147
  course-work, 116
  self–, 116
  see also examinations

Assessment of Performance Unit (APU), 66, 71, 101, 104–5, 143, 172, 202

assimilation, 130, 137

association, 125, 148–9

autonomy, 24, 25, 84, 88, 91, 123, 156, 163, 169, 173, 174, 183–4, 186, 188, 190, 193, 199
  of teachers, 55, 63, 64, 65, 76, 77, 88, 100

balance, 112

'basic skills', ix, 8, 32, 34, 50, 65, 91, 139

behaviour modification, 125, 126, 127, 149

bilateral schools, 44

biology, 1

birthrate, 44

'bulge', the, 44

Business and Technician Education Council (BTEC), 114

carpentry, 34

central schools, 38, 40

Certificate of Extended Education (CEE), 113

Certificate of Pre-Vocational Education (CPVE), 69, 114, 115

Certificate of Secondary Education (CSE), 46, 64, 122, 113, 114, 116, 202

Civil Service, 111

Classical conditioning, 125

Classics, 10, 32, 45, 92

cognitive conflict, 137, 185

cognitive content, 95, 144

cognitive development, x, 3, 7–9, 12, 21, 95, 96, 123, 124, 128, 129–39, 140, 143, 145, 149, 182, 184

cognitive domain, 86

commerce, 68, 75, 85, 112, 119

common curriculum, ix, 11, 71, 94–101, 102, 108, 119

community, 69, 81

comparative education, 2

competence, growth of, 138, 139

competent newborn, 136

Comprehensive education, ix, 7, 33, 43, 44, 45–50, 52, 53, 64, 65, 73, 97, 115